A Jericho Writers Guide

GETTING PUBLISHED

How to hook an agent, get a deal and build a career you love

By Harry Bingham

PRAISE FOR A PREVIOUS EDITION

'A **hugely expansive resource** giving you everything you could possibly need to know about the publishing world and how to get there. Eminently readable too'

—Intheamazone

'This could well be called 'The Idiots Guide to Getting Published'... **Getting Published tackles all the hard, almost fathomless questions head-on** and in a sympathetic, hand-holding way, as well as being brutally honest.'

—Richard Cox

ABOUT HARRY BINGHAM

Harry is the author of a dozen novels and several works of non-fiction. He's been published all over the world, been prize long- and short-listed, had his work adapted for TV and has won global critical acclaim. Best of all: he loves writing as much as he ever did. He's also the founder and owner of Jericho Writers.

If you want to explore Harry's fiction, your best bet is to start with *Talking to the Dead*, the first book in the Fiona Griffiths series.

A Jericho Writers Guide

GETTING PUBLISHED

How to hook an agent, get a deal and build a career you love

By Harry Bingham

Jericho**Writers**

Published by Jericho Writers, 2020
www.jerichowriters.com

Copyeditor: Karen Atkinson
Formatting: BB eBooks
Cover design: Kelly Finnegan

CONTENTS

INTRODUCTION

You've reached the last full stop. Your finger presses that final key, then withdraws, astonished. You've reached the end! Your novel (or non-fiction book, or children's novel, or whatever) is complete.

It's hard to describe your emotions. In amongst them is the thrill of arrival. A Channel swimmer grazing his knees on the rocks outside Boulogne must feel something similar. It wasn't so long back that this project looked so dauntingly *huge*. So many miles to swim. So many words to write. The logic said that, if you just wrote so-and-so much every day, then you'd get there in the end, but as you gazed out over all the miles of empty space, the logic seemed impossible to believe; it simply ignored the multitude of ways in which this project could have spiralled off into uselessness or failure.

Another part of you feels pride. You did it! You say that little sentence over and again to yourself and it feels amazing every time. Putting aside your family and other loved ones, this is probably the biggest single achievement of your life. Sure, you've passed exams, secured jobs, won promotions – but so does everyone. Writing a book is a bigger, tougher, more serious challenge altogether. Maybe you know someone else who's written a book, but quite likely you don't. You certainly don't know many. You're special, and you know it.

And then, of course, there's another feeling bubbling up as well. Excitement. You'll send the book out to agents, you'll get taken on, you'll get a book deal – in your home country to start with, but then overseas too. And how about a movie deal? You aren't into counting chickens, but some of your scenes would be just amazing on screen and you've written a part that most actresses would die for.

Needless to say, when you tell people that you've finished your book, you keep most of these thoughts private. You tell people that there's still a long way to go, you know you need to revise a few things, that it can be tough to get an agent, that you aren't taking anything for granted. Yet, all the time your lips are saying exactly the right things and in exactly the right tone of voice, your thoughts are racing twenty miles ahead. The thrill of seeing your name on *The New York Times* or *The Sunday Times* bestseller lists. The pleasure of your first book review. Just how you'll introduce your book on Oprah. Or on some TV culture show. What you'll say to Jonathan Franzen when you best him at some awards ceremony.

The joy of finishing a manuscript is to be relished. I've known it many times myself and hope to feel it again a good many times before I hang up my pen. It's a milestone of huge significance in a new writer's career. The only moments that compare with it are the pleasures of getting an agent, getting a book deal and – ultimately – seeing your book on the shelves of a real-life bookshop.

Yet completing a manuscript is the start, not the end, of a process. Revising a manuscript is tough. Getting an agent is tough. Getting a book deal is tough. Negotiating the whole publishing process so that you end up with a book you love and which is being marketed hard and well by people you enjoy working with – well, there may be times you wish you'd become a Channel swimmer instead.

Worse still, you'll often find yourself adrift in an industry that everyone but you seems to understand perfectly. Issues you didn't even know existed – the difficulty of getting into a three-for-two promotion; the near-impossibility of getting reviews for paperbacks – suddenly rear up to thwart what you had thought would be an ordinary part of the publication process. Such things afflict first-time writers particularly. By definition, first-timers have no experience to fall back on. On the other hand, many professional authors aren't vastly better off. An editor at a leading publisher might handle a couple of books every month. That means that, in six months, they'll have handled more books than a committed writer is likely to produce in a decade. And, of course, that editor is surrounded by other editors, has instant access to salespeople and marketers, and can call on any amount of expertise in design, PR and everything else. No wonder you feel like the novice in the room. That's what you are.

This book is a guide for every writer who's completed (or completing) a manuscript and doesn't know what to do next. It's a guide for writers who have found an agent but never got a book deal. It's a guide for those who have had the sheer delight of a book deal – and the sheer misery of a book that bombed with no clear reason why.

This book is your instruction manual and survival guide. It won't make the publishing process easy or certain. Nothing short of being an A-list celebrity will achieve that happy outcome and, even then, it won't always. But it will tilt the odds in your favour. It will arm you with the information you need. It'll tell you about the pitfalls that lie ahead. It will draw a map of an industry that too often leaves its writers politely in the dark.

If you want to rattle straight on to the substance of the book, then please feel free to do just that. If you're the sort that likes to have 'i's dotted and 't's neatly crossed, then bear with me for a another second or two.

First off, this is not a book about self-publishing.

I love self-publishing. It's an approach I use now myself (with some, but not all, of my work). Self-publishing has become an amazingly professional discipline within the space of just a few years. If your aim is to make a living from your writing, self-pub is now arguably more credible than traditional publishing. So I'm not in any way dismissive of that whole approach, but this book is about getting published the traditional way: with a literary agent (probably) and a traditional publisher. If you want help with self-publishing, you need to pop this book quietly back on the shelf. I hope to write a beginner's guide to the subject before too long, but in the meantime, get your hands on work by David Gaughran, Nicholas Erik, Tammi Labrecque and Joanna Penn.

Those guys will sort you out. You can trust what they say 100% – perhaps even 110%, if you like exaggeration and have shoddy arithmetic.

Second, you should use this book just as you want. There's no need to read it cover to cover, if you don't want to. The book is broadly arranged to follow the publication process itself, so you can jump straight through to whatever part of it is currently baffling and enraging you. Do, however, keep the book at hand. Parts of the book which don't seem relevant now may become relevant soon. As you start to get more experience, different sections of this book will echo differently.

Third and last, a word or two about me and about the experience and philosophy which underpin this work. For the first ten years of my career, I worked as an investment banker. I enjoyed what I did, but I didn't love it. As a child, I'd always wanted to be a writer, but writing hardly seemed like a practical way of paying bills.

Then my wife got ill. I quit work to look after her. As I sat by her bedside (in a darkened room because her vision was problematic), I tapped away on a laptop, drafting the book that would one day become *The Money Makers*, my first novel.

I finished the book and got an agent. I was surprised by how hard it was to get an agent, because I was pretty sure my book was OK, but eventually two agents offered representation at the same time. I chose one of the two; she sent my book out, an auction ensued, and a very nice book deal was the happy result.

That, in a way, was the high point of my involvement with the industry. For sure, I went on getting some very attractive book deals. I sold five novels, all to HarperCollins. I sold a couple of 'how-to' books on writing and publishing to Bloomsbury (and this book is a completely revised version of one of them). I sold a couple of popular non-fiction books to a different bit of Harper-Collins. I then switched to crime and sold the (currently six-volume) Fiona Griffiths crime series all over the world. I've also worked on some projects as ghost-writer or editor; I've edited an anthology of short fiction; I've done some other things too.

I like what I do, and I fully expect to continue writing and selling books for a very long time to come. I've sold books in North America and Australia, France and Germany, China and Japan, and a ton of smaller territories too. I've had book clubs making me their book of the month. I've clambered onto bestseller lists. I've had some nice reviews (written by geniuses) and some stinkers (from idiots). I've been longlisted and shortlisted for some great awards. I've had my work adapted for the screen. I've recently signed a potentially huge new TV deal as well.

All the same, my early cheerful belief that all I had to do was write good books and the rest would follow has long since evaporated. Publishing is *hard*. It's hard enough for publishers, but at least they can spread their risks over a whole host of titles. It's a lot harder for authors, whose risks are firmly pinned to a single frail manuscript.

I see those risks more clearly now because, fifteen years back, I set up a consultancy which aimed to help first-time writers. The business started out small and now – rebranded as Jericho Writers – is among the largest in its industry. We offer editorial advice and use dozens of professional authors and commissioning editors to deliver that help. We cover every branch of writing from craft books and picture books through to fantasy sagas and highbrow literary fiction. Where work is strong enough to present to agents, we help with that part of things too. We also offer courses and mentoring and events and literary agent search tools and … well, if it's useful to writers, we probably do it.

Perhaps nobody in the world has helped more newbies through to publication. I'm proud of that.

Running Jericho Writers has vastly extended my knowledge of publishing. For one thing, it's opened my eyes to the problems that first-timers routinely face in navigating the industry. Agents who are dilatory. Agents who are useless. Agents who are outright scammers. These aren't *normal* problems, you understand: most agents do a good, thorough, professional job. At the same time, the problems aren't exceptional either. At Jericho Writers, we simply hear too many stories of woe to set them aside as once-in-a-century exceptions.

It's the same thing with publishing generally. As I've come to know the authors who work for us, I've seen again and again how challenging it can be for a writer to build a lasting career in this industry. I've gained some experience of what works and what doesn't. Equally, as I've deepened my connections with agents and publishers, I've learned ever more about the commercial logic which can be so perplexing to outsiders. I've spoken to dozens, even hundreds, of industry insiders – editors, marketers, booksellers, books-page editors, and more – about their own roles and how they see the world. All that experience, theirs and mine, informs every page of this book.

So much for my experience – but philosophy matters too. This book is written emphatically from an author's perspective. I know that you didn't come to writing to make money. You came to writing from a sense of passion. A story you wanted to communicate. Characters you couldn't get out of your head. Information and insights you wanted to share with the broadest possible audience.

I have that perspective too. Writing for me is a passion from which I happen – miraculously – to make money. Yet that doesn't mean that the commercial side of things doesn't matter. On the contrary, I detest it when writers are treated badly, or sidelined, or pressured into agreeing to things which aren't in their (or often their publisher's) best interests. I hate it when writers are told half-truths because editors want to avoid the discomfort of conveying a few hard truths. I hate it when authors feel like they occupy the lowest rung of an industry that should really set them in the place of honour at the top. This book is written from a perspective that honours the writer's artistic impulse but also passionately believes in the author's right to treatment that is fair and respectful of their commercial aims.

I offer no guarantees. Even forewarned and forearmed, you'll find the publishing industry tricky. Good writers often fail. Bad ones sometimes thrive. No handbook will put an end to those outcomes. All the same, you should use this book as your guide and compass. It will tell you what to expect, how to proceed, what choices to consider. If the outcome is less than positive — well then, at least you'll have made the best possible choices available to you. You'll have nothing to regret. If the outcome is fantastic, so much the better. I'll be cheering you all the way to the #1 bestseller slot of *The New York Times* – and every fellow author will cheer you too.

Godspeed.

HARRY BINGHAM
Jericho Writers

Part One
GETTING READY

MOTIVES AND EXPECTATIONS

Why do you write, and what do you hope to accomplish?

The question seems so obvious that no one ever asks it. Writers write because they like it. Because they want others to read their work. Because they want to make some money. Different writers may weight those three things differently, but it would be a rare writer for whom one of those three motivations was altogether absent.

The question matters, all the same, because the motivations are different, and they need to inform how you proceed with your work and the expectations you set yourself. Some examples will illustrate the point. (I should also say that all the case histories in this book are real. I've changed each individual's name but have otherwise stuck closely to the truth.) So. The examples:

> **EMMA**, *literary novelist*. Emma started out as a short-story writer. She got some very positive feedback on her short stories and was encouraged to write a novel. She did so. She got an agent. The agent managed to secure a $5,000 deal for the book with a small, but highly esteemed, literary publisher. The book got two or three nice book reviews. It did not earn any royalties over and above the initial advance. Emma continues to work full-time as a doctor, as she had always intended. She is currently searching for a publisher to take her second novel.

> **RICHARD AND JENNY**, *mental-health memoirists*. Richard and Jenny are a husband and wife team who collaborated on a memoir about Jenny's history of mental health problems. The book was acquired by a publisher specialising in

mental health issues for no advance, but a share of royalties. The book has sold a few hundred copies only, but Richard and Jenny know that their readers are almost certain to be ones for whom the book came as inspiration and help. It hasn't reached many readers, but it's reached the right ones.

JOHN, *commercial novelist.* John has a high-paying job as a management consultant. His first book – an adventure romp about a high-class thief – was bought for a good five-figure sum by a major US publisher. The book went on to sell around 150,000 copies, which meant there were decent royalties over and above that initial advance. The book also sold worldwide. John's publishers have commissioned further titles from him, and John continues to write them – without, however, choosing to give up his existing job.

All these authors feel thoroughly pleased with what they've accomplished. Emma wanted a commercial book deal, because of the quality standard it represents, but the money itself was immaterial. She's probably never earned so little money for so much work in her life. She doesn't have a huge readership and is most unlikely ever to get one, but, then again, her work is quiet, beautiful and unflashy. It's not the sort of thing to cause a splash, but Emma wouldn't dream of adapting her tone to the market. She writes what she wants to write and is happy to see that acknowledged by a good, well-respected publisher, and to receive some nice reviews and some appreciative feedback from her readers.

If, however, Emma had ever thought about building a career from her work, then she'd made a colossal error right from the start. It's not that literary fiction *can't* sell for decent amounts, just that it's only likely to earn significant money if it works hard to call attention to itself. Among the most dazzling debuts or near-debuts of recent times, one can think of Jonathan Safran Foer's *Everything Is Illuminated*, Zadie Smith's *White Teeth*, and Marlon

James's *A Brief History of Seven Killings*. Each of those books (one American, one British, one Jamaican) banged every drum there was to bang. They were funny. They were raucous. They showed off a wide range of technique. They were jubilantly modern in their celebration of ethnic and cultural diversity. Just in case there wasn't enough going on, Zadie Smith thumped an attempted suicide right there on page one to grab and hold the reader's attention. Safran Foer handed his opening credits over to one of the most hilarious and bizarre versions of English ever to hit the printed page. Marlon James blitzed up Jamaican slang, biblical sonorousness, and dozens of other voices in a vast and ambitiously over-the-top confection.

All these three are accomplished novelists. Nevertheless, it wasn't quality alone that determined their success. They produced novels that deliberately created a din, that insisted on being given attention. Emma didn't want to write like that. It's not her style. The outcome that she's enjoyed reflects the way the market operates and it's an outcome she's been entirely happy with.

For Richard and Jenny, the memoirists, a large audience might have been positively unwelcome. Their work traipsed across sensitive territory. If they had been asked to alter their work into a warts-and-all misery memoir, then no matter how large the potential sales through mass-market outlets, I think they'd still have said no. Other things mattered more. They've secured the readership they wanted, with a publisher who understands their project.

As for John, he doesn't take his work too seriously, but he enjoys it. If he can combine writing and a career, he'll go on doing just that. If his book sales ramp up from where they are now, then just possibly he'll put the career on hold and pay more attention to his writing – but he's a smart cookie, and he knows how precarious the writing world can be. I suspect he'll hang on to the monthly pay cheques for some time yet. If I were him, I'd do the same.

FINANCIAL CONSIDERATIONS

The list below attempts to put some very crude figures to these thoughts. It's crucial to stress that in books, perhaps more than in any other industry, it's hard to set benchmarks for the price of a particular product (and your book will, of course, be considered as just that – a product). First of all, the market is always changing. Then too, books are so wildly variable that no table can offer more than the very crudest indication of possible outcomes. Although the table already includes some quite broad bands for the range of possible advances and likely sales, there will be plenty of books that fall outside those bands. In short, please don't hang your hat on these numbers! They're intended as the roughest of rough guides only. (And indeed, if and when you get an agent, they won't tell you what advance they're hoping to achieve for your book. That's not because they're mean and won't tell you. It's because they're experienced enough to know that their private guesstimates may be way off the mark. And since we're tidily tucked away in parentheses at the moment, let me also add that this section is likely to raise as many questions in your mind as it answers. Don't worry. We'll get to everything in due course.)

Oh yes, and I've given guidance for typical US advances today. If you're British, the advances will be somewhat lower – but not nearly as much lower as you might think, given the size of the respective markets. Because this book has a global audience, I've tended to work with US dollars. You'll just need to make the adjustments in your head if you need to translate to pounds or Aussie dollars or the like.

Poetry
Typical advance: $0–$1,000
Typical sales: 50–500 paperback (pb)

Children's novel
Typical advance: $1–$20,000
Typical sales: 2–25,000 over pb and e-book

Niche literary fiction
Typical advance: $0–$5,000
Typical sales: up to 3–5,000 over hardback (hb) and pb

Specialist non-fiction
Typical advance: $3–$10,000
Typical sales: very variable, depending on segment

Mainstream non-fiction
Typical advance: $10–$75,000
Typical sales: 5–10,000 hb, plus maybe five times that in pb/e-book

Mainstream literary fiction
Typical advance: $10–$50,000
Typical sales: 5–10,000 hb

Mainstream commercial fiction
Typical advance: $30–$75,000
Typical sales: 10,000 in hb, plus five to ten times that in pb/e-book

Poetry, the first item on the list, is included for the sake of comparison more than anything else. Poetry occupies, at best, a semi-commercial corner of the publishing industry. If you don't have a major reputation already (and preferably a Nobel Prize to boot), then you are likely to be published only in a tiny print run by a specialist publisher who subsists in part on government or charitable funding. There may be some money involved in the deal, but, if you choose to celebrate your success with a meal out at a nice local restaurant, you'll probably have eaten and drunk your way through your advance before you get to coffee and mints.

When it comes to the wider market – novels and non-fiction, children's and adults – the possible outcomes splay out into a range so wide that it's hard to find meaningful benchmarks. I've distinguished between 'niche' and 'mainstream' as a way to separate out large publishers from small, and 'big' books from 'little' ones. A big book can usefully be defined as any book that is expected to grab a real slice of retail promotional space. That is, it can expect to grab serious levels of promotion via the supermarkets and other big hitters. A little book is one that will be distributed to many or most bookshops, but which doesn't feature in any promotion. For many types of book – a 'how-to' on dog grooming, let's say – there's no chance of being included in a promotion, no matter how good the book might be. Indeed, such a book will get almost all its sales via Amazon.

You need to be cautious in reading these ranges. A range of $30,000–$75,000 might imply that the average advance is smack in the middle of those two numbers, or about $50,000. Except that advances will cluster towards the bottom end of the range in pretty much every case, so the median payout will be less than you might guess. Sorry.

As for publishers, there are essentially five major publishers that straddle the English-speaking world. They are Penguin Random House, Hachette, HarperCollins, Macmillan, Simon & Schuster – the ranking is in terms of gross market share as it stands today. As I write, Simon & Schuster has put itself up for sale, with HarperCollins the most likely buyer. The one-time Big Six, currently the Big Five, is shrinking down to a Big Four.

You might be perplexed by that statement. Big Four? What about all those other names, the ones you actually see on the spines of your books? I'm thinking of names like Delacorte, Bantam Dell, Grand Central, Little Brown, Putnam, Sentinel, and bazillions of others. The answer is that each one of those names is an imprint – a brand name, effectively – of one of the big houses. These big companies are by far the best-funded publishers around and the ones best placed to pay out large advances.

After the Big Five, you get to a raft of independent publishers. Some of these are substantial. Some of them are excellent. Some are both. Kensington is a big US independent with an impressive backlist. Bloomsbury in the UK, best-known for Harry Potter, also runs a substantial trade publishing operation.

And of course, size isn't everything. Faber has revenues of under £20 million ($25 million), which makes it a minnow in normal corporate terms. But in publishing terms? Well, Faber is *Faber*, once the home of T. S. Eliot and publisher of no fewer than eleven Nobel prize-winners. I was once offered a deal by Faber, which I turned down because I was offered more money elsewhere. But still. I got a tickle of excitement from that offer just because of who it came from. Money isn't the only metric.

CAREER DEVELOPMENT

The final point to be made is that the table refers to debut advances. As soon as you have a sales record, your future advances will be determined largely by the number of books that you've sold in the past. Quite likely, that means your advance will be headed *down*, not up. That will strike almost every reader as bizarre. Surely, once you start to establish yourself, you'll begin to gather a readership, you'll get more reviews, you'll sell more books, and you'll start to prosper.

Impeccable as such logic seems to be, it's not correct. Fiction publishers lose money on a significant proportion of all books they sell, perhaps 70%. Obviously enough, they don't knowingly publish loss-makers, but it's hard to tell in advance which book will sell and which won't. The result is that most authors will see sales that lag behind their advance. These authors are likely to see a large drop in their advance when they come to negotiate a renewed book deal, or they may get no deal at all. Only where an author achieves sales well in excess of expectations is their advance likely to climb significantly.

I'll give you some examples of how this can work – all true.

One case involved an author of classy historical fiction. She's had great reviews. She is represented by a very well-connected agent. Her first book sold well, and her second book did better. She and her agent thought it would be a good idea to talk to her publisher about an advance for her third novel, then partially written. Because of broader market difficulty with this kind of fiction, both author and agent were expecting a reduction in the advance offered – perhaps a 30% cut. In actual fact, the publisher came back offering an advance that was a full 70% lower than before, an amount so derisory that in any other industry the offer would have represented an only semi-polite way to tell somebody that they weren't wanted. Yikes.

Or take another example. A Jericho Writers client came to us with a well-written and unusual memoir. We helped him get it into shape, then took it to a very capable agent, who took him on and sold his book for an excellent £75,000 to one of the biggest publishers in the true-life-story area. The book sold so-so in hardback, but it wasn't really a hardback sort of book. In paper covers, the book leapt straight on to the non-fiction bestseller lists and stayed there for weeks.

Now, unusually, the author in question had a second volume of memoir as good as the first. I've read both books and can genuinely say that there was nothing to choose between them. Alas, the publisher decided that a few weeks on the bestseller list weren't enough to justify a further advance, so they didn't offer anything at all for that second book, which has remained unsold and unpublished.

Facts like these will shock almost any industry outsider. They should shock you. And alas, it's rare that agents or publishers discuss them fully with authors. Consequently, it's commonplace for authors to import to their new career the assumptions and beliefs taken from their old one – assumptions that suggest talent will be rewarded, that seniority and experience will be appropriately valued. This approach, unfortunately, can easily prove unhelpful.

I speak from experience. My first novel sold for a good, strong sum. It was energetically and successfully marketed by my publisher, HarperCollins. The book was accepted into a number of major promotions and sold well. The second book sold less well – perhaps the cover design was not quite right? Perhaps the book itself was not quite as well-judged as the first? Nevertheless, that second book was one of the summer books of the year in Britain's biggest high-street retailer and a film company sought to option it. The book was hardly a dud.

Fresh from experience in a more normal career, I assumed that I was doing well. My next book was better than either of my first two. I'd built a platform. The next steps would be onwards and upwards, right? Full of confidence, I bought a new house. I didn't move anywhere crazy, I just assumed that my income wasn't about to plummet. Bad move. In fact, the advance I was offered for my next couple of books was almost 40% lower than for the first pair. Looking back, and knowing what I know now, I'm astonished at how generous that offer was. The truth is, Harper-Collins must really have liked my work and remained willing to pay over the odds to keep me. Nevertheless, that plummeting advance meant I was now in a house too expensive for my income and I was forced to sell it. (Fortunately for me, a crazy property market meant I made money anyway.)

So much for some stories of disaster. Here's one with a totally different flavour.

A friend of mine sold a crime novel to a major publisher for $10,000. That sum represented the sale of world rights: that is, the publishers had the right to sell that book across the world in any language. The sum paid was right at the bottom end of what any such publisher would normally offer for a book like that.

But –

The book was superbly marketed. It had a killer twist. The author's backstory had some resonances with the one in the book, which made it easy to find publicity. The author was very capable and driven and made the most of that launch. The result was that the book sold well over a million copies worldwide, got listed in a ton of award shortlists, and launched an extremely strong, global career. In short, while authorial careers are certainly precarious, they aren't only downwardly precarious. Phew!

WRITERS' INCOMES

Another way to look at these matters is by looking at author incomes. I'll present the data in a second but, first, a word of caution.

These surveys are generally anything from bad to terrible. Those that I've seen are clunkily constructed, often with questions that are unclear, intrusive, or burdensome. Response rates are low and, because the sample is self-selecting, it's not clear how representative the answers are. A further problem arises because of self-published authors. It makes no sense to exclude such writers, because they form a large part of the market and make up a large proportion of the authors earning at any income threshold you care to name. At the same time, there's an extremely long tail of indie authors who earn little or nothing. That long tail just drags down the overall stats, without illuminating anything much.

In brief, I don't much like the data, but for what it's worth, the Authors Guild in the US, together with some partner organisations, surveyed 5,000 published authors in 2018. Here's what they found:

- A small majority of respondents said that writing was their primary occupation.
- About half were traditionally published only. About a quarter were self-published only. The balance did a bit of both (which is, by the way, a highly rational approach and one that I commend to you in the fullness of time.)
- The median income of these authors was a miserly $6,080. (That sum relates to the portion of your income which re-lates only to writing and writing-related activities. If you also make a living as an accountant or a gardener, that in-come is excluded.) In theory, that's down from a 2009 figure of $10,500, except that the approach to survey col-lection was so different, I don't think it makes sense to compare one to another. The 2018 median income from writing alone was just $3,900. (The broader total includes such non-book-related items as speaking fees, editorial work, and the like.)

- If you ignore the part-time or self-published component of the survey, and look only at full-time, traditionally published authors, incomes look a little better – though at $20,300 annually, you are going to need a trust fund, a rich partner or a sideline in computer fraud to make ends meet.

The same basic picture applies in the UK and elsewhere. Despite the weakness of the data, I think there's little doubt that trad-published authors are badly paid, and that earnings have been in long-term decline. There is also a very long tail of writers who earn essentially nothing at all – trad-oriented writers who fail to get a book deal and self-published authors who never make any meaningful sales.

Again, all these figures relate to medians. Thus, to say that the median income from writing is £4,000 means that there are exactly 50% of writers who earn more than this figure and exactly 50% who earn less. Because there are a handful of super-well-paid authors around, the average (or mean) figure is significantly higher than these medians, just as the mean income in any room would jump if Jeff Bezos happened to walk into it. The median is a better reflection of likely outcomes, however.

THE IMPORTANCE OF PASSION

This section opened by asking about motives and expectations and has spent nearly all its time discussing money. In a strange way, however, that takes us back to the heart of the question. There can be money in writing, but for most people, most of the time, there isn't very much. Authorial careers tend to be short and precarious. There's no sick pay. No health coverage. No unemployment support. No pension. Which, when you think about it, is liberating. You didn't start out writing your book to make money or pay the mortgage or buy that yacht you'd always dreamed of. You started it because of a passion to write, to communicate, to spin dreams and inform others.

Good. You need to hold on to those motivations, as they're the only ones which can reliably sustain you. That's not to say you should give up thoughts of commercial success altogether. On the contrary, this book aims to give you a road map that will maximise your chances of selling books to the very limits of your potential. But selling books is as much about the desire to communicate, to connect with readers, to pass on your vision to others as it is about making money.

Because most authors will want to get as many readers as possible and (secondarily) to earn as much as possible from that readership, this book will concentrate on the centre ground of publishing: the territory of agents, major publishers, retail promotions, and all the rest of it. But not all authors will make it to that centre ground, and nor should they necessarily want to. At the opening of this part, I mentioned three authorial trajectories: Emma, Richard and Jenny, and John. All four authors have done well, in terms of what they have got out of writing. The satisfaction is primarily artistic in Emma's case. For Richard and Jenny, their satisfaction came from having grappled some meaning out of their own personal battles, and from having been able to put that experience to use in the service of others. John, the only one to have clambered securely on to that centre ground, finds that he gets a kick from writing, he gets a kick from his fans, he likes the diversity that writing has brought to his life, and (even for a talented management consultant) the money is welcome. None of the four, however, has chosen to become a full-time professional. Most writers don't. The centre ground of writing isn't the only territory that matters, and this book will pay plenty of attention to the more remote corners of the landscape as well.

It's important to remember these things as you read on. All authors need to find a meeting point between what they want to write and what the market will buy. You can't neglect the latter, because if you do, you'll remain unpublished. But you mustn't even think of giving up on the former, because that will void your writing of the one purpose that you can entirely rely on: your own passion, the very thing that brought you to writing in the first place.

Is Your Book Ready to Go?

A typical agent will receive approximately 2,000 submissions a year. From that pile, he (or, more likely, she) will offer representation to perhaps two clients. Some agents will find themselves taking more than that, but others may go a year or more without taking anyone from the slush pile. The sheer difficulty of getting representation has given rise to a belief that the whole damn industry is a conspiracy of the metropolitan elite where people with big houses in the country throw commissions out to their friends whilst excluding everyone with the misfortune to have only one surname.

If there is such a conspiracy, then I have yet to find it. The simple truth is that quality sells. There are some caveats that we'll come to in due course, but the caveats are much less important than the headline itself. Quality sells.

When manuscripts don't sell, when they get rejected by agents, it's almost always because the darn things were never good enough in the first place, and that in turn means that writers are sending them out prematurely. The purpose of this section is to give you pause. Is your manuscript genuinely ready to send out as it is? Does it need more work? And, if so, are you capable of doing that work on your own, or will you need outside assistance?

PAUSING FOR BREATH

Every now and then, we at Jericho Writers receive an enquiry which says, roughly, 'I've completed the first three chapters of my novel. Do you think I should contact agents now or wait until I've written a little more?' The answer, emphatically, is that you need to wait. (With fiction, that is. The situation with non-fiction is a tad more complex – more of that shortly.) You don't just need to wait until you have bustled your way to the final full stop. You need to wait until your novel is perfected. To properly professional writers, the first draft is just that: a working draft which may need to be completely rewritten. Indeed, I know one prize-winning author whose working routine is: (1) write a complete first draft of her novel; (2) read it, then throw it away; (3) write a completely new draft; (4 – optional) repeat steps two and three; (5) work on the final draft to bring it all the way up to the required standard. Not every author is quite as committed to rewriting as that, but I don't know any quality author who isn't a serious rewriter and self-editor.

One of the most important tips here is also the simplest: take your time. Once you've completed your manuscript, read it through once, then put it away in a bottom drawer. If you can, spend the next few weeks doing something entirely different. Go on holiday, take up sailing, run a marathon, have an affair. Come back to your project once enough time and life have elapsed to give you a sober view of it. Then reread your work from cover to cover. Jot down thoughts as they occur to you, but avoid getting stuck into any actual editing yet, because the process will distract you from the big picture.

With luck, the reading process will shift your mindset. Any writer, as they're ploughing ahead with a first-draft manuscript, needs to keep themself motivated. That can often mean living in a warm haze of self-deception, in which every sentence seems brilliant, every plot point inspired. Good. There's nothing wrong with that. I've been there myself, and plenty of others are the same. When it comes to rewriting, however, you need to turn from Mr or Ms Indulgent to Mr or Ms Savage. You need to scour your work for its failures. You need to anguish about sentence construction and pick away at flaws in plot and character. If you aren't as ruthless as you were once kind, you simply aren't exposing your work to the kind of scrutiny it needs.

What's more, you need to set no prior limits to how much rewriting may be required. I know one leading author who wrote four novels which remained unpublished before selling her fifth. I myself deleted the opening 60,000 words of my first novel, because I realised that my writing had developed through the course of the book, and the opening material wasn't as good as the stuff later on. With my second novel, I realised that my first draft was rubbish, so I deleted the whole damn thing and started again from a blank screen. I'm not advising that you need to take action as radical as this, but you mustn't rule it out in advance. What matters is quality and only quality. If you don't care enough about excellence, your lack of care is certain to show. Agents and publishers have thousands of other manuscripts to choose from. Make them choose you.

As the roughest of rough guides, I'd suggest that reaching that final beautiful 'THE END' represents an approximate halfway point. If you spend as much time on revising and perfecting your work as you did on writing it in the first place, then you'll have got it about right. As you develop your skills, the time spent revising may drop. In any case, you should forget about time spent. Effort doesn't matter; quality does. If what you produce is excellent, then the time you've taken to get there has already been rewarded.

GETTING HELP FOR FREE

Different writers work differently. In my own case, I wrote my first novel chapter by chapter. Because I had three stories running in parallel, I didn't even write the book sequentially. I wrote it in three separate strands, then assembled them all by spending two days in the living room on my hands and knees shuffling the chapters into an order that I was happy with and building a giant spreadsheet to keep track of it all. I then revised the novel intensively. I handed it out to family and friends (beta-readers, in the jargon) and solicited comments.

I thought hard about getting external professional feedback on my work but decided against it. I went straight out to agents. The first six said no. I didn't know it at the time, but my query letter was disastrous and some of those first six would have rejected the manuscript without reading so much as a sentence. I thought again about getting professional feedback, but again decided against it. I went to six more agents and obtained two offers of representation. (Actually, three, but one of the offers was from someone I am convinced was a lunatic.) In any case, with two sane offers, I was up and running.

I mention this experience because I need to flag up a conflict of interest. I'm the owner of Jericho Writers. Among many other services, we offer tough, expert editorial advice to first-time writers. So it is, in principle, in my interest to sell you our (very excellent) editing help.

So yes, I have a conflict. But let me be clear: although there are huge advantages in getting third party advice, that route is not right for everyone. It wasn't right for me. It may not be right for you.

With that caveat in place, let's review the options. The first and most obvious source is family and friends. These people are likely to come up with a few helpful observations. A plot issue here. An aspect of character there. Such things matter and can help improve a book.

But you need to be realistic. There are only two sorts of people who have a genuinely expert grasp of editorial work: those with real editorial expertise inside a publishing house, and those who have written and sold work themselves. Unless your friends and family are all novelists and editors, you are unlikely to get anything approaching systematic and rigorous feedback. It's not enough that Uncle Fred has written an academic text on management theory or that dear Aunt Hephzibah has taught English for years. Those things do not equip them to edit your novel. By all means, solicit comments, but don't assume that they represent the final word on anything.

While we're still in brutal realism mode, let's just slay another myth. Agents do not give feedback to non-clients. If you send your material out to agents hoping to get feedback on your work, you will be cruelly disappointed. Agents receive 1,000 manuscripts for every one they take on. If they gave editorial advice to the 999 rejectees, they wouldn't have time to wash or eat, let alone do their job. Every now and then an agent may reject a manuscript with a personal note that adds a few words of editorial explanation but, most likely, you'll just get no feedback at all.

SEEKING EXPERT PROFESSIONAL HELP

Many writers will decide to move beyond the mere beta-reader and onto proper, professional feedback. Good. That feedback, in my opinion, is and has always been the gold-standard way for improving a manuscript. Not one of my books has ever been published without that input (usually supplied free by my publisher). None of my books will ever be published any other way. No manuscript is good to go in its first draft. But no manuscript is beyond improvement even in its twentieth draft. An expert outside eye – sympathetic, but rigorous – is the best way to make those difficult last yards from good to dazzling.

So, what are the options? What do you need? And what should you look for?

Well, to start with the last question first, you are looking for someone with real editorial experience. I'd say that a more confident, later-stage writer will tend to do well with editors of a publishing-type background. Those guys are good at helping a nearly publishable manuscript go the final distance. If you're at an earlier stage in your career, then you may well prefer the services of someone whose background is primarily authorial. After all, an author is a practitioner. An author's day job is to solve the exact same problems that are in front of you right now: weak characters, sloppy pacing, inconsistent plotting, and all the rest of it. If you're not sure whether you're late-stage or early-stage – well, don't worry. Good editors are good editors, and if you feel the fit is right, it probably will be.

Things get a bit more delicate when it comes to what the various editorial options are. The main flavours on offer are:

(1) **Manuscript critique**, also called manuscript assessment or manuscript appraisal or, in some contexts, structural editing. A critique is pretty much what it sounds like. You'll get a detailed report on what is and isn't working, plus constructive advice on what to do next. The emphasis of the report will be, inevitably, on the things that aren't yet working. That sounds mean-spirited, except that there's no point paying someone to tell you all the things that are great. Think of a manuscript critique as a professionally drawn-up snagging list for a major building job. You don't especially like what it's telling you, but you certainly need it.

(2) **Developmental editing** is a slightly blurry term which is usually defined as one round of manuscript critique combined with extensive marginal annotations/corrections. Unsurprisingly, this is an expensive service, sometimes as much as $0.05 a word. Quoting stuff in cents makes it sound blessedly cheap, but on that basis, a 100,000-word manuscript will cost you $5,000 to put right. Yikes!

(3) **Line-editing** is just what it sounds like. Someone goes through your manuscript and cleans it up at a sentence-by-sentence level. That should cover the tasks involved in copyediting (typos, spelling, punctuation and the like), but it's broader. A good line-edit will make baggy sentences economical, confusing ones clear, and soggy ones crisp. It's like the ultimate manuscript wash-and-brush-up. Think of it as a crisply laundered suit and a very nice haircut.

(4) **Copyediting** is like line-editing, but narrower in scope. Yes, a copyeditor may silently correct a particularly clunky sentence, but for the most part, a copyeditor will limit

themselves to correcting typos, misspellings, erroneous punctuation, awkward repetitions, manuscript inconsistencies and the like. You can think of it as the nice bit of house-tidying you do before your mother-in-law arrives. Not strictly essential, but a nice welcoming touch.

(5) **Proofreading.** I've listed this as a kind of editing for the sake of completeness, but nothing more. Proofreading is the last whizz-round you do after the manuscript has been typeset for print (or formatted for e-book) but before it's been published. If copyediting is what you do when you are preparing for your mother-in-law's visit, then proofreading is what you do when you actually see your mother-in-law's car pulling into your driveway. Bit of fluff on the floor? Pick it up. Weird stain in the kitchen? Cover it with a teapot.

Assuming that you are hell-bent on traditional publication, you don't really need either of the last two things. If you get a publishing deal, then your manuscript will be copyedited, typeset, formatted and proofread, all for free. It's part of what your publisher does. The only exceptions would be if you have an unusual problem at the text level – you're dyslexic, say, or you are an excellent but non-native speaker of English. In either of those cases, you might possibly want a professional to look over the manuscript before it goes out to agents.

But before all you dyslexic Norwegians go charging off to pay for copyediting, you need to pause. Copyediting is essentially a cosmetic task, and there's no point in doing it if the basic structures aren't in good order first. I've come across people who have paid $1500 and more for a copyedit when I knew for a fact that the underlying manuscript had major structural issues. Put bluntly, until those underlying issues were fixed, the manuscript would be unpublishable no matter how many nice suits and fancy haircuts it wore.

That same issue pushes back into line-editing and developmental editing too. Both services are expensive because of the line-by-line, word-by-word work involved. And if your manuscript isn't structurally sound, all that work is at risk of being wasted.

All that might sound odd to you: after all, here I am, the owner of a major editorial service company warning you of the risks of buying editorial help. And yes, I am. But what I'm really saying is that your starting point should always be the manuscript critique (or assessment, or structural editorial review, or whatever the heck you want to call it). That service focuses on the big issues of plot, character, point of view, pacing, theme and everything else that goes up to make up a great book. It's that service above all that helps a book to shine. If you care to get outside help, it's there you should start. If you want to go ahead and purchase line-editing or some hi-spec developmental package, then feel free. But for the most part, I'd say that you should get that manuscript critique, rework the manuscript, and then take stock as to whether or not you need all the other bells and whistles. You probably don't.

Finally, before you toddle off to get yourself a manuscript assessment – and did I mention that Jericho Writers is an excellent source for such things? – do remember to check exactly what you're getting. Some services are cheap but deliver a report of just one or two single-spaced pages. A report that brief is pretty much valueless.

Our own experience at Jericho Writers has been that an editorial report needs to be at least 3,000 words long to be of value. (I'm assuming here that the underlying manuscript is a full-length adult novel of at least 60,000 words; shorter manuscripts may well need less commentary.) If you aren't getting that kind of in-depth report, the editor is almost certainly missing stuff that you really need to know.

I'd also say that you need to be able to interrogate the editor once you receive your report. That doesn't need to be a two-hour Skype call or anything like it. Truth is, the editorial report should tell you everything you need to know. Yes, you may want to understand exactly what an editor means by X, or whether she thinks that doing Z could work instead of the Y approach she recommended. But really, those are just clarifications.

Now, you just need to figure out what to do next.

HOW TO WORK WITH EDITORIAL FEEDBACK

The first thing to say is simply – you're allowed to cry.

That's not a joke. You really are, and some people do. I've been a pro author for two decades and getting editorial feedback is still, amazingly, an emotional process. I don't actually cry, but hearing an editor dismiss a particular thing you've laboured hard to achieve is always bruising. It's not just that your ego takes a knock; it's also that you hoped your work was done and the editorial report makes you aware there's weeks more to do yet.

So let those feelings out. Yell. Scream. Kick a pillow. Take a walk. Go for a swim. Eat a hamburger as big as your head.

A day or two later, you should be able to go back to the editor's notes with a little more calmness. Remember that your editor is an adviser offering an opinion, not a superior officer issuing orders. You are free to pick and choose which suggestions to follow and which to leave.

Very approximately, I'd guess you'd want to take 60% of your editor's suggestions and implement them very much as proposed. With another 20% or so, you may understand the editor's reservations about your current draft but take a different approach to solving them. And with the last 20%? Well, heck, you're the author. This is your book. Sometimes, you'll just want to say, 'Yes, well, I hear what you say, but I like it like this, so I ain't changing.' Take that approach too far and you'll probably have a lousy book. But there are risks in being over-obedient as well. You are an author. Your writing should have force, personality and idiosyncrasy. Those things are a sign of good writing. And if that sometimes means saying no to a capable, intelligent and sympathetic editor? Well, so be it. Me, I do it all the time.

OTHER SOURCES OF HELP

Getting one-to-one feedback on your manuscript is the only way to get commentary that is entirely focused around you and your work as it stands now. Nevertheless, there are a whole host of other support services, some of which may be helpful. Of these, the ones you're most likely to be interested in are:

Online courses

Once you've written a complete manuscript, or are a good way into a particular project, distance learning courses are likely to be frustratingly non-responsive to your needs. That said, there are some really brilliant self-editing courses which centre themselves around the work you've already done. (We run a spectacularly good one of these, but it's always booked up, so that may not help much. Sorry!) Likewise, and especially if you're at an earlier phase of your writing career, then any course on how to write a novel will help build your basic technical skills. Those things will inevitably feed through to your work in progress, so your manuscript will improve, as it were, via the backdoor.

Mentoring

If you have already completed (or largely completed) your manuscript, then I'd suggest a manuscript critique as an essential first step. Occasionally, and depending on what you learn from your editor, it may be that you want to rework your manuscript in the company of someone who knows what they're doing. Buying some mentoring time, most likely from your existing editor, can be a really great way to do this. It means that when you strike out in a new direction, you have someone looking over your shoulder making sure that the direction you've chosen is roughly right.

MA/MFA courses in creative writing

Most people reading this book are likely to have gone beyond the point of considering a university-level creative writing course, but the option exists and has become strangely popular. One obvious benefit is that you get to go back to college to explore your creative side. If your tutors and fellow students are inspiring and delightful, you'll have a good time, you'll become a better writer, and you'll end up with a deeper appreciation of literature.

On the other hand, most of these courses believe that it's their job, first and foremost, to encourage students in their creative endeavours. That culture has its merits, but it can seriously mislead students as to the standards demanded by the publishing industry – or the kind of books that the publishing industry is interested in.

Such courses can also leave students shockingly ignorant about even elementary matters to do with the business. On the day of writing this, for example, I got an email from a master's degree graduate of a well-known creative writing school asking me whether I thought that self-publishing or approaching agents was a better first line of attack. I mean, that's a perfectly logical question – and, to emphasise, self-publishing is a perfectly reasonable strategy – but what the heck is a creative writing school doing with its students if it hasn't explored those issues in depth already? I was shocked at how unprepared that graduate seemed to be for his chosen profession.

It's also rare to find a creative writing course which is as serious about genre fiction as it is about literary fiction. There's just no excuse. Is Elmore Leonard not a serious, wonderful author? And what about Gillian Flynn? Or Patricia Highsmith? Or John le Carré? Or Aldous Huxley, Ursula le Guin, Margaret Atwood, Neil Gaiman? Genre fiction is, in the end, just another name for the fiction that people most like reading. The idea that a course on writing should ignore such work is just ridiculous.

So I have my concerns. But for literary writers for whom self-expression is or may be more important than commercial publication, then an MFA or MA course may prove joyous and fulfilling. Just check the course out carefully before you go. (You may also want to check out Jericho Writers' own Ultimate Novel Writing Course[1], which doesn't confer any kind of degree, but which does attempt to model the kind of course we'd want to go on ourselves.)

Writers' conferences

Writers' conferences provide an excellent way for first-time writers to meet professional authors, agents and editors. Most such conferences offer a good mix of keynote speeches, workshops and informal opportunities to make contacts. Most will also offer participants a chance to pitch their work directly to agents.

That all sounds like a rich, useful, practical brew, but a good conference should have a generous splash of inspiration, exhaustion and sheer damn fun. There's something about the synchronicity of everything that creates the magic. You go to a plotting workshop in the morning and finally solve the thing that's been bugging you for five months. You see an agent who likes your work. (Yay!) You see an agent who doesn't, but has something really insightful to offer. (Sort of boo! But also sort of yay!) Then you go to two more really helpful workshops – on prose style and marketing – before collapsing into the grateful arms of a bottle of Pinot Noir in the company of three writers you've never met before but who feel like real friends by the end of the evening. You end those weekends feeling clearer, brighter – and astonished that the whole thing only took two or three days. I can't quite explain the time-tunnel nature of it all. All I can tell you is that it's a real phenomenon.

In the US, the conferences with the best reputations are probably the Writer's Digest Conference (though the parent company has gone bankrupt, so changes may be afoot), the San Francisco Writers Conference, and the Novelists, Inc. (NINC) Conference, which gets rave reviews from everyone who attends (though you

---

[1] https://jerichowriters.com/ultimate-novel-writing-course

do need to be at least somewhat of a pro before you can go). In the UK, there's less on offer, so I don't even feel too guilty about mentioning our own Festival of Writing, which is not just the biggest event of its kind in the UK, but also by a million miles the best.

Before you rush off to book your tickets, however, a word of realism. Yes, these conferences will add to your understanding of the industry, and you should have a brilliant time. But they're not magic. If your work isn't strong enough, then no matter how entertaining, witty, personable and polished you are when meeting agents, you will not be taken on. It's the manuscript that matters.

CONCLUSION

If you've written your manuscript, paused for breath, then revised and edited as hard as you possibly can, you should now be ready for the next step: going out to the market. We'll turn our attention to that in a moment, but first we'll quickly review what's needed for a good non-fiction book proposal. If you've already completed your book, or if you're writing a novel, you can skip the next section and move on to the one after.

How to Assemble a Proposal

If you are writing a novel, you need to complete it before you think of going out to agents or publishers – there are some exceptions to this rule, but very few. If you are writing non-fiction, however, things are more shaded, and it may not be necessary to write your book in full – or even a single word of it – before writing to agents or publishers. This section is about the non-fiction book proposal, and how to judge what you need in order to put it together.

NARRATIVE-LED NON-FICTION

Some non-fiction nestles close-up against the novel in terms of structure and impulse. A memoir, for example, needs rich characters, a strong sense of movement and story, and vibrantly described settings to succeed. That's pretty much a tick-list for writing a decent novel, except of course that the memoir needs to be true. The same goes for most travel writing and for many biographies. With all such works, you probably need to have written the entire book to convince an agent or publisher to take you on.

This rule isn't absolute, however, and there are exceptions. If, for example, you are a journalist and you have a stunning story to tell – let's say you had some unique access to and experience of the Trump White House – you can sell your book on the basis of two or three opening chapters and a quick outline of what will follow. The same is true if you have a plausible writing back-ground (which doesn't include business or academic writing) and you are writing the biography of some obviously interesting person. For example, if you're a TV writer and are collaborating with a famous mountaineer about a story of triumph and disaster in the mountains, again you can probably sell the book off three chapters and an outline.

On the whole, though, the rule is the rule. I know one writer who ghosted a memoir of the first woman to serve in the French Foreign Legion. That book sold for an enormous advance but did so off a 'book proposal' that was almost one hundred pages long. In other words, the writer (who was very experienced) was at pains to make sure that her proposal left nothing out in terms of story. There were gaps as regards characterisations, settings and a host of incidental details – but the agents and publishers were able to read the story at length and knew that the author's prior track record guaranteed an excellent execution of the complete book. In such a case, a debut author would have been very well-advised to write the whole damn thing before seeking to sell it. The same goes for any type of story-led non-fiction.

POPULAR SUBJECT-LED NON-FICTION

There's a further category of non-fiction, which is subject-led, but where tone and treatment is crucial. My own *This Little Britain*, for example, was a book which looked at all the ways in which British history diverged from that of its neighbours; my subjects ranged from the early adoption of the rule of law to why English spelling is quite so bananas. That's clearly a book which would be interesting to publishers in principle, but the project's success relied entirely on my ability to deal with a broad range of subjects in an engaging way. The result was that I assembled a book proposal which comprised:

- **An introduction**

    The introduction was, in effect, both an outline of what the book would look at and a justification for why such a survey was important and worthwhile – a manifesto for the book, if you like. The introduction was written with not only agents and publishers in mind but also the ordinary reader. The introduction in the book proposal was almost precisely the one that wound up in the book.

- **A handful of short chapters**

  These amounted to some 12,000–15,000 words in total. In the case of *This Little Britain*, the chapters were picked largely at random. In a more structured work, it might be necessary to include the first three chapters. The crucial thing, however, is that you include enough material to allow publishers to form an opinion on whether you'll be able to convey complex material in an entertaining manner.

- **A two-to-three-page outline of the book**

  If the introduction and the sample material are strong enough, the outline may not matter much. In the case of *This Little Britain*, the book's range of subject matter was so broad that I simply hadn't bothered to research it all at the proposal stage. As a result, many of my individual chapter outlines were cryptic in the extreme. They were broad gestures at the territory, not attempts to set out the precise lie of the land. This technique worked fine: I honestly don't think the publishers who bid for the book either noticed or cared. Why would they? I'd delivered half-a-dozen chapters that were funny, authoritative and thought-provoking. I'd indicated a host of further subjects that I wanted to tackle. That was enough.

If you are writing a book in any popular subject-led non-fiction area, then a book proposal on these lines will serve you just fine.

If you're not sure whether yours is a 'popular' title or not, then have a think about whether you can plausibly see it on the front table of a major store chain. If you can, then it's popular non-fiction. If you can't, it may still be 'popular', in the sense that your style needs to attract people who aren't technically specialist. And remember, if you want a wide audience who will read your book for fun, you must write in a popular way. No shortcuts, no excuses. Yes, you may have all the knowledge and authority in the world, but if your book feels like a chore to read, no one will read it. So entertain. It's your job.

TECHNICAL SUBJECT-LED NON-FICTION

Where a book proposal concerns a fairly narrow and technical subject, it can be fairly brief. A decent proposal might do no more than:

- Outline the market.
- Identify the main existing texts.
- Explain why your proposed hook brings something new and important.
- Outline your qualifications to write it.
- Summarise in a few pages the proposed outline of your work.

If a gap in the market exists, and if you are amply qualified to fill it, you may not actually need to supply a single specimen chapter of the intended book. The very first version of this book, for example, was commissioned by Bloomsbury on the basis of a proposal that contained no sample material at all. My future editor agreed that there was a gap in the market. My qualifications to write the book were strong. The outline proposal covered everything necessary. That was all she needed to know.

Now, it's true that I came to this book with a publication history, but that only mattered because of my subject matter. If my book had concerned fly-fishing, or computational techniques in statistics, or the history of croquet, no one would have expected me to come brandishing a publication track record.

Most proposals will need you to say something about the market for your book. That's hard, because you don't have access to reliable sources of data, but you can do your best. That means going to Amazon, perusing your subject area and (over at least a month) getting a sense for the bestsellers in your category. Do note that Amazon's sales ranks are very volatile, especially in their lower reaches, so you do need to check a book's rank a number of times over the course of a few weeks in order to get a fair sense of its steady state position. You can then use that data to guide your comments about the market. Yes, publishers will then be able to assess the market more accurately than you, using their own data sources, but the fact that you've made a serious attempt to scope things out will count heavily in your favour.

Finally, although getting the book proposal right matters a lot, once you've got a contract you should feel free to depart from the precise terms of the proposal, if you feel that would help the book. I doubt if any of my four works of non-fiction have followed my book proposal precisely. I'm also sure that none of my editors noticed or cared. All that matters, in the end, is that you are following roughly the lines that you first sketched – and that the final manuscript is as wonderful and compelling as it can possibly be.

THE IMPORTANCE OF ANGLE

The issue of angle is extremely important. Since there are a zillion books already written, all subject areas will already be crowded. My book on British history, for example, was exciting because it found a new way to look at the past. If I had simply been reprising facts familiar from countless existing histories, I wouldn't have got anywhere.

There are, of course, a few books with no obvious predecessors: Dava Sobel's *Longitude* was one such book; so was J. D. Vance's *Hillbilly Elegy*. But even those books exist within a broader genre (history books, works on contemporary American society), and your book has to be able to bustle its way to the front of the mob.

At Jericho Writers, people often come to us with a manuscript that addresses some popular 'how-to' area: diet, perhaps, or leadership/motivation. The writing may be perfectly good. The writer may be somewhat authoritative: perhaps they practise as a dietician or as a motivational trainer. The subject is clearly important enough to merit a book, since shedloads of books are sold in these areas each year. Very often, however, the angle is completely missing. We tell the author that their book isn't distinguishing itself from countless other titles in the genre, many of which have celebrity endorsement, or are familiar from TV, or already have bestseller status in the much larger US market.

The writer is often incredulous. 'But what I'm saying is *true*', they tell us. 'My stuff *helps* people.' They're probably right. But being right is not an angle. When a potential reader is browsing the dozens of available diet books, they're not going to know whether your arguments are true or not. They're going to look at the title, then the cover, then the blurb. They might dip into the 'Look Inside' area on Amazon as well. That's it. That's how long you have to convince the reader that your strategy is the right one for them. That means you need to think about your book the way a brand-strategist thinks about canned beans; the way a copywriter thinks about a TV commercial.

And if you don't think about angle, an agent will. If your book doesn't have one, a good one, it'll be turned down flat. And quite right too.

WHICH AGENT? WHICH PUBLISHER?

Most authors, well before they even finish their work, will start to Google 'literary agents'. They'll pore over the various sites and listings, trying to sense which of these sacred names is going to be The One. Depending on taste, they may also start to highlight names, compile matrices, compare websites, make phone calls or (who knows?) fashion an array of voodoo dolls out of candle wax and matchsticks.

I'm entirely in favour of all these activities and was as prey to them as anyone else at one stage in my career. On the other hand, I'd gently suggest that there are some elementary steps that may be useful supports to the voodoo-doll and sacred-name procedures. The very first step is simple. Ask yourself: do you even need an agent?

WHO NEEDS AN AGENT?

Not everyone needs an agent. There are some who emphatically **do** need agents, who persist in sending their work to publishers and who will be doomed to failure until they shift their focus. But there's also – inevitably – a middle ground where there's room for doubt. Here's what you need to know:

You do need an agent, if ...

... you are writing any kind of mainstream book. A mainstream book is anything that you might see in a prominent position in a major bookstore or supermarket. If you've written a novel (for adults or kids), you need an agent. If you've written a work of popular non-fiction, you need an agent. Travel books, memoirs, popular science, biographies, popular history and some 'how-to' titles all need agents. The reason why you need an agent for work of this sort is that the major publishers of books like these don't even look at unagented work (or if they do, they do so only in an absent-minded and neglectful way). Without an agent, therefore, you are cutting yourself off from the most important possible market for your work.

You don't need an agent, if …

… your book is highly specialist. An agent will take a commission, usually of 15%, on any money they make on your behalf. If your book is a specialist one – *The ABC of Snowmobile Maintenance, Avant-Garde Knitting for the Experienced Knitter, A Primer on Early Medieval Manuscripts* – it's not going to sell for very much money. 15% of not very much money isn't going to keep an agent in champagne and Marc Jacobs for more than a few seconds, so they will have no interest in representing you. But plenty of publishers specialise in books just such as these. Motor publishers who want books on snowmobiles. Craft publishers who love knitting. Academic publishers who go all pink and giggly when a primer on early medieval manuscripts plops through their letterbox. In all such cases, you need to cut out the agent and head straight to the relevant publisher.

You might want an agent, if …

Needless to say, there's a middle ground where it's unclear whether an agent should or should not handle your work. Snowmobile maintenance texts only appeal to a small audience, but what about a *Field Guide to American Flowers*? As it happens, a client of ours wrote such a book and got a deal by going direct to a specialist publisher. On the other hand, I could imagine an agent receiving a proposal like that and thinking, 'Not my usual area, but there must be a lot of flower-lovers out there, and maybe I could sell this guide for a lowish advance and pick up a stream of royalty earnings over the years as well.' If that agent happened to be in need of a new pair of Marc Jacobs at the time, then that might just have been enough to clinch the deal.

Children's picture books are another area of unclarity. There are some good agents who specialise in such texts. Equally, publishers are happy to look at unagented work. Do you need an agent or not? Well, no, you don't *need* one, but you may nevertheless *want* one. It's up to you. If in doubt, my advice would be to get an agent. Once you've established a decent name in the field and started to learn the ropes yourself, you may well feel better off managing your career by yourself. I know a very successful author of children's picture books and novels who took exactly that route.

ASKING A BANKER ABOUT BONUSES

One last word before leaving this subject. If you're unsure about whether you want an agent or a publisher, never make the mistake of approaching agents and publishers simultaneously. If an agent is interested in taking you on, they'll be extremely disconcerted that you've made prior approaches to publishers. If those publishers have already said no (perhaps because you approached the wrong editor in the wrong way at the wrong time), you'll have impaired the agent's chances of securing a deal and the agent will therefore be more likely to reject you too.

If, by chance, you approach a major publisher with a mainstream novel and get it accepted (a rare but not impossible occurrence), then you have the opposite problem – and a nice one to have. Although you'll be delirious about the acceptance, you'll also suddenly realise that you have no idea what you're doing and that you really, really need an agent. At that point, however, it's easy. All you need to do is contact a handful of agents, tell them you have a significant offer from a major publisher, and ask if it's possible that they'd like to represent you. Although agents will certainly want to read your work and make sure that they like it too, the commercial proposition is an easy one, as they know there's money to be made. It's a bit like asking a banker whether he fancies a bonus: the answer is likely to be yes.

Though this sequence is rare, I know one very high-profile author who took this route. A publisher waded through the slush pile, found her work, loved it and made an excellent offer. The author thought, 'By heck, I'd better get me an agent,' so she did just that. Her agent did what any competent salesman would do and auctioned the book off to the highest bidder. The initial publisher still loved the book and raised his offer to crazy new heights, but he was still outbid. The moral of that story from the first publisher's point of view is never to bother with the slush pile, because, even if you do find jewels, they'll be snatched from you anyway.

TARGETING AGENTS: THE RULES

One of the questions we're asked most frequently is some variant of this one: 'I've written a novel which I'd classify as a—. Please can you suggest which agents are interested in works of this kind?' Sometimes the blank is filled in with something fairly generic: 'a historical romance' or 'a political thriller'. Sometimes, however, those blanks are filled in with an astonishingly specific array of descriptors: 'A religio-political drama set in the court of Ferdinand of Aragon and incorporating certain philosophical arguments connected with the ethics of the later Reconquista'. Sometimes we honestly get the impression that, if we were to come back saying that we knew of an agent specialising in religio-political dramas in the court of Ferdinand of Aragon, but one with no prior expertise in Reconquistan ethics, the author concerned would stomp off in a huff, looking for someone who *really* understood his market.

These queries are essentially misconceived. The truth is simply this: agents aren't very specialist. My own agent will happily handle commercial fiction and literary fiction and non-fiction. He handles thrillers and women's fiction; serious non-fiction and popular bestsellers. He needs to *like* the book in question. He also needs to believe that he can find a publisher to take it. But that's it. My previous agent operated the same way. So do a large majority of all other agents out there. The simple truth is that, if agents tried to specialise too far, their supply of saleable manuscripts would dry up very rapidly indeed, leaving them cold, poor, ragged and hungry.

Having said that, it's worth taking any obvious and easy steps to direct your work to those most likely to take it. Good-quality online search tools (like AgentMatch, available from Jericho Writers) will collate all the publicly available information on given agents and make that data searchable. So you should be able to narrow down by genre and the agent's attitude to new clients – are they actively looking to take on new writers, or are their lists already essentially full?

These tools will let you develop a longlist very fast indeed. The question then is: what should you do with it? Your longlist is very likely to have more than sixty names. Quite likely over a hundred. That's too many to approach. Ideally, you want to generate a list of about ten to twelve agents, perhaps fifteen tops.

If a dozen agents turn down your novel, then a dozen professional assessors of manuscripts have, in effect, ruled your manuscript unsaleable. If that's the case, you need to fix the manuscript. Even if you did find an agent to take you on, publishers are more likely to agree with the first dozen agents than they are with the solo contrarian voice. Remember that there are unlikely to be more than six to eight strong publishers for your novel, and those firms will be even more demanding of your work than Planet Agent will be. So, if you can't get a solitary 'yes' from among a dozen agents, your attention should almost certainly turn back to your manuscript, not to more submissions.

OK. So you know what you want to do – but how do you whittle your sixty to a hundred names down to a manageable shortlist?

The short answer is that you search through your longlist and look for points of contact. Your book is set in Rome/Rio/Albuquerque, and Agent X was born in/grew up in/has represented a book about one of those fine places? That's a point of contact.

You love Author X and Author Y is his agent? Assuming that Author X is a relatively unknown author, that's an excellent point of contact. If Author X is just John Grisham or Patricia Cornwell, then I'm not sure. Most experienced agents will have at least one superstar or near-superstar name on their list, and an awful lot of the query letters addressed to that agent will reference that one mega-name. By doing the same thing yourself, you risk looking lazy rather than sincere.

In searching for points of contact, the main thing is to stay broad-minded. Maybe you're selling fiction, but if the agent represents interestingly relevant non-fiction, you could certainly use that. Or if you happen to share an interest in (say) Victorian-era steampunk, you might want to approach that agent, even if your own MS is a near-future thriller. The point is that tastes can echo through any number of genres, and if you sense some commonality, that's enough to work with at this stage.

And that's it! Use a good online search tool to create your longlist. Then look for points of contact to create your shortlist. Bingo. That's all you need to do.

Even if you perform this task perfectly and you have written an excellent manuscript to boot, don't expect a 100% success rate. Some agents will reject your manuscript for essentially random reasons: the book you've written just doesn't happen to be their sort of thing. They're dealing with something highly similar. They're too busy to breathe. Or whatever. Don't worry about it. This is a tough industry. We've all had rejections. And you only need one acceptance.

BIGGER OR SMALLER? OLDER OR NEWER?

There aren't all that many genuinely large literary agencies on either side of the Atlantic. In both London and New York, there's a smallish handful of big agencies, followed by a whole slew of middling ones – perhaps with three to five actual agents on the staff, plus a slightly larger number of people in support. Down at the lower end of the spectrum there are a number of one-man and one-woman bands, where the agent will also be opening envelopes, answering phones and sweeping the floors. The oldest established agency has been going for more than ninety years, while new ones are springing up all the time. (They're also disappearing, of course. Because of the general pressure on the industry, which tends to concentrate more and more money in the hands of fewer and fewer bestsellers, the pressure on literary agents has been acute at times too. It's not size, however, but quality that confers immunity to such pressure. Some of the best agencies are one-woman shows.)

On the whole, established agencies will have a longer list of clients, easier access to celebrity and established authors, and perhaps less appetite for new clients. On the other hand, even established agencies will have newer agents working for them, and those agents will be working hard to build their lists and make some sales. Equally, there'll be plenty of smaller agencies who are kept busy by their existing clients and who will need to be dazzled by a manuscript to take on a new author. If a particular agent hasn't been in business long, she'll certainly be looking to take on new clients, but then again she'll also be keenly aware that she needs to build her reputation with publishers, so she'll want to go out to them first with submissions that are very strong rather than marginal.

In short, although it's probably true that younger/smaller agencies are a little greedier for new clients than older/bigger ones, it's by no means a reliable rule. It's also not true that the letterhead of a big agency on a submission to a publisher will create shock and awe amongst those who receive it. A young, inexperienced agent at a large agency won't have a lot of shock and awe at his disposal. An agent who's in business on her own will, if she has a strong reputation, command plenty of respect.

In the end, though, it's not about respect; it's about the quality of the manuscript. If a newbie agent sends a manuscript out to six to eight properly selected editors, and that manuscript is fantastic, then the publishers will respond the way any market normally would: it'll push the price for that manuscript rapidly upwards. Likewise, if a very well-known agent sends out a manuscript that isn't quite strong enough, no one will bid for it. Fifteen years ago or more, it would have been common to find capable agents boasting that they'd never failed to sell a manuscript. I don't think I know any long-serving agent of whom that is still true. Publishers have cut their lists and become more conservative. It's not uncommon for a manuscript to be rejected by a publisher, with a note from the editor containing only praise for the writer and the writing, with a plaintive addendum to the effect that the folks from marketing weren't convinced. Those folks from marketing have nixed a lot of good books.

I generally advise mixing your submissions up somewhat: approach some larger agencies and some smaller ones, some older ones and some newer ones. There's no overwhelming logic in operation here. If you want to do it some other way, then feel free. The only real purpose in mixing things up is that, if you do get more than one offer of representation, you may be in a position to compare and contrast the feeling of being one client amongst many hundreds in a larger agency, or one rather more significant client in a smaller one.

WHAT PERCENTAGE?

Not too long back, most agents charged 10% or 12.5% on commissions earned on home sales, and 20% on commissions earned on overseas sales – that 20% in effect representing 10% for the home agent and 10% for their overseas counterpart.

As median advances declined, agents noticed that their pockets were jingling with rather less change than had once been the case. So agents started to push their commissions upwards, and a majority of agents now charge 15% of home sales. This has, of course, been adverse for authors. It does, after all, seem harsh to be paying 50% more commission when median advances have been in steady decline. That's not exactly rewarding success.

On the other hand, you can't fight the market. Every now and then, I've come across first-time writers selecting agents according to how little they charge. That's crazy. A good agent is the most important ally a writer will ever have. Really good agents may charge 10% or 12.5% if they are looking to attract clients to an expanding business, but most good agents charge 15% – and should be able to deliver far more value than that to their prospective clients. If you get more than one agent offering to represent you, then you can certainly ask – gently – about commissions, and it's quite likely that you'll be able to negotiate a little give in that 15%. But don't obsess about it. It's not worth it. Go with the best agent, not the cheapest one. Selecting your agent is a very big decision, and quality matters.

LONDON, NEW YORK, DUBLIN, SYDNEY?

For most people, it'll be obvious which publishing centre is right for them. If you are American or Canadian, and living in North America, your agent will almost certainly be based in New York, or one of the good agencies scattered elsewhere across the country. If you're a Briton living in the UK or Europe, you need a British agent who, most likely, will live or work either in London itself or very close by.

That's the easy bit. But if you don't fit into one of these super-easy categories, the issue of where to send your material becomes a little more complex. The following rules will be correct in most instances, but you need to be guided by common sense and some understanding of the market, not simply by the rules. But the rules first:

If you are Irish and are writing Irish-interest material

You should approach Dublin-based agents or publishers.

If you are Irish but are writing general interest material

You will be looking for a publisher based in London. That sounds a tad colonial, I know, but all the big publishers are based there, and you want their scale. A London-based publisher doesn't absolutely require you to have a London-based agent – any half-capable Dublin agent will know the British publishers well – but you should look for the best agent for you, not the closest agent to you. Oh yes, and don't make the mistake of thinking that, because your work might be set in Ireland, it's of Irish interest only. Maeve Binchy is as Irish as a leprechaun dancing on a shamrock, but her work is of universal interest and absolutely the kind of thing that any London publisher would love to acquire.

If you are from South Africa, Australia, or New Zealand or, indeed, you hail from anywhere in the Commonwealth apart from Canada

You have a decision to make, which could run one of three ways:

(1) If you reckon there is a healthy local market for your work, you can approach local publishers or literary agents. Selling to a local publisher doesn't have to mean giving up on your global ambitions. If you sell world rights and are confident that your local publisher will make a real effort to sell those rights to publishers elsewhere, then you are effectively getting an agent and a publisher all in one go. You've got a decent hope of there being a local market for your work if it is clearly of a type handled by local houses. If you can offer some specific local interest into the bargain, then so much the better.

(2) If you reckon that the local market for your work is a little skinny, but your work has the quality and breadth of appeal to succeed elsewhere, then you can try a London agent. British agents won't care that you live half a world away. However, because authors who live half a world away are less available for PR and are going to be consid-

ered somewhat less newsworthy by the British press, the hard truth is that you are probably at something of a disadvantage compared with British or Irish authors. Not a huge disadvantage, but a real one nevertheless.

(3) If you reckon that the local market is going to be too skinny for you, you can approach agents in New York. There tends to be a slight expectation that Commonwealth authors will look to London first, and it's probably true that UK agents will be more accustomed to an international outlook than American ones, but these are fairly minor factors. If you have strong US connections via family or work, they should trump anything else. And in certain areas – say, fantasy/sci-fi – the North American market is livelier than the British equivalent, so that would also be a strong reason to snub the queen and salute the president. The queen will survive.

If you are British or Irish and living in North America, or if you are North American and living in Europe

The world is your oyster. You could go either way. You are probably better off dealing with an agent located in the same continent as you, but if there are reasons for doing otherwise, then do otherwise. If you want to send your material to agents in both locations, go right ahead.

If you are Canadian

So far, I've treated North America as a unit with New York as its hub. That's too simple. Canada has its own excellent publishing industry and looks almost as much to the Commonwealth market as it does to the American. Many Canadian authors will secure a Canadian agent or publisher as a first step, then proceed from there. On the whole, I'd advise you to look for the best agent for your particular work and ignore the question of where the agent is based.

If you are Indian or African

It's perhaps worth emphasising that the publishing industry today is somewhat discriminatory – that is, it discriminates *in favour of* authors who aren't middle-aged white Europeans or Americans. A dazzling first novel by a Nigerian author may well sell for more than the same novel written by, for example, me. Indeed, I have had agents explicitly tell me that they are looking for brown-skinned authors (to use their own surprising phrase). That's a barmy state of affairs if you ask me – I'd like a world where authors are judged only on the merits of their work – but it's certainly better than the other way round.

It's also, just to be clear, absolutely fine if your novel is written in something other than Standard British English or Standard American English, but it must be fluent. Unless you are entirely comfortable in English as a spoken language, you are unlikely to have the fluency needed to write a novel. If you have that fluency, however, then drawing on your local version of English (Indian-English, Jamaican-English, or whatever) may greatly enrich your work.

And if those rules don't deal exactly with your situation, then use your head. If your work is good enough and your approach is professional enough, it probably doesn't matter all that much which door you knock on first.

TARGETING AGENTS: FANTASY AND SCIENCE FICTION

Fantasy and science fiction is an altogether more problematic area. There's a ludicrous snobbery which pervades the industry about this kind of speculative fiction. No matter that the *Iliad* and *Odyssey* fall into this category, that *Beowulf* does, that *Le Morte d'Arthur* does, that Dante's *Inferno* does. And Shakespeare's *The Tempest*. And *Gulliver's Travels*. No matter, in fact, that many of the greatest works of world literature have been solidly 'speculative' in nature; the snobbery has solidified into something so pervasive that it's virtually impossible to find a way over or through it. There are some genuinely interesting fantasy authors writing today (for example, Neil Gaiman and Guy Gavriel Kay). Russell Hoban's stunning 1980 novel, *Riddley Walker*, is dystopian science fiction – and a classic of post-war fiction. Though Haruki Murakami is normally categorised as surrealist, he's only a fingernail's thickness from being an out-and-out fantasy writer.

I, therefore, don't share this snobbery about speculative fiction, but I do, in part, understand it. For one thing, it's one of the genres that have been most fully invaded by self-publishers, leaving an ever-narrower slice for the traditional firms. One agent told me recently that she thought, if Philip Pullman were a debut author, the *His Dark Materials* trilogy might now prove unsaleable. Shocking, but true.

In any case, selling good-quality fantasy/sci-fi to trad firms is harder than it should be. One good trick is to look at your book and see if you can reclassify it. A light science fiction novel might be reclassifiable as a techno-thriller or a near-future thriller. A novel set in a post-apocalyptic future might 'explore the same territory as Margaret Atwood's *The Handmaid's Tale*'. Fantasy novels are often able to masquerade as 'young adult fiction'. Sad as it is to say, these dodges are normally advisable, so long as they're plausible. If your 'techno-thriller' involves space suits and warp drives, no one will believe your reclassification.

If reclassifying your work isn't possible, you simply need to make the rounds of agents in the normal way. You'll need to do more work than usual in establishing which agents are potentially fantasy/sci-fi friendly. You may well need to go to more than the usual ten to twelve agents in order to get a reliable read as to the market for your work. Fifteen to eighteen agents might be a more realistic number to target – but, again, I would urge you to make sure that your manuscript is up to scratch before you send it out. The ultimate reason why most fantasy manuscripts are rejected is not that agents are snobs, it's that a lot of fantasy manuscripts just aren't good enough. Don't let yourself fail for that reason.

TARGETING AGENTS: NICHE AREAS

Having stressed early on that most agents are generalists, I should also acknowledge that there are some niches, where specialists do operate. Sports books, TV tie-ins, cookery books, illustrated work and other specialisms do exist. If you've written a book in an area that you feel might have a niche of its own, then there's no way to check whether there's a specialist agency operating other than by checking AgentMatch or other similar tools. If such a specialist does exist for you, then by all means send them your work, but don't necessarily despair of using a non-specialist. The lack of a clear route just means you have more options.

TARGETING PUBLISHERS

If you decide that your work would be best sold direct to publishers, the task of identifying those publishers is more complex than with agents. There are two basic techniques to use, which are best used in conjunction.

First, use Google. Smaller publishers are upfront about what they want. Just try to find publishers in the right area. Second, you should also go to the relevant section of a bookshop, or the right category list on Amazon. Spend time looking for books in a similar area. Don't be too pedantic. Your book may be specifically about knitting, but any craft- or sewing-related title is relevant. When you find related titles, look at how the book is packaged and marketed – that information may well suggest some useful revisions you could make to your text – but also note down the publisher's name and address. You'll find that information on the page of tedious-looking small print at the front of the book, or you can just look up the publisher/imprint you find on the book's Amazon page.

Oh, and do home in on the specific address you need. If you just send your work to a general email address for giantpublisher.com, it may not find its way to the specialist editor at the specific imprint you are looking to reach. If in doubt, use the phone.

When you approach publishers, you need to think about the work from their point of view. Let's say, for example, you've written a book on classic motorbikes, and you've discovered a publisher that has the titles *Classic Cars*, *Classic Planes*, *Classic Ships* – but nothing yet called *Classic Motorbikes*. Clearly, you're in a potentially strong position. But take the time to study those other titles. If they all have a certain format – a jaunty prose style, text boxes full of trivia facts, comparison charts and the like – your book needs to fit that basic mould. If it doesn't, the publisher won't want it.

And on that subject, don't expect publishers to have the imagination to leap from the text that you've submitted to the text that you could supply if you had a contract to make the necessary changes. I yield to no one in my love and admiration for all publishing kind, but I'd no more rely on their imagination in such a context than I would hand my wallet to a jewel thief. You get to do the work. Then they get to say yea or nay. That's not fair, but there it is.

AVOIDING BANDITS

Because of the vast number of people seeking to be published, there are inevitably also fraudsters preying on them. In particular, you should avoid:

- *Agents who advertise aggressively on the internet*. Real agents don't need to advertise. I once found a US 'agency' that advertised on the internet. It accepted every new writer as a client. Those clients are then asked to pay a small sum – $90, typically – for a 'critique'. These critiques are computer-generated and all positive. Often there are follow-up requests for further relatively small sums of money for minor tasks. Then there's often a suggestion that self-publishing (with a sister company, though they don't tell you that) is the right course of action for you. These outfits are scams, pure and simple. Avoid them.

- *Agents who ask for money upfront.* It's rare to come across this now, but, when one dodgy agent goes bankrupt or (as happened in a recent case) flees the country, another one will sooner or later pop up in their place. Real agents don't ask you for money – ever. I have never, ever given a penny to any agent or any publisher that I've had dealings with except, in the case of my agents, the commission due on money they've rustled up on my behalf. If you're asked for cash upfront, then – it doesn't matter what they call the payment or say it's for – just say no.

- *Publishers who advertise on the internet.* Real publishers get their books from agents or direct submissions. Publishers who advertise are one of two things. They may be perfectly reputable companies who help with some of the chores of self-publishing. (Lulu.com would be an example of these.) Most of the rest are vanity publishers, only a Rizla paper away from being out-and-out bandits. If you're aiming at commercial publication, avoid all these people. You can always come back to self-publishing as an option later.

Here is a short way to remember this advice: if an agent or a publisher asks you for money, just say no. If you like, you can enrich your refusal with certain earthy Anglo-Saxon words of your choice.

PROTECTING YOUR COPYRIGHT

This section is short, because the issue it deals with is a phantom one. Although it's something that bothers many new writers, it really needn't trouble you at all. If you're not worried about copyright theft, then just turn the pages and move on. If you are, read on …

How do I protect my ideas?

You can't. There is no legal mechanism in the US or the UK or anywhere else at all for doing this. And just as well, since there are said to be only seven plots in the world. Shakespeare, for one, was a serial recycler of ideas.

How do I protect my manuscript itself?

In all signatories to the Berne Convention – that is, the entire known universe aside from Betelgeuse IV and North Korea – the copyright in artistic or literary works (which includes any novel or any book of non-fiction) belongs to the creator. You don't have to sign documents, register at the Post Office, send sworn affidavits into the Library of Congress, chain yourself outside Parliament, or video yourself writing the book to claim copyright. The copyright is yours from the moment that the words tumble from your fingers on to the page. I myself, in common with almost every professional author under the sun, have only ever taken two steps to protect my copyright. Those steps are:

(1) *Write a book.* That's what gives me the copyright in the first place.

(2) *Sign the contract that is put in front of me.* Publishers will take care of the rest.

We'll deal with publishing contracts in a later section, but any standard contract will secure a statement of copyright for you in every book that is published under the terms of that deal. You don't have to raise this subject with your agent. You don't need to make a fuss about it with a publisher. You just need to check that your contract contains reasonably standard copyright terms – which it will – and then sign it.

What does copyright registration do for me?

By writing the book, you own the copyright in it. That sounds neat and simple, but it's a bit more complicated than that.

If someone simply pirates your text, it's pretty obvious that they've done so – the same sequence of 70,000 words isn't going to arise by coincidence – so you have a legally easy and legally valid claim for breach of copyright. OK, that's simple enough. But suppose someone's piracy was a little more subtle. So instead of just replicating your text word for word, a pirate took your story and rewrote it in their own words. Names have been changed. Some settings. Some minor plot issues. But let's suppose that someone actually took the heart of your story and reproduced it as theirs.

In such a case, you might have a claim for breach of copyright, but you would have to prove that the putative pirate had actually read your book. And how would you do that? Short of obtaining incriminating video or having the ability to hack into the pirate's Kindle data, you wouldn't be able to.

Step forward copyright registration. If your book has been registered with the US Library of Congress Copyright Office, any court will deem that the pirate *has* read your book. That still doesn't determine whether the level of copying involved is excessive. (Jane Smiley used King Lear as the model for her *A Thousand Acres*. Even if *Lear* were still in copyright, it would be hard to argue that the copying was excessive.) It also doesn't do anything to determine the extent of damages. If you can't show that a pirate has dented your sales, a court might agree that a breach of copyright had occurred but that any damages would be minimal or even nil.

So registration doesn't tackle all the issues that matter, but it does tackle one. Your publisher will take care of it for you. You don't need to be in a rush to register. You can just let the publisher do their stuff.

Why copyright doesn't actually matter

And look. There will be people reading this who are certain that the moon landings were faked, that the CIA arranged 9/11, and whose cellars are full of bottled water, tinned food, shotgun shells and gas masks. These guys will want to approach the US Copyright Office (www.copyright.gov) and register their work there.

And fine. If you feel better doing it, then do it.

But bear this in mind. Owning and protecting your copyright does not give you access to some supra-national force of gun-toting crimebusters. It gives you access to one thing and one thing alone: the ability to sue your supposed pirate in a court of law. Since most pirates are based in Russia, or in other dodgy locations, or a highly effective at concealing their location, that ability to sue someone may not help you much.

And I do know this:

You will never succeed in eliminating pirates. Or rather: if your work is decently successful, you will never succeed, because pirates make their money by selling your $9.99 e-book at $0.99 in a pirated version. The price of success is piracy.

And Penguin Random House is a large company. They've got a lot of successful books and a lot of corporate lawyers. But PRH's books get pirated as much as anyone else's. PRH's lawyers chase those rogues around the internet. They swat one nasty little nest of bad guys, and another group will pop up somewhere else. And if PRH can't solve the problem, nor can you. It is almost inconceivable that the situation will arise when it will make emotional and financial sense for you to go to court about a breach of copyright. So yes, although the protection is there, it is much more theoretical than real.

So leave the whole issue to your publishers and forget about it.

(And yes, I know, the moon landings *were* faked.)

COPYRIGHT PROTECTED NOTICES

Finally, please, don't go writing 'copyright protected' warning notices all over your script when you send it out to agents. Don't put that little © symbol on every page. Certainly, don't ask an agent to sign a Non-Disclosure Agreement ('NDA'). Unless the circumstances are exceptional, you'll just look like an idiot if you do.

Just write the book. Make it good. Then send it out.

MANUSCRIPT PRESENTATION

Your manuscript should be tidy and well-presented. Your name and contact information should be on the title page. You should put your name and the title in the header or footer. You should never use single line-spacing. Use 1.5 line-spacing or double. The 'Paragraph Format' menu on your word processing package will tell you what that means, if you don't already know. You should avoid any howlers in your opening pages. If you commit a grievous sin later than that, it'll probably be attributed to a moment of sloppiness, not something more serious. Don't call your novel 'novel.doc', because an agent may have five such files open on their laptop at any one time. Use a simple convention like yourname-title-documenttype, to label your documents. So, for example, farewell-to-arms-hemingway-novel.doc. Or farewell-to-arms-hemingway-synopsis.doc. That way, a busy agent will easily be able to manage their open document pile.

In truth, that advice is all you really need. No manuscript that obeys those rules has ever been rejected because of a format or presentation issue. Nevertheless, because I know you won't be satisfied without a much longer list of dos and don'ts, here, for your delight and delectation, is just such a list.

Font selection. Don't be freaky. Use a standard font. Times New Roman is an excellent default option. Georgia or Garamond are frequent substitutes. Unless you're very old-school, don't use Courier – it's just weird. It's common to see Arial used, which is a sans-serif font (that is, there are none of those little strokes at the tops and tails of the letters). This may work for manuscripts that are assertively modern, but I'd recommend you use serif-based fonts: they're easier to read over an extended period. That's why sans-serif fonts are mostly used for headings or as attention grabbers in advertising.

Font size. Use a font size of 12. Not 10 or 11: they're too small and strain the eyes. Not 14 or larger: that makes you look like a child. 12 is just right.

Line-spacing. Use either 1.5 or double line-spacing. You should simply be able to select all the text in your document (Ctrl-A on a PC, Cmd-A on a Mac), go to the 'Paragraph Format' menu and select the appropriate option. If you don't know how to do this, then ask somebody who does. Agents don't want the text to be properly spaced because they're going to making a host of editorial changes in between the lines. They want the text spaced so their eyes don't explode.

Chapter breaks. It doesn't matter too much, but a page break at the end of each chapter is standard. You can number chapters any way you like, start the text halfway down the page, and play around with other minor format issues if you like, but you don't have to. My chapters begin with a number or heading at the top, centred, in bold and one or two font sizes larger than the main text. The text begins a few lines down. If you want to get fancier than that, it's up to you. But nothing weird.

Page numbering. Your pages must be numbered. Must be. If you don't know how to insert page numbers in your word processing program, ask someone who does. They can go anywhere: top or bottom; left, right or middle. No one cares.

Headers/footers. Not a huge issue, but I do suggest that you use headers or footers with your name and the MS title. If you know how to put the header/footer text in dark grey rather than black, you may want to do that too. But don't get hung up about it. No one else will.

Title page. It should have the title. Your name. Your contact information (address, phone number, email address). The presentation can be stylish, but, if you think that your presentation is definitely stylish but just possibly weird, then play it safe. There's nothing wrong with a title in a large font (go crazy – try out 36 or 48), your name a few lines below that (in a smaller font size, 12 or 14), and then your contact info in the bottom right- or left-hand corner. You can have the word count on your title page as well, if the fancy takes you.

Paragraph breaks. Business letters and documents have a complete blank line to separate paragraphs, but paragraphs themselves are not indented. (That is, the first line of the paragraph begins on the left-hand margin like everything else.) You, however, are not writing a business letter or a business document. You are writing a book. That means that there is no blank line to separate paragraphs, but the first line of every paragraph should be indented. To achieve that indentation, you can either use the tab key in your word processing program, or you can set the 'Paragraph Format' menu so that you choose 'First Line' in lieu of 'None' in the indentation dialogue box. In terms of how far to indent your first line – well, it just doesn't matter very much. Less than 0.2" is too small to register. More than 1.0" is heading off into Possibly Freaky territory. I'd suggest that anywhere between 0.3" and 0.5" looks nice.

Margins. Go with the default page margins, or at any rate don't try to squeeze too much text on a page. An inch at top and bottom, with an inch or so at the sides, looks nice.

Indicative cover designs. What a great idea it would be to offer the agent a sample cover design to help them imagine what your book would appear like in print. You're not saying that your chosen image would have to be the cover, you're just giving the imagination something to work off. If you have access to a colour printer and some semi-pornographic graphics involving purple skies and women with tight clothes and implausibly long legs, then so much the better ... Needless to say, if you so much as catch yourself starting to think along these lines, then take a cold bath until you stop. Hit yourself repeatedly over the head with this book or an e-reader of your choice, whilst repeating, 'I shall not be freaky when it comes to manuscript presentation.' If you've got a genuinely lovely and appropriate black-and-white line drawing that will reproduce well, then you can think about including it. But, if in doubt, don't do it. The manuscript is what matters.

Avoiding howlers. I've already said that it's a waste of money to get your manuscript copyedited, and it is. But attention to matters of detail is a genuinely reliable indicator of manuscript quality. If a writer has taken sufficient care over word choice, sentence structure and the rest, then they are almost certain to have cared about such things as punctuation, consistency and spellings as well. That does therefore mean that while a few errors will creep into your manuscript – and it's just fine if they do – you need to avoid any hint of more widespread inattention. Given the importance of first impressions, you should take particular care over the first few pages. That means don't write *its* when you mean *it's* or vice versa. It's a criminal offence to get this wrong. Don't write *whose* when you mean *who's*. Don't anywhere talk about your 'fiction novel'. (All novels are fiction. Just call it a novel.) Don't make any errors of the sort that would make any self-respecting pedant want to hurl hard objects at you. If your own spelling or punctuation is poor, then ask someone competent to do it for you. Better still, learn the rules, then apply them diligently. You are unlikely to succeed until you do.

SOME THOUGHTS ON DIALOGUE

'Have we covered everything?' Harry wondered aloud.

The image of his first editor hovered in front of him.

'Dialogue formatting,' she said. 'You must cover that.'

'What, all that tiresome stuff about inverted commas?' he replied. 'How double inverted commas were once standard in the UK, but have now given way to single inverted commas? How Americans still prefer the double sort?'

'Well, yes, now that you mention it. But really, I meant how all the commas and capital letters work. And what about that thing about quotations inside dialogue? Like if I wanted to quote your comment about, "How Americans still prefer the double sort?" I'd have to dress it inside double inverted commas ... except funnily enough, if I were American, when I'd have to go for single inverted commas to distinguish them from my ordinary doubles.'

She thought a bit, then added, 'Hold on. I am American.'

In deference to the ghost of my first editor, let me add that you should also get your dialogue formatting right. The little snippet above gives you most of what you need to know. Please notice (1) that every bit of dialogue starts a new, indented paragraph, as does any action paragraph, such as the second line of the text above; (2) that commas, question marks and so forth live inside the inverted commas, not outside; (3) that you do not need a capital H in 'he said', even if the preceding bit of dialogue ended with a question mark or an exclamation mark; (4) you don't end a bit of dialogue with a full stop if you are running straight into a 'he said' or 'she said' – you use a comma instead; but (5) you do end a bit of dialogue with a full stop (as in the last line or so of the final paragraph above) when the sentence that follows is not a 'he said', a 'she said' or an obvious equivalent.

If you apply those rules consistently, you're doing fine.

ONWARDS! ONWARDS!

All this, in a way, is to give too much attention to the subject of presentation. The takeaway message from this section is a simple one. Take care to present your manuscript in a smart, professional way, then stop stressing. Your manuscript will not stand or fall on how pretty it looks. It will stand or fall on how well it's written. That's where you should concentrate your time, care and attention. The rest is just a question of ordinary professionalism.

TITLES, OPENING LINES, OPENING CHAPTERS

It's said – on the basis of what research, I have no idea – that the average house-buyer makes their purchase decision within a few seconds of seeing a property. And for sure, any seller takes plenty of care in ensuring good 'kerb appeal' – that is, making sure that the property looks good from the most casual of external inspections.

It's the same with manuscripts. On the one hand, no manuscript will be taken on by an agent or a publisher unless the whole thing is in good shape. In that sense, you have to be as worried about the plumbing in your bathroom as you do about any weeds in your front garden. On the other hand, your manuscript is, in the first instance, going to be rapidly assessed by somebody who will be expecting to reject every new submission in that morning's inbox. You can't allow imperfections to manifest early. Your manuscript must do as much as it can to capture an agent's attention from the start.

TITLES

Titles are odd things. There's one perfectly sound argument which says that, at this stage, titles don't really matter at all. Of my first seven books, only one went to print with the same title that it wore when I first sent it to my agent or publisher. In all the other cases, the titles were changed, often several times, prior to publication, and sometimes for the oddest of reasons. For example, the title I initially gave to my fifth novel was *The Russian Lieutenant*. My agent liked the title. So did my editor. So did the sales team. It looked as though I was about to notch up only my second ever title-success. Then we got a huge offer from one of the old-school book clubs. They wanted to place a huge order but told us that they couldn't sell a book with the word 'Russia' or 'Russian' in the title. It wasn't a political matter; it was just their readers were put off. So *The Russian Lieutenant* became *The Lieutenant's Lover.* I didn't mind too much either way, but it was symptomatic of how fast and randomly titles can change.

Agents and editors know all this. In that sense, they shouldn't care too much what title appears on the document you send. It also shouldn't matter to a potential home-buyer whether the front garden is littered with leaves in autumn, yet matter it does. Strong titles do help.

It's clear enough what a title needs to do. A good title will:

• Be highly consistent with your genre.
• Offer some intrigue – for example, launch a question in the mind of the reader.
• Encapsulate 'the promise of the premise' in a few very short words, distilling the essence of your idea down to its very purest form.

That first element, genre-consistency, is the most essential and the easiest to achieve. It's especially crucial now that so many books are being bought on Amazon, because book covers on an Amazon search page are no more than thumbnails. So while the cover has to work well in thumbnail form, the title also has more work to do.

In consequence, your title has to say to your target audience, 'this is the sort of book that readers like you enjoy'. It has to invite the click-through. That's its task.

The intrigue is harder to do, but also obvious. '*Gone Girl*' works because of the go girl/gone girl pun, those double Gs, and the brevity. But it also works because it launches a question in the mind of the reader: Who is this girl and why has she gone? By contrast, '*The Girl on the Train*' feels flat. There are lots of women on lots of trains. There's nothing particularly evocative or intriguing in the image. I don't think that book was much good, but I don't think the title stood out either. (The book sold well because of some pale resemblances between the excellent *Gone Girl* and its lacklustre sister. The trade, desperate for a follow-up hit to *Gone Girl*, pounced on whatever it had.)

The third element in a successful title – the 'promise of the premise' one – is very hard to do, and just isn't often done well. Personally, I've seldom nailed this one, and I've probably had a slightly less successful career as a result. So what works? Well, below are some examples of titles that do absolutely nail it.

The Girl with the Dragon Tattoo

Brilliant! That title simply ditched the over-serious Swedish original (*Män Som Hatar Kvinnor* – 'Men Who Hate Women'). Rather it took the brilliance of the central character and captured her in six words. She was a girl (vulnerable), and she had a tattoo (tough and subversive), and the tattoo was of a dragon (exotic and dangerous). That mixture of terms put the promise of the book's premise right onto the front cover and propelled the book's explosive success.

You'll notice too that the title also completely excludes mention of Mikael Blomkvist, who is as central to that first book as Salander is. But no one bought the book for Blomkvist and no one remembers the book for Blomkvist either. So the title cut him out and did the right thing in so doing.

The Da Vinci Code

Brilliant! Dan Brown is a limited writer, but it was a stroke of genius to glue together the idea of ancient cultural artefacts with some kind of secret code. Stir those two things up with a bit of Holy Grail myth-making, and the result (for his audience) was commercial dynamite. Better still, that dynamite was right there in the title. The *Da Vinci* part namechecks the world's most famous artist. The *Code* part promises that there are secret codes to be unravelled. Four words delivering the promise of the premise in full. And one of those words was 'the'.

I Let You Go

This was Clare Mackintosh's breakout hit, about a mother whose young son was killed in a hit-and-run car accident. The promise of the premise is right there in four very short words ... and given a first-person twist, which adds extra bite to the hook in question. A brilliant bit of title-making.

So that's what you're seeking to do. Easier said than done, in my experience. But one tip: you need to look at the book from the outside, not the inside, when you consider titles. You have to think of what you're communicating to a reader who has no idea about your book, your protagonist or you. That's the communication that matters. If you find a perfect title, but it misses some inner essence of your book – well, who cares? The reader doesn't know what that inner essence is anyway. Go for the great title.

When you send your book out, you don't need to tell agents or anyone else that your chosen title is provisional, because all titles are provisional until they go to print. If the title you've selected has already been taken by another book and another author, then use your common sense. There's no copyright in titles, so there's nothing illegal in duplicate titles. If you've called your book *The Copper Moon*, and you discover that a minor author in the 1960s had a book by the same title, don't worry about it. Stick with what you've got. If on the other hand, there's realistic scope for confusion between your book and something else currently on sale, you should change your title.

OPENING LINES

It is – or has become – conventional writerly wisdom that first lines matter a lot. It would be traditional for me at this point to trot out some well-known first lines of fiction and encourage you to imitate their literary and commercial excellence. Obedient as I am to my reader's every expectation, I herewith submit a handful of such opening lines for your review:

'Lyra and her daemon moved through the darkening Hall, taking care to keep to one side, out of sight of the kitchen.' – Philip Pullman, *Northern Lights*

'It was a queer, sultry summer, the summer they electrocuted the Rosenbergs, and I didn't know what I was doing in New York.' – Sylvia Plath, *The Bell Jar*

'As Gregor Samsa awoke one morning from uneasy dreams he found himself transformed in his bed into a gigantic insect.' – *Franz Kafka, Metamorphosis*

'It was a bright cold day in April, and the clocks were striking thirteen.' – George Orwell, *1984*

'I am an invisible man.' – Ralph Ellison, *Invisible Man*

'Granted: I am an inmate of a mental hospital; my keeper is watching me, he never lets me out of his sight; there's a peephole in the door, and my keeper's eye is the shade of brown that can never see through a blue-eyed type like me.' – Günter Grass, *The Tin Drum*

'The human race, to which so many of my readers belong ... ' – *G. K. Chesterton*, The Napoleon of Notting Hill

'You better not never tell nobody but God.' – *Alice Walker*, The Color Purple

These are all, self-evidently, strong opening lines, and, if you have a strong opener, then good for you. It'll help matters, if only just a little.

But don't go crazy. It can be an error to chase too hard after that golden opening line. Too hard a chase tends to end up with an opening sentence that smacks more of contrivance and effort than of real talent, and your first sentence needs to lead on to a first paragraph and a first page which cohere and sound good together. If your novel isn't the dazzling opening sentence kind of novel, then don't worry too much. Most novels aren't. I once began a book with the word 'Rain.' End of sentence, end of paragraph. I did that partly because Elmore Leonard says that you should never start a book with the weather so I thought I'd do just that. But no one ever told me my first sentence was weak or should be changed. And if 'Rain.' is a good enough way to start a book, then whatever way you've chosen is probably fine too.

OPENING PAGES

If I sound relaxed about that opening line, I'm more hardline when it comes to opening pages. Plenty of writers worry about submitting the first three chapters to agents because 'my story only gets going later on'. That, let's be clear, is not acceptable. When I first read *War and Peace*, I remember thinking that the story took about a hundred pages to get going. In *The Good Soldier Švejk*, I'm not sure that the story ever actually gets going, though it's entertaining to watch it try.

These days, whether you are writing genre fiction or commercial fiction, you must grab the reader hard and early. If the reader doesn't have a strong sense of the story by the end of chapter 1, you need to rewrite it – or perhaps, better still, just start with chapter 2. Equally, if you are writing non-fiction, the purpose and importance and momentum of your book must be apparent early on. If you play fast and loose with this injunction, then your book will very likely not sell and, however good the rest of it may be, it probably doesn't deserve to. (As it happens, I'm editing this text, having just given feedback to a couple of Jericho Writers members on their opening pages. In both cases, I told them to delete most of the text. I walk my talk.)

Nor can you commit mortal or venial sins against the Gods of Good Prose in those opening pages, while a reader is making up their mind whether to read further. Once they've made the decision to read on, the odd embarrassing slippage may be forgiven. Early on, you can't afford to give anyone the excuse to stop.

And if you don't know what a mortal or venial sin is, then don't worry. I'm about to tell you.

QUERY LETTERS

When I came to send my first novel out to agents, I thought I knew what I was doing. I was confident that my novel was a strong, saleable proposition. I had also spent ten years in finance, during which time I had learned to pitch. Pitch hard, pitch pushy. So I wrote a query letter that briefly introduced the novel and outlined the brand concept that would unite my future *oeuvre*. I don't quite remember what else went into that letter – though I do remember that I made free use of bullet points and was more than willing to share my thoughts about the American market – but I'm pretty sure it would have been a leading contender for that year's World's Worst Query Letter Award. The first six agents who received my package either sent standard form rejection letters or didn't bother to reply at all. Utterly mystified, I sent my package out to a further six agents and this time my fishing line came back with two little fishes wriggling on the hook.

The moral of this story is twofold. First, query letters matter. Second, they don't matter all that much. The one absolutely central, critical, crucial and decisive point is that your manuscript is excellent. If your manuscript is strong enough, then even the World's Worst Query Letter is unlikely to prevent you from getting an agent, though it may certainly delay your journey there. As for the query letter itself – well, there's just no need to write a bad letter. This section will tell you how to write a good one. But all a query letter really needs to do is not to be so awful that it stops anyone from looking half-seriously at the manuscript itself. The same is true of the synopsis. It's well worth avoiding some basic mistakes, but you don't need to get into a pickle over minutiae. If your covering material is decent, and your approach to agents is businesslike, then your success will be determined by your manuscript itself – which is just as it ought to be.

WHAT A QUERY LETTER NEEDS TO DO

A query letter has one main role: to not be so bad that it puts anyone off looking at the manuscript itself. If an agent turns from the letter to the MS, then the letter has succeeded. That is a fairly low hurdle to clamber over. If you care to set your sights a little higher, you may want to make the agent turn *with interest* from the letter to the MS. That's a bit more of a challenge, but still hardly insuperable. One senior agent once told me that the best query letter she'd ever received ran like this:

> *Dear Sirs,*
>
> *I have written a book and am looking for a literary agent.*
>
> *Yours faithfully,*

Personally, I'd say that was a little on the skimpy side but, as you can see, this bar is not set particularly high.

Assuming that you want to write a slightly longer letter, what should that letter seek to accomplish? There are no rules here, but I'd say that a good template for a query letter might run like this:

- Use the right name!
  Address your letter to a named agent, not to the agency (unless you are told to send it to the Submissions Department, or whatever). Double-check spellings. You can bet that a Jon or a Jayne notice every single time they are addressed as John or Jane. And not in a good way.
- A one- or two-sentence introduction to the book: title, word count, genre.
- A somewhat longer paragraph (or two) introducing the book at greater length: the theme, the setting, the protagonist, the premise – but not a detailed plot exposition.

- A shortish paragraph introducing you.
- A sign-off.

Thus, if I had not been attempting to win my World's Worst Query Letter Award, the letter I sent out for my first novel might have looked something like this:

Dear Jane Agent,

I'm writing to introduce my first novel, The Money Makers, *an adventure yarn of some 180,000 words.*

The novel opens with the death of the multi-millionaire Bernard Gradley. Angry at the indolence of his three sons, Gradley has written his will so as to force them into action – and competition. Each son is given three years to make a million pounds, starting from scratch. If one succeeds, he inherits everything. Should they all fail, Gradley's millions go to charity. The book is a fable of modern-day treasure-hunting, and one that becomes complicated by growing emotional and ethical dilemmas as the young men get closer to their goal.

I am 31 years old and worked in the financial industry until recently. I am currently caring for my wife, who has been struck down (temporarily, we hope!) with a neurological illness.

I'd be delighted if you felt able to represent me. I look forward to hearing from you.

Yours,
Harry Bingham

That is, I hope you agree, a fairly simple letter. If you are capable of writing a saleable manuscript, then you are surely capable of writing a query like the one above. It's not, however, entirely devoid of subtlety. Although the letter mostly presents the novel as a good old-fashioned adventure romp, the final sentence of the second paragraph strikes a slightly different note: hinting that the book, though fun, isn't without its more thoughtful side.

Likewise, that dart into parenthesis – '(temporarily we hope!)' – has a twofold job. First of all, it's a marker of social awareness. It's a big thing to tell a stranger about a major disease that's affected your wife, and the little lightening of mood is a way to signal, 'Don't worry, I'm not going to get all heavy on you.' Furthermore, the willingness to vary the tone of a fairly neutral business letter suggests a certain degree of authorial confidence.

Those are little things, no doubt, but I'd say that any agent who's halfway interested in a good old-fashioned yarn will have her interest piqued by such a letter. Instead of turning to the manuscript itself with a weary sense of duty, she'll turn instead with a slight quickening of interest. That's hardly winning the war, but it's a tiny opening victory, which is all you can hope to achieve at this stage.

Finally, you should also note that the letter says almost nothing about plot. It doesn't need to. Your synopsis will do that. The letter doesn't even grapple with all the subtleties of the premise. (What if more than one son makes a million pounds? Is Gradley's money divided or does it go to the son who has earned the most?) Indeed, the letter entirely neglects to mention that Gradley had a daughter, but excluded her from the competition altogether, for reasons of his own. These things don't matter – or, rather, they don't matter at this stage. In describing the book, you have only three golden rules, which you must follow to succeed.

Golden Rule the First is that you must be brief. Unless your work is literary fiction or the kind of non-fiction that simply requires complex explanation, I'd say your book description should come in at no more than 150 words. Quite possibly less. If your query letter is, in fact, delivered via an online submission form, you may be character-limited anyway. But whether you are or not, short is nearly always better. The *Money Makers* letter above uses just ninety words to describe a book of 180,000 words. That's fine.

Golden Rule the Second is that you have to explain what the book is. That is, you need to deliver the various co-ordinates of genre, premise and storyline that allow the agent to say, 'Oh, it's *this* sort of book.' In some cases, you can do much of that by simply defining genre and setting. If I were describing my Fiona

Griffiths novels, I'd do a lot to set the scene by explaining that they are police procedurals set in Cardiff. But most books aren't as easily pigeonholed, so you'll notice that the first paragraph of my *Money Makers* description simply explains the premise. That's enough to allow the agent to understand, very approximately, what they are dealing with.

Golden Rule the Third is that you need to say something about what the emotional rewards will be from reading the book. In this case, I've made it clear that the book is an adventure story – an action book, but without violence, in effect. I've also made it clear that the book is a little more thoughtful than that 'adventure' description might suggest; that there are some emotional and ethical issues underlying the romp. In effect, I'm saying, 'Yes, this would be a great beach read, but with just enough about it that you won't be mortally embarrassed to be seen reading it.' And in many genres, of course, the rewards are going to be clear. A rom-com needs to be romantic and comic. A thriller needs to thrill. These things may be obvious, but you still need to hint at them in your description.

WHAT A QUERY LETTER CAN HOPE TO DO

In smaller agencies, it'll quite likely be an agent who deals with the morning post. In larger agencies, it'll be support staff. If you feel cast down by the idea of mere support staff opening your letter, you shouldn't. Although agencies pay badly, they secure a high calibre of recruit, often youngsters with the ambition of entering the profession in due course.

In addition, all agencies are aware of the need to take on new clients. Although an agency can survive perfectly well off its existing clients if it doesn't take any new ones on for a year or so, writers are seldom immortal. Unless an agency refreshes its stock of clients, it will wither and die.

That's not always the impression those agencies give. It's a commonplace of rejection letters that 'the agency is not actively seeking new clients at this time'. That statement is, almost always, a lie. True enough, the agency is unlikely to have declared at its last board meeting, 'We must get new clients *now!*' An agency isn't going to put up ads in Times Square, start handing out flyers on the subway, or grab passers-by and interrogate them about any plot ideas they may have; so in a sense the agency can honestly say it isn't actively seeking new clients. But it's on the lookout for them, nevertheless. Indeed, the weary old formula about not actively seeking new clients or not having slots available on its list (as though there are any such things as slots!) is simply a con. It's a way of fobbing an author off in a manner that is calculated not to rile them too much.

(I think these circumlocutions are unintentionally confusing; unhelpful to writers who, in their ordinary lives, expect people to say what they mean. Sometimes what people mean may be disappointing or upsetting. Fine. So be it. Writers are as robust and capable of dealing with disappointment as any other group on the planet. More plain-speaking, please.)

In any case, the point is that agents want clients. If support staff are tasked with looking at new submissions, they are trained and monitored carefully. Query letters can be useful indicators of excellence, and staff will be trained accordingly.

This means that, although a straightforward letter, such as the sample one above, is a perfectly fine method of introduction, some writers may wish to set their sights a little higher. In particular, if you are a literary author, you may well want to make sure that you strut your stuff in the query letter as much as you aim to do in the book. If you are a superbly well-qualified non-fiction author, then making that authority fully apparent in your letter is also highly advisable.

The reason for this is that very often a manuscript may miss its target but may nevertheless succeed in advertising your essential competence. I've come across several really talented writers who have received a letter that said, in essence, 'We can't sell this manuscript and therefore can't offer you representation, but we think you're a class act. So please come back to us if you have something more commercial to offer.' On at least one occasion that I know of, just such a letter led to the author in question launching a nicely successful career with his second manuscript.

Indeed, it's worth being clear at this point that it's common for agents to say, 'We like *you*, but we don't think that this manuscript is yet right for the market, so we'd like to talk about some possible alterations.' When I wrote the proposal that would eventually turn into *This Little Britain*, a book of popular historical non-fiction, I got precisely that response. The agent I spoke to told me that he liked the concept and liked my prose style but felt that I needed to make the book more easily digestible if it were to sell. Over a period of about six months, I reworked the proposal. My initial draft, which would have had chapters of some 10–15,000 words, morphed into something significantly lighter in tone and made up of a lot of bite-sized 2–3,000-word chapters. During this period, the agent I was working with was not formally my agent. We didn't have a contract and he was not representing me. Only when I sent him a proposal that he believed to be saleable did we sign on the dotted line with each other. Thanks to my concept and writing ability, and his nose for the market, we ended up with a proposal that sold in a keenly contested auction, very swiftly and for a lot of money.

The anecdote illustrates one of the single most important aspects of an agent's function: they know the market and are there to relay it to you. Because of my work with Jericho Writers, I'm more keenly in touch with the market than nearly any other writer out there. All the same, I don't know as much as any properly competent agent. Their day job is selling books into that market. They are constantly in touch with editors and publishers, sensing what's in demand, what's not. An agent who likes your work enough to talk to you about revising it is someone who needs to be listened to very carefully indeed. You may not like the idea of the proposed revisions, but writers need to compromise. You need to find an intersection between what you want to write and what the market wants to buy. You don't get to make the rules.

Whatever else you do, you should keep your letter fairly brief. Most letters will fit comfortably on to a page (or the email equivalent). Some few will spill over to a second sheet. No decent letter will be any longer than that. And, of course, no letter that's halfway competent will commit any of the sins covered in the section that follows.

THE MORTAL SINS

You are a writer. Your query letter is trying to pitch your skill with words. You are hoping to make a living by putting words together in an entertaining and compelling fashion. So your letter must read well. You can no more afford sloppy sentences or clunky constructions in this letter than in the manuscript itself. Yet such errors are hideously commonplace. (I know this because we offer a free query review service to Jericho members and we get to see an enormous number of such letters.) Although first-time writers often complain that an agent may not even have read their work before rejecting it, why on earth should an agent waste their time on a submission which displays a feeble command of English? If I were an agent, I'd move on too.

Some of the sins are glaring:

- 'Its my first novel' – *should be 'It's'.*
- 'This is my first fiction novel ...' – *it's not a fiction novel; it's a novel.*
- 'My main character, whose got the power to ...' – *should be 'who's' or 'who has'.*
- 'The protagonist Rachel has to go away ...' – *there should be commas around the word 'Rachel'.*
- 'The hero should of been killed, but ...' – *'should have' not 'should of'.*

And so on. If you don't feel confident about such things, you aren't ready to send your work to agents. You *must* have an excellent command of written English. That isn't snobbery on the part of the industry; it's common sense. You wouldn't hope to be a dancer if you were too unfit to get out of bed; you wouldn't set out to be a cook if you were a klutz in the kitchen. Same with your writing. It's all very well to have a story that you want to tell, but telling it means using words – and that means using them skilfully or, at the very least, competently.

More commonly, the sins we come across are less glaring. They're still sins, however, and will debar you from the paradise that is agency representation. For example:

- 'The protagonist, Richard, has to go to battle and he fights hard but gets wounded and has to crawl away and hide in a cave and stay there until nightfall.'
- 'The adventure drama is one of suspense and intrigue which culminates ultimately in a showdown that pits the forces of good and evil against each other but in a way that maybe puts more shades of grey in there than you usually see in there.'
- 'Joanna is hopefully a really sympathetic heroine (at least I think so), but she does have faults too, so she isn't all good.'
- 'Enfolded in silken luxury and with maidservants and marble palaces, her every waking hour is a blissful annunciation of peace until the dread hour when Evil comes to stalk in on her.'

I hope I don't have to tell you why these sentences should make any self-respecting agent want to screech, but in among those shockers you'll find problems with punctuation, run-on sentences, poor use of abstractions, some horrible old clichés, sloppy use of colloquialisms, careless sentence construction, incorrect word choices and more. If I were an agent and encountered any of these sentences in a query letter, I wouldn't read the manuscript. I'd know for sure that any writer capable of inflicting those monstrosities on me has not written a book that I want to read. So check your query letter before sending it out. If you fear that your English may not yet be up to the right level of proficiency, you need to improve your skills with the written word before you even think of sending your work out to agents. If you need help, get help.

THE VENIAL SINS

Finally, there are a host of lesser sins, which don't have to do with command of the language, but which should nevertheless be avoided. Those sins – many of which I managed to commit with my early entry for the WWQL Awards – include the following beauties.

- *Overselling your book.* You don't need to push your work. Simply sending it to a sensibly chosen agent along with an intelligent introduction is enough. It's the manuscript's job to sell itself.

- *Overselling yourself.* If you are very well-qualified to write about a particular non-fiction topic, say so. If there is a particularly interesting connection between your experience and the topic of your novel, then make it clear. Otherwise, no one is all that interested in who you are. A swift sentence or two about you is plenty. The manuscript is the star, not you.

- *Talking about overseas markets.* You know nothing about those overseas markets. An agent does. So shut up about it.

- *Talking about the movie potential.* See above. Only doubled.

- *Talking about merchandising opportunities.* See above. Only trebled.

- *Talking about why the world needs this book.* Neither agents nor publishers are interested in ending world poverty. They are interested in making money. If they think they will make money by buying your book, they will buy it. If not, they won't.

- *Talking about how good it's been for you to write the book.* Agents don't care. Publishers don't care. See above.

- *Comparing yourself to exceptionally successful authors.* It's usually fine to say that 'this manuscript occupies the kind of territory normally associated with Patricia Cornwell' (or whoever), because that's simply identifying the kind of novel you've written. But don't say, 'I see myself as the new Patricia Cornwell,' or 'My prose style is reminiscent of John Updike.' In the first place, you're probably deluding yourself. In the second place, it's for an agent to make those kinds of judgements.

- *Talking about the excellent feedback you've had from friends and family.* Your mother loves you. Good. Keep it to yourself.

- *Grossly overstating the market.* 'My book is about pilots and aeroplanes – and we've all been on aeroplanes, haven't we?' Yes, and everyone who has ever flown is certain to buy all books that make mention of aeroplanes. Your logic is impeccable. What an excellent marketing ploy.

- *Mentioning the website you've constructed.* If you run an organisation that bears directly on the subject of your non-fiction book, then mention it. Because that organisation presumably gives you direct access to the target audience for your putative book, that fact will be highly relevant. But if your website is not directly connected with the book – or if your book is a novel, in which case no website is all that relevant – just don't mention them.

- *Wittering on.* It is no doubt a source of continuing delight and pleasure to you that you once won a story competition when at school. Your cute little story about running the parish magazine is certain to have the minister chortling to himself in the vestry. But now is not the time and place for such disclosures. Keep your letter short and taut.

- *Feeble attempts at humour.* It's much harder to write humorously than it is to speak humorously. Something that sounds good in your head when you post a submission off on Friday evening may sound horribly limp and contrived to the mildly hungover person ripping open your envelope at 9.30 on a busy Monday morning. If you genuinely have a wit and lightness of touch that comes over well in print, go for it. If not, leave well alone.

• *Excessive confidence.* 'I will call your office shortly to set up a meeting, where we can discuss this further.' Anything of this sort alienates the agent almost instantly.

• *Gimmicks.* Agents love gimmicks. Oh yes. Little novelty gifts. Letters that have the word 'SEX' in big capital letters, before that beloved phrase 'That got your attention, didn't it?' A query letter that talks about 'you' as the protagonist. ('You are in a locked room. Water is seeping up through the floor. You estimate you have half an hour to live unless you can find a way out ...' Excellent stuff!) All these things are wonderful, of course, and bring a depthless measure of hilarity and warmth into an agent's lonesome life. But couldn't you do more than this? How about mailing out a hard copy of your work along with a plastic dustbin which you refer to as a filing cabinet? What about making reference to your impending suicide? Surely you can rack your brains and find a good comedic use for some tomato ketchup or a toy gun? Agents really, really love all that. They love it so much that your manuscript will go straight into that plastic dustbin and never, ever come out.

YOUNG AND BEAUTIFUL

When Zadie Smith sent *White Teeth* to the well-known agent Andrew Wylie, her query letter ended, 'I'm six foot tall. I'm nineteen years old, and I don't exactly look like the back of a bus.' *White Teeth* was a stunning debut novel, but Smith's age, beauty and background substantially increased the advance that her agent (who was not, in the end, Andrew Wylie) was able to achieve. That's not because publishers go all wobbly-kneed in the presence of beauty, but because they calculate correctly that youth and loveliness make for some terrific PR opportunities. Sure enough, the newspapers couldn't get enough of their new literary star, and the book was launched with far more publicity than usually surrounds a debut novel. Though the book would have deserved to sell well, no matter who its author, its sales were certainly boosted by Smith's PR advantages.

These facts raise the question of how to deal with age and beauty in the query letter. Let's start from the happy assumption that you have recently excelled in competitions both for lingerie modelling and for nuclear physics. On the one hand, it helps to mention these things. On the other hand, you can easily come across as a pushy oaf if you do it wrong. Some delicacy of touch is therefore called for. So perhaps you attach a short bio that refers to your awards:

2009 – Nobel Prize for Physics (joint winner).

2008 – Miss Lingerie's 'Best Basque Wearer' Award (runner-up).

That would do fine. If the things you want to stress aren't quite as tangible as that, I'd recommend that you hint at – rather than shout about – your assets. 'I am a personable and confident twenty-year-old,' for example, would be a good way to indicate that you cause photographers to faint with longing. The truth is that, no matter how gorgeous and talented you may be, you will only get taken on by an agent if your manuscript is up to scratch. If it ain't good enough, it ain't good enough. An agent is almost certainly going to want to meet you before they agree to represent you, and once they've made your acquaintance, they'll know all about your physical charms and will certainly let publishers know about them in full. In other words, you can let the agent boast on your behalf. At the opening stages of your approach to agents, you can afford to play it fairly cool.

Being young and beautiful is by no means the only PR asset a person can have. At the time of writing, I'm trying to find a home for a client of mine. The client isn't particularly young. He's white, British and middle class, like so many others. But he has had an exceptionally well-travelled life and, whilst writing a book about kidnap, he was himself kidnapped in the Niger Delta. That, to put it mildly, suggests a hook for a future PR campaign. Another client worked for years as a TV presenter before she switched her attention to writing. She too had an obvious PR asset that was well worth a mention. Your query letter needs to allude to such things in a way that is clear, but not crass.

Let's now look at the much more common issue of writers who aren't young and gorgeous. The fact is that good writing tends to come with maturity. Many terrific writers have first picked up their pens in their fifties and sixties. With such people, I suggest that the query letter simply sidesteps the issue. If being sixty-two is a slight disadvantage – and that's all it is; it's not a killer blow – say nothing. Let an agent fall in love with your manuscript, then deal with everything else later. There's simply no need to disclose anything negative about yourself in the letter. After all, and as I've said (almost) often enough, it's the manuscript that matters.

THE SYNOPSIS

Nothing, but nothing, stresses a writer more than their synopsis – and there's no need. Synopses are easy, and arguably the least important part of the overall package. You won't sell a book because of a good synopsis, but nor are you likely to fail to sell it on account of a bad one. But every element of the package contributes to the impression you make, so it's worth getting it right.

First, be clear what it is. A synopsis is not a blurb. It is not there to pitch the book. You are not trying to advertise something, entice interest, get the pulse racing, or anything else. A synopsis is a simple plot outline of the book itself.

That doesn't sound too interesting, but you have to consider this from an agent's point of view. Let's suppose you have sent a query letter and a chunk of text to an agent. The agent has read both and is interested. Good. But what next? Plenty of books look interesting at the opening chapters stage but fall apart sometime in those difficult middle sections. Yes, an agent could simply read the whole damn book to find out that it doesn't ultimately work. But that's hours of work to invest in a project that is still more likely to fail than succeed.

That's where the synopsis comes in. The purpose of a synopsis is to set out the basic story arc of the book in a way that is brief and clear. Does the story work? Is there tension? Is there emotional movement? Is the climax and resolution satisfactory? An agent can read a couple of pages of the synopsis and get a good general sense of whether the book is likely to work. That doesn't mean that the synopsis provides a final answer – only the manuscript can do that – but if a synopsis strongly suggests that the basic direction of the book is flawed, the agent can save themselves the chore of reading the whole damn thing to find out.

That said, plenty of writers get the synopsis wrong. There are good books out there with lousy synopses. And terrible books with synopses that sound OK. Agents know this, so although they do care about the synopsis, they are also cautious about placing too much reliance on it. The synopsis is a tool. An indicator. Nothing more than that.

So that's what a synopsis is for. Here's what you're aiming to deliver:

- Your synopsis should be about 500 words long. Annoyingly, different agents ask for different lengths. Personally, I think that's just irritating, and I wouldn't go to the bother of creating (say) a 400-word version, an 800-word version and a 1000-word version just to meet the requirements of the various agents on my shortlist.

- Your synopsis should provide a summary of the book's plot. That includes the ending. If you really, really can't bring yourself to reveal the final twist, you can say something like, 'And in a dramatic final scene, Tariq discovers the truth about why Alby has been lying.' Mostly, though, you should just tell the whole story. Hold nothing back.

- You should introduce the main characters.

- Your synopsis can, especially with a literary novel, introduce some of your thematic concerns.

- You should write in fairly neutral language: you're telling, not showing. So rather than say, 'Amelia has tears running down her cheeks ...', you'll say, 'Amelia is upset at this revelation, and ...'. Needless to say, that's not how you'll do things in the manuscript itself.

- You should write competently, of course.

- If the book is non-chronological in structure, then your synopsis should be non-chronological too. It should follow the pattern of your book.

- The synopsis should tell the story, not talk about the book. So don't say, 'At this point the novel introduces Tara, who is ...'. Say, 'Tara is ...'.
- The synopsis doesn't have to contain every plot element of significance. It can't and it won't.
- Most of the rules in the section on 'Manuscript Presentation' apply to the synopsis too, but it's fine to use 1.5 line-spacing or even less for the synopsis.

Occasionally, you'll see people advising you to produce detailed notes on each character and their development, detailed chapter outlines, and more. I can't see why on earth any agent would ever want that, and I can't see why you should waste your time with such things. If those things are useful to you as a working tool, then fine, but don't start sending them out to agents.

Knowing what you are aiming to achieve is all well and good, but I haven't actually told you how to go about achieving your goal. The answer is pretty simple: you ignore your manuscript. You put it away. You do not have it on screen or in a bundle of tear-stained paper at your right elbow.

A synopsis is all about paring your story back to the very bone. It's about ignoring plot detail and dropping any mention of mechanics. Secondary characters should mostly disappear. Complex emotional detail will all be sandpapered away. Yes, the result will seem simplistic and bland – I've never read a synopsis that felt any other way – but that's the point. You want broad-brush simplicity. The complex mechanics and delicately weighted emotion of your novel have no place in a synopsis.

And the reason why your manuscript should be nowhere close to you when you write your synopsis is that you already know your story perfectly well. So proceed as follows. Give yourself the following headings:

1. Status quo.
2. Inciting incident.

3. Developments.
4. Climax.
5. Resolution.

Then fill in your synopsis using that as a skeleton. The 'developments' section will probably account for about 250 words, but that short chunk will represent maybe three quarters of your manuscript. You can't possibly hope to do your manuscript justice at that level of compression, but you're not trying to. You're simply trying to display the bones of your story. Giving extra weight, proportionately, to the front and back of the book allows the agent to see properly how your tale starts and ends; what the overall story arc feels like.

As you do this, make sure that you don't simply list events. ('Zoe tells Jacinda that they can no longer be together.') Make sure you also register emotional reactions. ('Jacinda is heartbroken and …') That way, even at this scant and bare-bones level, the reader has a good sense of the emotional curve of the book.

If you manage a synopsis which ticks all the boxes on the list above, you're doing fine. If you spend more than a day on the exercise, you've got too much time on your hands. Quite honestly, an hour or two should be all you need.

OLIVIA, MEET LORD GZHANEZ

Many agents like to wait till they have a good pile of submissions in their inbox, then zap through them as fast as they can one Saturday morning. The weak material will be swiftly rejected. Other work will need more consideration. Some manuscripts just dazzle from the very first page.

But – the names!

I remember a phone call with my editor once. He'd worked with me on several books by this point. We were talking about his reactions to the manuscript I'd recently delivered. And he was getting tongue-tied when talking about one of my characters. I said, 'You've forgotten the name, haven't you?' He admitted that he had, and I told him I didn't care. I often forgot the names of my characters as well. Not while I was working on the book maybe, but not long after.

And he was relieved. A lot of authors expect editors to know their books with the same deep intimacy that the author has, but they simply can't. Not just that, but an editor – or agent – is a machine for reading. They read huge numbers of works. And the names just pass in a dizzy blur of Alice, Bob, Cassandra, Dorcas, Ezequiel, Faatihah, and the good Lord Gzhanez.

That basic problem is at its most acute in the synopsis, when character descriptions are compressed to a couple of words and where characters run through the story at a gallop. So make it easy. Only give names to your major characters and put those in CAPS or **bold** or, if you want to go crazy, in **BOLD CAPS**.

Instantly, the agent's problem is solved. If they forget who your Olivia is or what she's doing, they only need to refer back up the page to where Olivia was first introduced. And if you're wise, those first introductions will include a thumbnail sketch of who the person is – 'Olivia (42), a computer scientist and compulsive gambler ...' That's all you need to do. And your putative agent will love you for it.

MAKING YOUR SYNOPSIS STAND OUT

If you want to make the synopsis stand out, you can attempt a little more. The thing that matters most about the story is sometimes *premise* and sometimes *shape*. A 950-word synopsis of a detective story, say, may be perfectly accurate but also quite complicated. It can be hard to read such a synopsis and get a sense of the overall arc of the story. So, before you launch into a synopsis proper, you could allow yourself a few lines which present the premise or shape of the book. You could set those lines in italics to distinguish them from the synopsis proper.

Thus, if you are introducing a thriller about diamonds, your intro might run something like this:

THE DIAMOND MERCHANT

Roy Harding loses $300,000 of diamonds in a hit-and-run raid in Amsterdam's de Clercqstraat. But why did the thief look like a senior Dutch politician? And why was the girl in the getaway car Harding's ex-wife?

That would be a good example of a quick outline of the premise. If you think that the shape of the book is more important, then your intro might run a little more like this:

THE SONS OF ADAM

Alan and Tom, raised as brothers, quarrel on the battlefields of WWI.

Alan comes to believe Tom is dead and goes on to found one of the world's greatest oil companies in his honour. But Tom isn't dead, and he has good reason to hate Alan. In the oilfields of California and West Texas, a second great oil company is born ... and a feud that lasts until D-Day itself.

(If you hate the sound of that second book, then please keep your thoughts to yourself. It's an outline of my third novel.)

Both introductions offer a snappy, memorable introduction to the most important aspect of the story. The detail that follows is there for anyone who wants to read on, but the introduction has already told anyone reading that you know what your story is and what's special about it. That means that your synopsis has already achieved most of what it needs to do.

But, as I say, most writers stress much too much about the synopsis. They don't need to. It's just not that important. Time, then, to think about approaching Planet Agent itself.

Part Two

PLANET AGENT

Approaching Agents and Publishers

Good. You've got your manuscript in shape. You've got a query letter. You've got a synopsis. You've done your research and picked the names of a dozen or so agents that you're intending to approach. You're ready to launch.

SINGLE SUBMISSIONS VS MULTIPLE SUBMISSIONS

Agents would really like it if you didn't go sending out your manuscript to all and sundry at the same time. They'd like it if you sent it to them on an exclusive basis. They'd like it if you allowed them to work at their own pace. They'd like it if they didn't have to compete with other agents. These things would all make their complicated lives very much easier.

Plumbers would also like it if you never got two quotes for the same job. Insurance companies would prefer you not to visit price-comparison websites. Thieves would like you to leave your windows open, and Bill Gates would be mightily obliged if you would update your software three times a year and pour hot goo into any iMacs you happen to come across.

You are not, however, obliged to spend your time caring for the needs of plumbers, insurance companies, thieves, Bill Gates or agents. You should behave in a responsible, professional way, but that doesn't mean you should be duped into behaving in a way which is grossly against your interests.

For one thing, Planet Agent is an orb that revolves more slowly than most writers would like. A really good agency might aim to respond to 90% of submissions within two weeks. More typically, an agency might take six to eight weeks to respond. If holidays or the major book fairs (New York, London, Bologna,

Frankfurt) intervene, then that eight could easily stretch to ten or twelve. You need to remember that the primary task of agents is to take care of their existing clients. Possible new ones are never a priority.

So much for the time lags. Let's say that your book is good and saleable, but not so obviously strong that every agent in town will be biting your hand off for it. It may well be that you need to reach ten or twelve agents before finding the one who's right for you. Multiply ten agents by six weeks, and you have already spent more than a year on the search. Multiply a dozen agents by a dozen weeks, and you have spent almost three full years chasing round after representation. If you have the genes of Methuselah, are starting out young, and are taking plenty of chewable calcium, then perhaps you will manage to fit in a decent career before osteoporosis sets in. For the rest of us, however, I'd advise a more pressured approach.

And competition is good. Normally, when you spend a lot of money on something, you will consider your choices very carefully before making your selection. Yet, although you may well end up handing over a lot of money to your agent in the form of commission payments, the difficulty of getting an agent in the first place means that you may well get desperately little choice as to where that money goes. Almost always, you'll end up saying 'yes' to the first agent who says 'yes' to you.

On the other hand, if you approach several agents at the same time, and more than one agent comes back to you with an interest in representing you, so much the better. Meet both. Talk to them. See who you like better. See which agency feels like a better fit for you. Feel free to ask awkward questions: is that 15% commission negotiable? How do they handle any possible film interest? How can they help your career development? What if you also want to write children's books/screenplays/non-fiction? There are other issues too; perhaps more significant ones. Different agencies handle film interest in different ways. Some agents are more thoughtful than others when it comes to career direction. And so on.

Plumbers don't particularly like you getting rival quotes, but, if you don't go ahead and get them, I bet you've got some very expensive plumbing. So yes. Make multiple submissions. I'd suggest dividing them into two waves of five or six submissions and leaving six weeks between waves. If you want to motor, a single wave of ten to twelve submissions is also fine.

FIRST THREE CHAPTERS VS THREE SAMPLE CHAPTERS

The standard package to send to an agent is a query letter, a synopsis and three chapters of your book. Some agents, however, take care to specify the *first* three chapters; others ask for 'three sample chapters'.

If you have written a novel, then, irrespective of what an agent asks for, you must send the first three chapters. If you cull some random chapters from elsewhere in the novel, they'll feel bafflingly incomplete. If your work is narrative-led non-fiction, the same still applies. If your work is subject-led non-fiction (such as this book, for example), it doesn't matter where those three chapters are culled from. Just pick whatever you think looks most powerful.

You can include a prologue without counting it as a chapter. If your chapters are unusually short or unusually long, you should adjust the three-chapter rule accordingly. You're aiming to send out about 10–12,000 words in total, ending at a natural break. That said, some agents like to mess around with their submission requirements, and you should (roughly) adhere to what the agent asks for, so there are no shortcuts. Check the agent's site. Deliver the package they request.

'NO UNSOLICITED MSS'

Some agencies state that they want no unsolicited MSS. ('MSS' is simply the plural of MS, which in turn simply means 'manuscript'.) The part of the formula that more often perplexes writers is the 'unsolicited' bit. What on earth does that mean? How is an agent going to solicit your manuscript from you, if they don't even know that you've got one?

One answer is that some agencies want you to send them a query letter before sending through your manuscript proper. The purpose of a query letter is effectively to say, 'I've got a great MS on the subject of _____. Would you like to see it?' If you get a positive response, your manuscript has been solicited, and you're welcome to send it. In a sense, there's no more to the 'no unsolicited MSS' message than that some agents don't want to have their inboxes flooded with massive documents.

On the other hand – and this is the less salubrious part of the answer – many agencies will feel that they are well enough connected already. They may have a good track record in poaching talent from other agencies. They may be good at persuading celebrities or high-profile academics to sign up with them. They may get plenty of good business from word of mouth. They may be good at identifying journalists who can be 'converted' into authors. They may have some good talent-spotters at creative writing schools. They may have strong links with an editorial agency. More likely, they'll be thriving because of a combination of many of these things. In such cases, then the 'no unsolicited MSS' message is really no more than an obscure way of saying, 'Please go away and stop bothering us.'

Personally, I don't much like this approach. The literary in-dustry feels closed to first-time writers and has been historically terrible at reaching out to more marginalised voices. Any approach which increases that impression is hardly welcome. On the other hand, you're under no obligation to work with agents who don't seem welcoming. So either send in your query letter and hope for the best, or simply turn to other, more generous, outfits. There are plenty of them.

APPROACHING PUBLISHERS

If you're writing to publishers instead – well, the same guidelines broadly apply, except that publishers can be more variable in what they say they want. Take a look at what they specify, then do your best to comply, at least roughly.

If publishers say that they won't look at submissions except via agents, you should take that statement at face value. Whilst, in fact, all big publishers do look at unsolicited work every now and then — perhaps a friend of a friend is an editor there, or knows someone who is — it's best to avoid these back channels. First, if your work is strong enough to secure an offer from a major publishing house, it's also strong enough to get you an agent. Second, if you are not represented by an agent, then it's all too common for editors to make some vague expression of interest, then just let the submission drift for months. I've known writers who have been in a state of limbo with major publishers for months and even years like this. The writer is puzzled by the inordinate delays, but worried about submitting the work elsewhere while it's still hanging in the balance. When push comes to shove, however, the work is nearly always turned down — and with no useful reason given. ('While we really admired your work, we just didn't love it enough to make an offer. We do wish you the very best of luck elsewhere.' Gee. Thanks.) No agent would put up with these delays, but you're in a weaker bargaining position, so there's nothing you can do.

In short, if you're approaching the mainstream: do it right and get an agent. A well-presented manuscript, a strong query letter and a professional synopsis or outline are your tools of entry.

COMMUNICATIONS FROM PLANET AGENT

You've sent your manuscript out to agents (or perhaps to publishers. This section will mostly talk about agents, because that's where the majority of authors submit their work in the first instance, but what follows is largely true no matter where you send your work.)

You know that Planet Agent rotates at one-fourth earth speed, so you know to adjust your time expectations accordingly. You have your fingers and toes crossed. You notice that you have substantially increased your intake of your drug of choice (builders' tea, coffee, red wine, cigarettes, dark chocolate, hash cookies, exotic vaping products, coca leaves, opium), but nothing you can't handle. You think you're keeping things vaguely under control – baby not dead; husband still speaking to you – but you have a creeping suspicion that you may be vibrating in public, you can't precisely remember the last time you used a bar of soap, and it has become somewhat disturbing that perfect strangers approach you in the street saying, 'Are you sure you're all right?'

And then your inbox pings with the name of a well-known agency ...

HOW AGENTS WORK

When it comes to decoding responses from agents, it helps to know how they work. Very roughly, agencies are likely to sort manuscripts into three groups:

Obviously unsuitable. Don't bother to read more than a page or so.

Marginal. Read the submission package before deciding to reject.

Intriguing. Read the entire submission package, before deciding to ask the author for the entire manuscript. When the manuscript arrives, it will be read in full.

The triage will often be handled in the first instance by support staff, but these staff are recruited and trained to handle the job well and properly.

In terms of ratios, different agencies work differently, but the 'obviously unsuitable' category perhaps amounts to around 80–90% of submissions. In these cases, the manuscript will be rejected because:

- The premise of the novel or manuscript is unappealing.

  There is not a lot of appetite for 'novels' that include large chunks of personal philosophising on life. Nor is there a big market for childhood memoirs, one third of which is made up of poetry. Nor does anyone want books very like (but not as good as) the books which were being published thirty, forty or one hundred years ago. And, of course, some agents just don't handle specific genres and plenty of writers just blast their work out without checking.

- The prose style is bad.

  It remains astonishing to me how many writers are careless about their prose. If you want to be a writer, you can no more be careless with your prose than a painter can be careless with his paints. Prose matters! You may think that no sane person can reject your manuscript without having read it in full, but, if your prose is weak then your manuscript is weak and it's not worth reading.

That's it. If the premise is potentially a marketable one and the prose style looks strong, then an agent or an agent's reader has to read beyond the query letter and a page or two of text to make a decision.

The quick rejections are the easiest. If a reader makes their way to the end of the three chapters and they're still happy, they'll quite likely refer the package to an agent for joint discussion. If they find something to bother them, on the other hand, a rejection is likely to follow. From your point of view, a rejection is a rejection and it doesn't make much difference whether the decision has been made relatively swiftly or relatively slowly. If, for example, your manuscript is nicely written but has profound plot problems, it may take three chapters (or more) to determine the extent of the plotting issues. That doesn't mean that you've 'done better' than someone whose perfectly plotted book is facing instant rejection because of poor prose quality. In both cases, the manuscript may need to be torn apart and reassembled.

If a reader and an agent both read a submission package and decide that they want to see more, they'll get in touch and ask to see the full manuscript. If you haven't got the full manuscript – or perhaps only the first three chapters are in shape to go out – you've created a problem for yourself. At this stage, an agent's interest is still only faint. If you send them work which isn't up to scratch, you'll be rejected. If you ask them to wait and come back to them in three months' time, you may have missed your window of opportunity. The moral of that story? Wait till you're ready.

If you're asked for the full manuscript, you're in the final stage of the triage. You may still be rejected. There are, after all, plenty of things that can go wrong from chapter 4, but, whatever happens, you'll know that you've made it into the top few percentiles of submissions. And, of course, the entire manuscript must excel. It's no use hoping that agents will see the potential in your work and take you on in the hope of a glorious future. Agents aren't in the glorious potential business. They're in the sales business.

THE STANDARD REJECTION

Most agencies will use a standard email for their rejections. That email will feel a little cold, because it is. It won't invite any further interaction. It'll say something to the effect that this is a subjective business and will wish you luck elsewhere, but a no is a no is a no is a no. That doesn't necessarily mean your work is a total disaster. Remember that maybe 90% of submissions (or more) will receive that standard email, so you can't tell whether you're at the top end of the range or plumbing its depths.

You should also be very careful about trying to intuit how good or bad your work is from the speed of an agency's response. A fast response could just imply that your package arrived in a quiet week. A slow response could mean that your work sat on a shelf somewhere for eight weeks, then was rejected out of hand.

In short, there aren't many clues you can get from a standard rejection. Bin it and move on.

THE 'NICE' REJECTION

Sometimes, authors will experience the strangely mixed joy of a 'nice' rejection email – that is one personally written by an agent and with a touch of regret. Such emails are much commoner after the full manuscript has been requested – indeed, I'd say it was bad form to ask for the full manuscript and then offer no comment.

If you get a response like this, you should assume that most of what an agent says is broadly true. So, if they say, 'We really liked this,' then they probably did. Perhaps they're being a bit more emphatic about their liking than was really the case, but they wouldn't go to the trouble of saying anything unless they really did have some positive feelings for it. Likewise, if they say, 'We just felt we wouldn't know how to sell this,' they are being nothing but truthful.

There are other common comments, however, which you should treat with some scepticism. My personal bugbear is the comment, 'We didn't find your central character sufficiently sympathetic.' What is that supposed to mean? Does it mean that

American Psycho is a rubbish book? That *Macbeth* is a rubbish play? That nobody could possibly build an appealing series of commercial novels around Hannibal Lecter? Indeed, James Bond – one of the most popular heroes of all – is a drug-taking, sadistic, sexually predatory snob.

The truth is the standards of editorial insight among agents vary wildly. The 'unsympathetic central character' nonsense has come to be a convenient euphemism which translates as, 'We didn't quite like your book enough, but we're not quite sure why.' I'd say that, in a large majority of such cases, a really good editor would be able to say precisely what isn't working with the book and what needs to be done to fix it. Making the central character someone who likes baking cakes and working with children is not the answer.

That's not to say that you can't or shouldn't make use of editorial comments from agents, but treat them with caution. We often receive manuscripts from clients who have been told by an agent that X is the problem. I'd say that about a third of the time X really is the problem and the agent has (succinctly, but accurately) identified it. About a third of the time, there is a problem and X is one of its manifestations, but the underlying problem is deeper and has more ramifications than the agent's short summary suggested. And, in about a third of cases, X simply isn't the issue at all. There are issues, for sure, but concentrating on X just won't get the poor old writer any closer to the target. Indeed, by concentrating on the wrong thing, the writer may move further from the target, not closer.

So, as with all things editorial, you need to ask whether a particular comment rings true with you. If you find yourself thinking, 'Dammit! I knew X was a problem, but I hoped I'd hidden it,' then the comment in question is spot on. If you find yourself thinking, 'Well, I hadn't thought this was an issue, but Agent Badger here tells me that it is and who knows more about books, really, me or Agent Badger?' you may well want to take the goodly Badger's advice with a small spadeful of salt.

In summary, 'nice' rejection letters are a genuinely positive sign. You may also glean some specific, helpful, relevant insights to your work. But don't start treating these bulletins from Planet Agent as infallible. They're not.

THE INVITATIONAL REJECTION LETTER

If an agent really likes something but is sure that he can't place it as it stands, he's in a slightly delicate position. He can't tell you that, if you change certain specific things, then he'd be happy to represent you, because he can't responsibly offer representation until he's got a complete, saleable manuscript in front of him. On the other hand, he doesn't just want to send you away with a 'nice' rejection letter, because he does see potential in your work and would like to work with it.

In such cases, you'll often get a response which invites further collaboration. Below, for example, I've included a real email from an agent to an author. (Well, OK, I've changed the names and a few other things, but I took a real email as my model.) The email is long. It's thoughtful. It's got a clear plan of action. All these things are clear signs that the agent is genuinely interested in collaborating.

Dear Wilma

Forgive the delay in getting back to you with my thoughts but it was the London Book Fair last week which seemed to take up all of my time.

Anyway, I have now read Romeo and Juliet *and enjoyed it a lot.*

It is great escapism, in the way Webster is, and there is an enthusiasm to the writing which one can't
help to be swayed by. [...]

In order to live up to this potential, I do think, though, that the book needs quite a bit of work, namely in terms of the archi-tecture of the story ... At the moment, the storyline/s aren't tight enough so that the whole thing feels too baggy and at the centre there is no one strong narrative strand that gives the whole story narrative tension and momentum. I would suggest that you need to rework and make more of the main rivalry to be found in your book – i.e. that between Tybalt and Romeo – because it seems to me that it is this which is/should be your main narrative focus. If you can set this up earlier, and then play this out as the story progresses, slowly cranking up the tension to a big climax, it will help give the whole book focus. [...]

The background is the rich and wealthy. Juliet is really the only character who isn't from this life. [...] Is it worth making her the centre of a love-triangle between Tybalt and Romeo? This might give the book a more obvious 'centre'. The other area you need to work on is Romeo's characterisation. [...]

If these comments strike a chord, then I would be delighted to see a revision of the manuscript along these lines. If you'd prefer to try your luck elsewhere, then let me wish you the best of luck with that. Whatever happens, I enjoyed reading this!

Yours
Wilmot

It's worth noting that the agent is talking about some pretty big changes here and offers no guarantee that he'll accept the finished work. That means that you, the writer, will need to decide what to do. In this instance, the writer decided that Wilmot was completely right about Juliet, largely right about Romeo, and mostly wrong about the Tybalt/Romeo rivalry. So she amended the book as she felt was right, not as the agent himself recommended in detail. She did, however, succeed in creating a tight central story and felt the resultant book was very much better.

Wilmot is currently reading the manuscript. It won't bother him that Wilma hasn't followed his exact recipe for improvement. As a matter of fact, he probably won't even look back at his original letter to refresh his memory about what his recommendations were. All that really matters to him is that, when he reads the manuscript through, it seems to sing. If Wilma's changes have got it to sing, Wilmot just got himself a new client. If, for whatever reason, Wilmot ends up turning the book down, Wilma will go on to other agents, confident that she has a much stronger product to pitch.

There's one last possibility to think about here as well. An agent may well get back to you not with editorial commentary exactly, but with detailed thoughts about the market for your intended work. Very often, the thrust of those comments is likely to be 'dumb down', 'make accessible', 'sharpen focus'. Many authors resist such suggestions, but you need to be careful. When it comes to purely editorial matters, you are, ultimately, the boss of your own work. Others advise. Only you can pronounce. On matters to do with the market, however, agents know what they're talking about and you don't. Even if you hate the message, you would do well to ponder it hard – and, if necessary, go to a bookstore and ponder it there.

THE SOUND OF SILENCE

Agents and publishers are often poor when it comes to the common courtesies. I once worked with a client who wrote a capable, professional adventure yarn. It probably wasn't quite strong enough to attract the biggest commercial publishers, but it was certainly strong enough to give some of the smaller publishers food for thought. He wrote a calm, professional query letter to around a dozen publishers who sold work of this kind, then sat back to wait ... and wait ... and wait.

In an email to me, he commented:

I have still had no luck with the small publishers. Mostly, they don't bother with the common courtesy of replying to emails, which I find rather irritating and arrogant. I don't understand how people who make their livings from the work of writers seem to feel free to simply be rude to them. Yes, I know they are busy. We're all busy.

He's right. Publishers and agents do make their living from writers. Rudeness should be unacceptable, irrespective of whether the writer involved is a client or not. The trouble is that the industry has evolved a blunted sensitivity to these things, so that what would be rudeness in any other context has come to be seen as perfectly normal. That doesn't make it acceptable, however. It isn't. Just don't take it personally.

You may also find yourself occasionally encountering rejection letters which seem needlessly spiky. For example, although Jericho Writers doesn't often act as an agent, we do occasionally present clients' work direct to publishers. We did so recently with a true-crime story, written by the villain himself, and with lots of hands-on input from an accomplished literary novelist. The resulting manuscript was an eye-poppingly good read. We sent the work to various publishers, all of whom were active in the true-crime market. Our query letter made it very clear what kind of manuscript we were dealing with.

One of those publishers responded promptly but acerbically, asking us with contempt whether we really thought that this publisher's readers would be interested in such a 'crude and unsympathetic' character as the one portrayed in the book. Their rejection was intended to sting, and it did. One would be tempted to say that their comments were fair enough. There's no question that our client, as he came across in the book, was unsympathetic. But – duh! – he was a criminal! And this was a publisher who specialised in books about criminals! What on earth did this publisher believe the criminal fraternity to be like? A true-crime imprint that restricted itself to books about gentleman thieves and art-collecting contract killers might, you'd think, end up with rather few titles to its name. It was a daft rejection letter, and intentionally, pointlessly rude. (This particular story ended well. Another true-crime publisher snapped up the book and was delighted to do so.)

The point to bear in mind, however, is that you may well encounter slowness, rudeness, prickliness and a degree of non-responsiveness that you can only hope to encounter in the outside world if you try to get customer services help from your telecoms provider. I'm afraid to say, that's life – or, rather, that's life as a writer. Shrug it off and move on. It's not you, it's them.

AREN'T WE MISSING SOMETHING?

As you tick off the subject headings in this section – the standard rejection, the nice rejection, the invitational rejection, the sound of silence – you may start to feel that perhaps we've missed something. And we have. Every now and then, it does truly, genuinely happen that an agent (or publisher) asks to see your full manuscript – and they like it! They want to take you on!

You start to uncross your fingers and toes. You get out the hoover for the first time in – how long? – and are slightly alarmed at what you find on the floor. (A few chocolate wrappers, fine. But what are all those chewed up leaves? And why do those biscuit crumbs smell so funny?) Life returns to normal. Your baby has grown rather alarmingly but is still alive and healthy. Your husband is still speaking to you, and perfect strangers no longer have that worried look on their faces.

Most of the time, agents will break the good news via email or phone. It's rare for an agent to use that first communication to say outright that they'd like to represent you. Mostly, they'll say that they loved your book and would be eager to meet up. If you come over as hopelessly rude and arrogant, you might be able to convert an acceptance into a rejection, but nearly always an agent is asking to meet you because they want and expect to represent you. You can go to that meeting in good heart and cheerful confidence.

And, if you reacquaint yourself with a bar of soap before you go, so much the better for us all.

An Introduction to Planet Agent

Meeting an agent is a thrilling moment. It's your first proper entry into the literary community, the first time you're there by invitation. Enjoy it.

If you're youngish and scrub up nicely, then scrub up nicely. That's not because agents are swayed by such things for their own sake, but because they know that publishers know that the print and broadcast media prefer people who are unafraid of exposure. If you're not young or if you look like something made of dough and old mattresses, it's not a big deal. People are after your words; the rest of it is secondary.

Aside from that, be prompt and pleasant. You are potentially about to enter a business relationship that will endure for years. But remember, the manuscript is the main thing and the agent already likes it. That's why you're here.

Curiously enough, although you are likely to be nervous at this first meeting, it's the agent who has more reason to be. For sure, you'll be giddy with excitement, but the agent knows that your manuscript is marketable and that you may well have sent it to other agents. That means that there's a whiff of competition around, whether or not you care to make that fact explicit. Although you need to present yourself well, the agent is also pitching to you. It's their turn to sell themselves.

You should expect a meeting of about an hour. There'll be some chitchat, some flattery, a cup of coffee and (if times are good) a cookie. Once the cookie is nibbled and the coffee has cooled, however, the agent will lean forward and say, 'So. What do *you* want to ask me?' This is not a good moment for your mind to go blank. Nor is it a good moment to start gabbling the first questions that come into your head. ('Do you ever get confused about how to pronounce the "r"s in "literary"?' 'What did you think of Keira Knightley in *Atonement?*' 'Have you ever actually read *War and Peace?*' 'Erm ... erm ... the capital of Colombia?')

As a matter of fact, it might be around now that you realise you don't actually know what agents *do*. Just as well, therefore, that this section is here to tell you.

WHAT AGENTS DO

Agents are there to sell

Agents are salespeople. That's the heart of their job. Like any good salesman, they are paid on commission. Like any good saleswoman, they know how to pitch and who to pitch to.

A large part of their sales skills is understanding the market – in this context, understanding which of the various publishing houses are going to see the most value in your work, because it's those houses who will bid the most for it. Agents also, however, need to know individuals. A certain sort of manuscript might be obviously right for (let's say) a leading imprint of Penguin Random House. But some of those imprints are huge, with numerous editors. Who is the right person for this book? An agent will want to choose someone likely to be passionate about the manuscript, but also someone authoritative enough to command widespread support in the organisation. One editor might be perfect for a book about a troop of commandos in Iraq. Another editor might be right for an affectionate memoir of farming life. Your agent needs to know who to pick for your book.

The agent also needs to pick the right sales strategy. Because books are more varied products than used cars or double glazing, there's no one way to sell a book. With a really commercial offering, an agent will almost certainly pick a small group of publishers – typically six to eight – and get the MS out to them all at the same time. Where a manuscript has an obvious preferred publisher, an agent may sometimes give that publisher a two-week 'exclusive', in the hope that a good deal can be tied up quickly. With manuscripts that are going to be a little more tricky to place, an agent may try a more select group of three or four editors in the first instance, or perhaps approach just one.

Agents are there to negotiate

In the most ideal of all ideal worlds, you'll have multiple publishers bidding for your book, in which case the main components of any deal more or less negotiate themselves. In other cases, the negotiations will be more one-on-one. If the agent pushes too hard, he risks the publisher walking away. If the publisher offers too little, she risks the agent taking the manuscript elsewhere. Either way, your agent needs to be an effective negotiator: dogged, but wise enough to close the deal when the moment is right.

Agents are there to sell your work overseas

Some work will sell well overseas. Most manuscripts, alas, are likely to pick up only pocket-money abroad. Nevertheless, your agent needs to secure whatever can be secured.

In a majority of cases, that'll be done through a network of 'sub-agents'. Thus, the XYZ Agency in New York might use the ABC Agency in London to sell its work there, the Agence DEF to sell work in Paris, and so on. Don't be confused by the term 'sub-agent'. A sub-agent is simply an agent: the ABC Agency in London has plenty of its own clients, and more than likely uses XYZ to handle its own activities in the US.

A good agency will make sure that it has excellent sub-agents in the major territories and will sell actively to the minor territories when the annual book fairs come round. A really good agency may also be selective. It might think, for example, that the ABC Agency would be the perfect outfit to handle your slim literary novel, but that the JKL Agency would be better if your next book was a rip-snorting bodice-ripper.

These issues, however, should barely trouble you. An agent is there to handle such things. You are there to pick up the cheques.

Agents are there to supervise

Every now and then, publishers mess up. You don't have much experience, so you may not notice if they do. An agent does, and it's their job to pick up any problems early and address them responsibly.

Agents are there as mediators

If you get into a disagreement with your publisher, the agent is there to mediate. That doesn't necessarily mean taking your side. Sometimes it'll mean telling you that you're being an idiot. Some of the time, your agent may deal with a problem directly with your editor. Other times, a really good agent will see the need to go racing up the chain of command at the publishing house and secure proper attention for the issue in question. When that happens, it's very good agenting – particularly if everybody ends up as friends afterwards.

Agents are there to manage your career

If selling is the heart of an agent's job, then career development is perhaps its soul – but you need to have a realistic idea of what's involved.

An agent isn't about to whip up movie deals for you. They won't get you a column in *The New York Times*. They won't come to you with a slew of interesting book commissions. They won't get you gigs on radio, place features in the Sunday press, or introduce you to leading broadcasters. What they can and should do, however, is ensure that any book ideas you have are properly considered and right for the market.

For example, once upon a time an author came to an agent with a number of ideas for a possible book. The author outlined the first idea – his best one, as he saw it. The agent said 'hmm'. He tried out his next idea. She said 'erm'. And so on down the list, until they had considered and disposed of the first five. The author then, rather gloomily, started to outline his final idea. He had long been a football fan and wanted to write about what that felt like ...

That book – *Fever Pitch*, by Nick Hornby – became a many-million-copy bestseller. It sold as well as it did because the author was an extremely capable writer, able to articulate the anxieties and contradictions of modern urban man. Yet it also sold because it was a book in tune with its time and its public. It sold because the market was ready for just such a book.

It's that kind of guidance that an agent can offer. You are the creative. It's up to you to originate and develop ideas. But your agent knows the market. He will know much better than you what editors are looking for, what retailers will be willing to promote, what markets are flourishing. Between the two of you, you need to find the sweet spot where the stuff you want to write intersects with what the market wants to buy. That's where success lies.

AGENTS AS EDITORS

It is also part of an agent's role to help you shape your work for the market, but explaining the way agents work editorially needs some delicacy. On the one hand, agents aren't looking for potential. If you send your manuscript to agents knowing that it's rough around the edges, it'll be rejected – and quite right too. Your work needs to be dazzling.

It's also true that many agents aren't editorially centred by nature. The most obvious alternative line of work for an agent is as an editor in a major publishing house. The fact that they've chosen to be an agent rather than an editor is normally telling. In today's literary economy, few agency business models allow time to work through countless new drafts of a manuscript. You should not assume that you and your agent will be going on long country walks, smoking pipes or discussing sentence structure in post-war American literature. That is not going to happen.

Having said all this, agents know that they can't send work to editors until it's glittering and perfect. If they go out to the market at all prematurely, they'll either fail to get a deal or they'll fail to get a deal as good as they ought to. Agents will also, as I've said previously, have a nose for the market that you can't have. It's not enough for a book to work in purely literary/artistic/intellectual terms. It must satisfy the needs of the market, no matter that the market can sometimes be crass or even downright barmy in its requirements.

What's more, agents will sometimes see that a particular manuscript has an X-factor, something so strong and uncommon that it merits extra input. For these two reasons – shaping something for the market and bringing something to its maximum degree of editorial potential – an agent may want you to make changes to your script.

Sometimes, those suggested changes will be very broad-brush indeed: 'This is a great story, but the cast list needs to be cut down and I really need to feel more emotion from the protagonist. I'd love to see the script again if you rework it that way.' I've witnessed editorial interchanges between agent and writer which could be summarised almost as briefly as that. These suggestions aren't really editorial ones, in the sense that the entire task of developing and implementing a plan of action is left to the writer. If you're an excellent writer, then you may not need more than this kind of nudge. If you're not, you may need to get outside help.

Other times, you'll get a more detailed plan of action – such as the plan outlined in the 'invitational rejection' letter quoted in the previous section. On still other occasions, you'll be told something about the market for the book and asked to reshape your book accordingly. In such cases, you're unlikely to be given any detailed set of editorial comments. The assumption will be that you're a competent writer and that, if you know where your work needs to end up, you'll figure a way to get it there.

THE AUTHOR AS PRODUCT

The final thing to say about agents is perhaps the most important. I was once chairing a workshop at the Hay Literary Festival, where we had a very capable editor and a senior agent on the panel. Talking about their different outlooks, the agent commented, 'The thing is, to an editor, a successful product is a book that sells well. To an agent, a successful product is an author whose career flourishes.' The editor nodded and agreed.

At the time, that shocked me – not least because the editor in question was my own editor from HarperCollins. Back then, I assumed that publishers still had some ambitions to create authorial careers, however hedged-in those ambitions might be by other realities. The truth, however, is that publishers now focus almost all their efforts on the book, not the career. That means that the only professional you'll have to nudge and guide your career will be your agent. For sure, publishers will play a massive part if your career does take off, because such breakthroughs can only come about from vigorous and imaginative publishing. Yet the focus of publishers will always be on the book deal that is actually signed. Only you and your agent will have a longer horizon. For that reason, it's very common for an author and agent to stick together for years and decades. You are most unlikely to have a relationship with your editor that endures nearly as long. (I've had two agents in my career. In terms of editors who mattered, I can count at least ten.)

So chemistry matters. An agent may tick all the boxes on competence, but, if you simply don't feel comfortable with him, it's not certain that you've got the right agent. Because it's so tough to get an agent, you may be more or less forced into signing up with him to start with, but don't feel locked in. If the time comes to change, change. Ultimately, the only person responsible for your career is you.

THE COOLING CUP OF TEA

Knowing all this, when an agent asks if you have any questions, you are now in good shape to put down your cup of tea and say, 'Yes.' The next section suggests a possible list.

Things to Ask an Agent

If you have only one agent interested in your manuscript, then the frank truth is that you're likely to accept an offer of representation, no matter what the agent says in response to the questions that follow. On the other hand, it can still make sense to ask them. One, because the agent's answers will let you know what to expect. Two, because those answers give you something to refer back to if you don't get the service that was initially promised. And three, because, once you've gobbled up your biscuit and agreed with the agent's lavishly flattering assessment of your work, you still have some minutes to fill in before it would be polite to go cartwheeling down the street kissing random passers-by.

Not everyone will need to ask all the questions that follow, but, if you adapt the list below to your own sweet ends, you'll be doing fine.

How many agents work here, and what's the set-up?

If you were half-awake when you looked at the agency's website, you already know the answer to the first part of this question, but it's well worth just exploring in a little more detail exactly how an agency operates. An agency with just two agents will typically operate with a fair degree of consensus and overlap. If your agent is away on holiday when some urgent issue comes up, then the other agent is quite likely to have enough background to give you a sensible response. That may be harder with a larger agency. On the other hand, a larger agency may have a level of specialisation that you think is helpful. For example, a slightly larger agency may have a 'Mr Thriller' or 'Ms Children's Fiction' on their team. That degree of specialisation won't run all that far – almost certainly, the agent who mostly handles thrillers will also handle material in other genres, and there'll be other agents in the agency with thriller writers on their books. Nevertheless, knowing the approximate set-up is a good place to start.

What is your own background?

Some agents will have spent their entire career in literary agencies. Others will be emigres from publishing, in which case you want to check that they have worked as commissioning editors at major houses. There may be other career paths that lead to a solid base in agenting (for example, a good book publicist might be able to make the switch), but feel free to probe. The core skill of an agent is knowing the publishing world very well. An individual can get that by being an agent, but not necessarily by being a member of an agent's support staff. They can also get it by being an editor, as long as their position was sufficiently mainstream. So, for example, someone who spent most of their professional working life commissioning textbooks for an academic publisher is not likely to know the industry well enough to represent general fiction. If an agent tells you that they worked for fifteen years at a publishing company you've never heard of, check that company out. There are plenty of large publishers whose names aren't well-known to the ordinary reader, so you don't need to worry if a name doesn't click with you right away.

How many clients do you have?

Most writers are shocked when they learn how many clients a well-established agent is likely to have – often somewhere north of one hundred. Few of those clients will write a book every single year. Many will, in fact, never write a book again: agents often handle the estates of dead authors whose backlists are still selling. Smaller agencies tend to have fewer clients per agent; larger ones to have more. But there are no firm rules.

How will you sell the book?

Via a mass auction involving eight or so publishers? Or via a more selective auction? Or using a more selective approach still? You should ask the agent to explain their thinking.

Will you accompany me to any meetings with the publisher?

Any agent will tell you that they expect to keep an eye on the publication process, but some mean it more than others. Asking them if they'd expect to accompany you to meetings is a good way to find out just what they're intending.

Are you happy getting tough with publishers?

A crucial question, although you won't really learn the answer to it until you reach some pivotal moment in your career. Nevertheless, you may be able to learn something from the agent's answer. Are they able, for example, to cite a recent dispute with a publisher where they hung tough and got results? Naturally, most disputes need to be resolved amicably, but there will be times when an agent needs to be willing to show teeth. If you get the impression that an agent is likely to fight shy of confrontation, then you may well have someone who's going to back down when you most need them to fight your corner.

How closely do you work with authors when it comes to developing new projects?

Creative ideas will come from you, but a good agent will want to winnow away bad ideas as early as possible and supply encouragement and direction for the good ones. When you ask this question, be alert to the kind of reply you get. All agents know what the right answer is and will do their best to give it. But the best agents will be talking about something that they do regularly and encourage; less capable agents may drop clues that this isn't something they routinely do.

Are you taking on me or my book?

An essential question. Let's say things go badly and the agent fails to sell your work. Are they still going to offer all their help and support as you develop your next project? You need them to say yes – and to mean it.

Do you ever 'terminate' clients and, if so, how does that process work?

A slightly strange question perhaps, but the issue is this. It happens far too often that an agent takes on a client, fails to sell the work, then wishes they'd never taken the client on in the first place. The businesslike approach would be to contact the client, to tell them that the business relationship isn't working, and – politely and respectfully – to end it. Alas, far, far too many agents prefer death-by-neglect. What happens is that the client stops getting quick answers to any emails, then the replies get testy, then there's a weird emotional outburst of some sort which the client has done nothing knowingly to provoke. The relationship is then terminated with tears and recriminations. This should be totally unacceptable behaviour, yet it's common enough that I hear of such things at least once or twice every month. Asking questions about this upfront may not help much, but you never know. Perhaps it might.

How do you handle foreign sales?

One of the clearest ways in which larger agencies have an edge over smaller ones is that it's easier for larger outfits to have specialist staff for overseas sales. Nevertheless, plenty of smaller agencies are well-equipped in this respect. Perhaps they've trained a member of the support staff to handle such things, or perhaps they have an arrangement with a specialist foreign rights agency. It's easy to overestimate the amount of cash which will come to you from abroad; nevertheless, you want the chance to grab as much of it as you can.

How do you handle film interest?

The biggest agencies have their own film and TV departments, so effectively you'd be getting all-in-one representation on both the books and the film and TV side. Smaller agencies tend to wait until they are contacted by some branch of the film/TV industry about a particular project and then pass that enquiry on to a specialist film agency. If any money emerges from the process, then you'll be paying your literary agent 10% for making that connection. Either way, large agency or small, the process will usually be reactive. Perhaps some of the best agents at the best-connected agencies may propose a project to a producer or director and toss your books into the mix, but this is a rare event. Mostly, what happens is that a production company will happen across your book (and they do keep an eye on publishers' forthcoming catalogues) and make an enquiry. The truth is, given how little money ever actually lands in authors' pockets from the movie business, you shouldn't be too exercised about the whole question.

Are you a member of the Association of Authors' Representatives (US) / Authors' Agents (UK)?

Nearly all agents are members of the AAR or the AAA. Those things are industry bodies there for the benefit of their members. They aren't there to look after your interests. Personally, I wouldn't much care whether my agent was signed up or not.

There's one last issue, not a direct question exactly, which is worth bearing closely in mind as you chat. It's this: does your agent 'get' your book? Does he love what you love in it? Is your understanding of the market the same? Do you both have a similar sense of how your career might develop? These are things to be felt out rather than interrogated directly, perhaps, but they're critical all the same. If your first book is literary fiction with a crime twist, and your agent wants to pitch you as a crime writer of class, then that could be confining into the future. On the other hand, the agent may have a sharper sense than you do of how the market will wish to pigeonhole your book. Worth investigating, anyway.

WHAT IF TWO AGENTS OFFER REPRESENTATION?

If you make multiple submissions (as you should), then it is possible that two agents will offer you representation at much the same time. This, in fact, happened to me when I was looking for agents with my first novel.

If you do get two offers of representation, then good for you. You now need to go and meet both agents and ask them a slew of questions, broadly along the lines of the ones above – and never forgetting to talk about any editorial issues which they have raised.

There is no hard and fast rule as to who you should pick. Or rather: the hard and fast rule is to trust your gut instinct. The two non-crazy agents who offered to represent me were (1) the MD of a large and famous London agency, and (2) one half of a two-woman agency that hadn't been in existence all that long. I met both people, and was very impressed by them both, but thought that I would feel happier with the dedicated attention of a smaller agency, so I ended up rejecting one of the best-known agents in London. I never felt that was the wrong decision. On the contrary: it was the right one. Somebody else might have made the opposite decision and felt it was absolutely the right course of action for them.

You should also feel free to negotiate. That 15% commission may be negotiable. You don't need to come over all aggressive about it. Just say in your sweetest voice, 'Gosh, I wonder if that 15% is negotiable at all. It's just that I suspect the other agent may be willing to offer me a discount.' If they say no, so be it. No one will be offended that you asked.

At the same time, don't go nuts. Don't try to start a bidding war or anything like that. It's far, far better to secure the services of an excellent agent at 15% than a mediocre one at 10%. A good agent will earn you way more than that 15% in the long run. If an agent refuses point-blank to consider any reduction in their take, then don't be offended or surprised. Agents have businesses to run and they do need to be properly incentivised to work hard on your behalf. If you have a slim literary novel for sale, and no realistic hope of a huge readership for it, then any move you make to reduce that agent's incentivisation is probably directly contrary to your own best commercial interests.

Signing up with an Agent

You've written your book. You've found an agent who loves it. You met her and liked her. You've handled any editorial changes. As far as the agent is concerned, your book is now ready to sell — which means that you and your agent need to sign a proper contract.

A TYPICAL CONTRACT

The contract you sign with an agent is likely to be simple and self-explanatory. The occasional agent may go in for a four- or five-page contract that's full of gobbledegook, but a more standard approach is a simple two page contract letter. That letter is likely to look rather like the one following. Comments in italics are, pretty obviously, my own. If you do receive a five-page monster letter, it's likely to boil down to the exact same thing.

> Dear Persephone,
>
> This letter confirms our agreement whereby you appoint us as your agents to act exclusively on your behalf for the sale of your work throughout the world, including but not limited to book publishing, motion picture, TV, radio and electronic publishing rights.

Note that your contractual relationship is with the agency, not the individual agent. That means if your agent goes AWOL – or mad, or dipsomaniac, or becomes a Trappist, or is sentenced to fifteen years' hard labour in a small Balkan state – you still have representation. Agencies, even the larger ones, can be terrible about honouring that obligation, though.

Do also note that word 'exclusively'. If you are thinking of writing for both adults and children, you might want to chat to your agent before signing up to this. (Is your agent capable of handling both kinds of material? Some are, some aren't.) Equally, if you intend to self-publish a proportion of your work (no bad idea these days), then you probably want to chat to your agent upfront. These things won't cause agents to have a meltdown. The most likely scenario is that you just tell your agent you plan to self-publish some work down the line, and they agree to remove the word 'exclusively'. Or just leave the issue for now, and sort things out by email nearer the time. It's no big deal.

Finally, it's worth observing that, as formulated here, you are giving your agent the right to negotiate movie rights. That's fine — it's what I do, for example — but this can work in a couple of different ways. If your agent is part of a large, full-service agency that includes a film and TV department, then great. You have everything you need under one roof. More commonly, though, your literary agency will handle only books, and they will sub-contract their movie business to an appropriate specialist firm. Your agency will likely split the overall 20% fee on such deals 50/50 between themselves and the movie specialist. You may think this sounds like a bad deal. Why not hire a film agent directly? Why not offer the film agent 15%, so they do better and you do better? Only trust me: it's not like that. You'll get a better, more focused movie agent if you go via your literary agent's firm. You'll get sane advice and real commitment when you need it. If at some point your needs change, you can always talk again with your agent.

We undertake to represent your interests to the best of our ability and will conduct negotiations on your behalf, subject to your reasonable approval in all cases.

Means just what it says.

We shall promptly remit to you any money due to you and which we receive on your behalf.

Agents are generally very prompt in handing over any money they get from publishers — but the cash always lands in their bank account first, not yours. When you do get payment from an agent, they'll have knocked off their commission from the total.

Our commissions, which shall be deducted from those disbursements, shall be as follows:

On home sales – 15%
On overseas sales, including translation rights – 20%
On film & TV rights – 20%
[On one-off journalism – 15%]

These fee levels are standard, though not quite universal. They are also, definitely, not prescribed by some industry body (as one agent once falsely tried to claim to me). The key point though is that agents get paid if they make sales. No sale, no fee. It's a good arrangement that aligns your interest and the agent's almost perfectly.

We have the right to reimburse ourselves from any money received on your behalf relating to any expenses that may be incurred on your behalf and only ever with your agreement.

You used to get deduction for things like photocopying and purchase of books. Those things have long gone. It's now rare to see deductions for pretty much anything.

This agreement may be terminated by either side, sixty days after written notice has been given.

Means just what it says.

After termination, we shall no longer undertake any new negotiation or representation on your behalf, but we shall have the irrevocable right to continue to receive the full commission above on all money due under all con-tracts which we have negotiated on your behalf, or which derive from them, or which are renewals or extensions of them.

This needs a tad more clarification. If you ditch your agent just after they've sold your sensational manuscript – The Secret Double Life of Prince Harry *– to MegaBucks Publishing Ltd, then your agent, quite rightly, thinks themselves entitled to all commission on that contract both now and in the future. This clause secures that right for the agent. The sixty-day termination clause needs to be read in that context. If your agent is in the process of negotiating a deal and you terminate, they have sixty days to get the thing done. And they will.*

Our right to receive money from these publishers and to deduct the commissions due may only be varied or revoked with our agreement in writing.

This is belt and braces from the agent. They're just saying that they're damn well going to hold onto those future payments unless they tell you explicitly and in writing otherwise. Which they won't.

We agree to continue to represent your interests with respect to such contracts unless you instruct us otherwise and our commissions shall remain due on any improved terms under such contracts, whether or not we negotiate such improved terms ourselves.

So if they negotiate that Prince Harry contract, they'll also remain committed to tending to it, now and into the future. In practice, their degree of commitment is likely to wane significantly if you've fired them.

You agree to hold us harmless for any breach of contract in respect of any agreements with publishers or co-authors signed by you.

If you mess up an agreement with a publisher, you can't pretend that your agent is at fault.

This agreement shall be governed by the laws of the State of New York/England and Wales.
Please signify your agreement to the terms of this letter by signing and returning both copies of this document.

Yours sincerely,
Peter Parminter,
Senior Agent, Parminter & Pickle Literary Agency

If you receive a letter that's significantly more complex than this, then feel free to ask for a full explanation of any clauses you don't understand. On the whole, though, the contract with your agent is not something to fret about. It's a simple and uncontroversial document. On quickly to more interesting things ...

LIFT-OFF

You've now written and polished your manuscript. You've secured an agent who loves your work. The agent now needs to send it out to publishers.

Sometimes, an agent will tell you exactly which editors at which publishing companies your MS is going to; sometimes they won't. Unless you have some industry background yourself, an agent isn't likely to discuss that decision with you. That's partly because they are the experts, but also because the agenting industry has evolved an attitude towards writers that's reminiscent of the way doctors of the 1950s treated their patients: with professionalism, but preferring an air of mystery to one of open frankness. If you want to know who your book is going to and why it's going to those people rather than others, then ask. It's not a secret and you have every right to be told. If you don't care too much, then that's fine too. Your agent has every incentive to get this critical part of the job exactly right. Luckily, as younger agents rise through the system, the air-of-professional-mystery nonsense is slowly evaporating.

As your manuscript noses off into the void, like some NASA probe voyaging out into the asteroid belt, you might suddenly notice that you know about as much about the books trade as you do about the asteroid belt – and have seen far fewer movies about it. So now, we turn to the book trade itself: understanding it and working with it.

Part Three
HOW THE BOOK TRADE WORKS

The Market for Books

Ten years ago, an earlier edition of this book quoted a 2009 article from the UK trade magazine, *The Bookseller*. The article reported:

> *Anthony Goff of David Higham Associates, acting president of the Association of Authors' Agents, confirmed that cuts in author advances had gone as deep as 70%. 'For big-brand authors their position is stronger than ever' he said. 'Elsewhere the reductions range from 5% to 70% — if it is much below 70% you are just dropping the authors. Publishers are cutting lists and there is less competition out there in the market, so there is a natural economics going on.'*

Now, OK, that was 2009. The financial crash had just happened. The world was still fingering its wounds and trying to figure out how badly it was hurt. But even at the time, no one I knew in the industry thought that things were going to magically reverse once economic growth came back. Everyone knew they wouldn't. The recent recession was simply amplifying and accelerating changes that were already in hand.

And? Well, the pessimists were right. The big houses are publishing fewer titles than they did. Sales have tended to coalesce around big-brand authors, with relatively fewer sales going to the mid-list. There has already been one major consolidation in the industry (with the merger of Penguin and Random House) and others are probable.

More interestingly — and this is under-remarked-on — the industry seems to generate fewer big brands than it did. So if you think of the biggest, most famous authors on the planet, you are quite likely to be thinking of people whose careers were established before the dominance of Amazon and the e-book. (Or, let's say, in the years prior to 2011, to be more precise about it.) Since then, you can think of plenty of books that have caused a sensation (*Gone Girl*, *The Girl on The Train*, *Where the Crawdads Sing*, and many others), but none of those authors (Gillian Flynn, Paula Hawkins, Delia Owens) feels like a new John Grisham, say, or a new Patricia Cornwell. Branding has made a significant shift from the author to the book.

But before we get into the weeds of why all this has happened, it's worth understanding how the market for books has evolved to be the way it is.

THE PRODUCT

In around 1439, Johannes Gutenberg invented a printing press that used a corkscrew press, oil-based inks and movable type to simplify and cheapen the business of reproducing the written word. William Caxton learned these techniques from Continental printers and returned to England in 1476 in order to set up a press in Westminster, where he printed Chaucer, Malory and other titles calculated to set fifteenth-century hearts a-racing. These books posed an unanswerable challenge to the old monk'n'quill technology, and books started to come down in price.

Their price would continue to tumble relative to incomes until, at the start of the eighteenth century, books became cheap enough that something like a mass-market product became possible. A new art form was invented – the novel – and for the first time the daughters of dukes, the wives of cloth merchants and the housemaids of both began to tremble, gasp and weep over the adventures of people who didn't really exist.

In the nineteenth century, steam–cylinder printing arrived – an event that's celebrated by no one today except a few Industrial Revolution technology buffs. For all history's neglect, the invention was arguably the most important advance in communications technology since Gutenberg himself. The invention took

Gutenberg's basic insight and mechanised it. Printing became even cheaper. The most popular book of the day — *The Bible* — was able to become a truly mass-market product. Mass-market newspapers flourished. So did mass-market novelists, to such an extent that it's guesstimated that one in ten Victorian Britons had read Charles Dickens, the most commercially successful novelist of his era.

The mass-market revolution, however, was not yet over. In 1934, the great Penguin publisher, Allen Lane, searched a station bookstall for something he could read on the way home. (He hadn't thought to borrow something from his host that weekend, a certain Agatha Christie.) He found nothing to his taste and decided that it was time for a whole new invention: the paperback. The new books appeared in 1935. They were priced cheaply but contained the same quality content as you'd have expected to find from any quality hardback publisher of the era. Within just twelve months, Penguin had sold 3,000,000 paperbacks.

It had now been five centuries since Gutenberg first slapped ink on paper, yet the essential product remained stunningly similar. Gutenberg would have been amazed at how cheap Allen Lane's paperbacks were. Allen Lane would have been astonished at how beautiful Gutenberg's printed volumes were. But the basic product simply hadn't altered in any of its essentials. Indeed, up to 2011, the book was perhaps the least altered technological product ever invented.

Then — thanks to the mighty confluence of platform (Amazon) and technology (the e-reader) — it became possible for books to slip free of paper covers altogether. A world of experiment was unleashed. Among the questions:

- Who would the new electronically reading public be? Would it be primarily early-adopter, higher-income, younger men? Or would the demographic be broader than that?

- How would people read? On specialist e-readers? Or on phones? Or what? The iPad was launched in March 2010 and sold a million units in less than two months. The first iPhones had taken three times longer to hit the same target.

- Would the ease of copying digital material mean that the price of e-books simply dropped to zero? Would kids just steal books via piracy sites and bring those same attitudes into adulthood too?

- Would the nature of reading itself change? Would the novel simply become some vastly old-fashioned art form? Would it be, for example, that no crime novel was complete without crime scene photos? Or music? Or 'choose your own adventure' type options? Or perhaps, the time-poor, screen-rich nature of modern life would mean that short stories (or stories written entirely via Twitter, or Wattpad) would take over? No one knew.

- Would the nature of publishing change? If people could just upload their own written work to Amazon, would anyone need publishers anymore? Would self-publishing go from a slightly eccentric niche activity to a wholly credible way to earn money?

- Conversely, could Amazon mess the whole thing up? If anyone could upload work to Amazon, then wouldn't Amazon start to resemble the world's biggest slush pile – a place where you had to look through 1000 terrible books before finding one good one? That worry was often phrased in terms of 'discoverability'. How would the good books be discoverable, when the bad books were so numerous? (And just to be clear, 'bad books' in this context was mostly code for ones which hadn't been created by traditional publishers in the traditional way.)

Today, those questions have some clear answers.

THE E-BOOK REVOLUTION

It turns out that e-books have changed some things a lot, and other things really not very much at all.

In terms of the things that have changed a lot, it turns out that people love e-books and audiobooks: versions of the written word which aren't merely sold online but *are* digital products down to their bits and bytes. One estimate, made by Paul Abbassi, the tech wizard behind Bookstats.com, suggests that about 70% of all adult fiction sold in the US *is* digital. If you add onto that figure the print books that are sold online, then perhaps three-quarters of all adult fiction is sold digitally.

Those are astonishing facts. They aren't just astonishing; they're also mostly unknown. The traditional industry has always collected its data using ISBN numbers – the little barcodes you see at the back of every normal book. And that's fine, in theory, because e-books can have ISBNs too. Except that ISBNs were invented by the industry for the industry; self-publishing authors never had any particular use for them. So the vast majority of professional self-publishers don't bother with e-book ISBNs. Which means that the data most cherished by the traditional industry (and breathlessly reported in the media) simply ignores the biggest, newest, most radical chunk of the market.

You can explore this for yourself. The market sector which has gone most completely self-pub is the romance one. If you look at the romance bestseller lists, you'll see that maybe 80–85% of the market is now indie-published. ('Indie' in this context means a self-published author. Since there are also indie bookstores and indie trad publishers, the term can get a little confusing.) The same is true of huge chunks of the SFF market. (SFF is science fiction and fantasy, by the way.) When you hear trad publishers comment that, let's say, military space opera is now completely dead as a sub-genre, you might want to pop over to Amazon to check. And when you do, you'll find that military space opera, and absolutely every other sub-genre and sub-sub-genre you can imagine, is vibrantly alive and well. It's just gone self-pub.

Equally, when you hear trad publishers comment that e-books have plateaued out at about 20% of overall sales, you have to add the silent rider that it's 20% of *their* sales. To indie authors, e-sales are likely to be 98% or more of the total. If you add in sale-equivalents via Kindle Unlimited (bear with me; I'll explain), then the digital sales of indies are often indiscernibly different from being 100% of the total.

Indeed, the most accurate way to understand what's going on is to view the market as splitting into three distinct chunks. There's a self-publishing chunk, whose home is, overwhelmingly, on Amazon, and whose sales are, overwhelmingly, of digital products. These products tend to be priced relatively cheaply. Books, especially fiction, are mostly written in series. The first book in that series is likely to be sold very cheap or just given away. Books are written and sold fast. For authors to produce four books a year is no longer uncommon.

Then there's an 'always trad' chunk which still does things in a wholly traditional way. These books will be marketed primarily to the chain bookstores and to the supermarkets. Print books, not e-books, will be front of mind when the publishers are thinking about price points, sales campaigns, and all that. And these things are broadly incompatible with all things Amazon. Take pricing, for example. Let's say that you are the sales director of Megabucks Publishing Inc. and you want to sell a $26.99 hardback to Barnes and Noble and a slew of supermarkets. What will you do? Well, you'll certainly offer some attractive discounts to the bigger buyers so that they can price-promote the book and still make good margin. But Barnes & Noble won't be thrilled to find you trying to push a $27 hardback through their checkouts while you're also offering the e-book version of the same thing at $0.99 or even $4.99. So you end up pricing the e-book at $11.99, which committed e-book readers will simply consider a deterrent to purchase. So, sure, you shift some e-books, but over the sales cycle of the book, you'll find that around 70–80% of units have sold in print form (whether online or not.)

In effect, the trad industry has to choose which horse to ride: the e-book and Amazon-led digital model, or the print and physical store-led traditional one. Those horses pull in different directions and the sales strategy that works best for print is incompatible with the one that works best for digital, and vice versa. Because the trad industry, for reasons good and bad, has largely opted to stay with the traditional sales model, it has also experienced levels of e-book sales that are quite misleading as a guide to the broader market.

And the third chunk of this emerging market? It's the digital-only imprints created (or purchased) by the big traditional houses. Those imprints have licence to ignore the chains and push for Amazon sales above all. Advances are low. E-books are priced at closer to the indie average (of, let's say, $4.99), but with plenty of price promotions to boost sales. The throughput of books is also faster. So Bookouture, the UK firm which first perfected this model, used to ask authors to put out a new book every ninety days. More traditional authors (myself included) had minor coronary episodes when this idea was put to us.

Those digital-first imprints have a real place in the maturing ecosystem, but I think it's worth being clear about a couple of points. First, the huge successes of the very first experimenters have mostly not been repeated. As the most effective sales-models become copied and endlessly repeated, nothing works as well as it once did. Second, you might think that being an Amazon bestseller would translate seamlessly to sales success in physical stores. It's the same darn story, after all. But no. Sales success does not translate. I know one author who has sold multimillion copies via a digital-first imprint. Her agent thought, sensibly, that it would be worth translating that success to supermarkets and elsewhere. The agent and author found an excellent, well-led and committed publisher to try exactly that. And – well, the author sold some copies, but at very ordinary mid-list levels. As far as I know, she is now hardly sold in bookshops at all.

THE COST OF A BOOK

Back in 2010, people wondered if the price of a book might fall to zero. That sounds like it might have been an apocalyptic prediction – terrifying, but basically bananas – but it really wasn't. After all, the music industry has seen the price of a song fall to something very close to zero: Spotify pays the rights holder about $0.006 per play. Indeed, the music industry is now actually grateful to the streaming companies, because though the cash is pitiful, it is at least non-zero. When online piracy was huge, it seemed possible that the price of a song would fall to $0.000.

The same risk was present with books. Book piracy is very simple. I once turned book pirate myself, by way of experiment. I took a published, copyrighted e-book that was protected via DRM (a kind of electronic lock). With a bit of guidance from my Evil Tech Guru, it took me about two minutes, maybe three, to break the lock and extract an easily copied version of the underlying file. If I'd gone over to the Dark Side entirely, I'd have popped the book on a website and started to distribute it for free.

(If you think ill of me for breaching copyright, I should probably add that the book in question was my own. I haven't yet sued myself, but I'll get round to it in time.)

So, yes, the risk was real, but it never really materialised. Partly, e-book prices did drop sharply, to a point at which the additional saving from outright piracy became relatively trivial. Partly, people don't actually like stealing. They don't like how it feels. They don't like the cumbersome tech involved. They don't like the poor quality of the downloads they often get.

In short, it turned out that Amazon's clean, slick, cheap and ubiquitous service out-competed the free but nasty services offered by the pirates. The trad world never quite admits it, but the main thing that saved Publisher Land from economic collapse has been Amazon. Its tech, its prices, its dominance. The result is an orderly market where books can be sold and authors make money.

THE NATURE OF BOOKS & READING

I mentioned earlier that, back in 2010, people wondered whether the novel-as-an-art-form was likely to change under the impact of the e-revolution. That question deserves an answer ... and the answer is basically *no*.

The kind of books that people like reading haven't altered at any fundamental level. I've never been asked by a publisher to augment my basic novel with any kind of electronica. No photos. No audio commentary. No 'choose your own adventure'. No nothing. If I came to my publisher with a headful of ideas for all the very cool things we could do ... they'd look mildly horrified and start, gently, to explain why these things are impossible.

That's not to say that new things won't emerge. Indeed, I'd bet that new things have already emerged but haven't yet become 'evenly distributed', in William Gibson's insightful phrase. But for current purposes? Just write a novel. Or a memoir. Or a diet book. Or the kind of thing that has always existed and always will. You'll do fine.

DISCOUNTING AND NARROWING

We've talked a lot about e-books, but the wider retail picture is characterised by two major forces, which were in operation long before Amazon grew to its current position of dominance. The first of those forces is discounting. Back in the good old days, it was often actually illegal to sell a book at a discount. That was the case in the UK until the early 1990s. It is still, more or less, true in France.

But not only has discounting become perfectly legal in every major English-language market, the nature of retail has changed too. Supermarkets built their books business around discounting. The big chains – Barnes & Noble, Borders, Waterstones – did the same. Consumers began to see half-price offers, three-for-two promotions, brand new paperbacks selling for less than half the theoretical price. Those forces conspired to push down the average selling price of a book in nominal terms, and to push it down quite sharply when you take inflation into account. And if you want to guess whether (1) publishers are earning less money, (2) retailers are earning less money, or (3) authors are earning less money as a result of all this, you won't be winning any prizes for a correct answer. (You may also be interested to know that publishers, despite the pressures, have earned record profits in recent years.)

The second force is even more dangerous. Supermarkets are designed to sell beans, not books. Where a decent independent bookshop might try to stock 10,000 titles, a typical large supermarket might stock a total of just forty. Of those, the majority will be either celebrity-led or written by authors who are already bestsellers, leaving precious few slots available for authors who do not already have huge sales. Given the huge market share of the supermarkets, that means that new authors are likely to find themselves excluded from 20% of the market before they've even started.

The narrowing of the book trade, however, goes well beyond the supermarkets. Much has been made of Amazon's 'long tail'; its ability to sell a range of titles that even the largest bookstore would struggle to load on to its shelves. Yet that long tail contains a nasty sting. If you're selling a non-fiction title, then Amazon will help you out. For example, if you have written a book on beekeeping and you call it something sensible, such as *A Manual of Beekeeping*, then anyone who types the obvious search term into Amazon will come across your book. Jolly good. For new authors of fiction, however, Amazon can be a deeply hostile place.

Amazon is good at selling bestsellers, or celebrity-led titles, or non-fiction, but it is not especially interested in performing that old-fashioned 'hand-selling' task of bringing new and unexpected books to your attention. In a bookshop, it's simple enough to call attention to the unexpected: you put titles on the tables and shelves, and let people browse. On Amazon, the river of attention always flows downhill, to the biggest sellers, the most obvious choices. If you look up a title written by a debut novelist, you'll find a section on the page which says, 'Customers Who Bought

This Item Also Bought' – followed by a selection of titles from famous authors. Needless to say, if you search for the books of those famous authors you won't then be led to the work of interesting debut novelists. Because of mechanisms like this, you can probably chalk up the online market as another place where you're not likely to sell your work in any volume as a first-time novelist. (I should probably say that indie authors have some useful tricks for maximising exposure and sales on Amazon. Some of those tricks really only work for indies though. And big publishers aren't always smart about using the tools available.)

So thank goodness for the bookshops, eh? Well, maybe. Until fairly recently, the big bookshops did what they could to funnel readers into a fairly narrow range of titles. They did this by price-promoting a bunch of big books at the front of their stores. They did it on a national scale, so those front-of-store tables looked much the same in Anchorage as they did in Albuquerque (or Penrith and Penzance, if you prefer). That was great for publishers. They just had to wave enough money and they could make a bestseller, but it was another major factor narrowing sales.

Today, the picture has been upended – again. By 2019, both Barnes & Noble and the UK's Waterstones were owned by the same private equity firm and run by British CEO, James Daunt. Daunt did something sensible – and revolutionary. He let store managers decide what books to stock. The front tables in Anchorage and Albuquerque were now shaped by local readers, not some stitch up between NY publishers and the central buying team at B&N. That has improved the world for readers, no question. But it terrified publishers, as their old sales strategies (hurl money at chain bookstores) no longer worked. It also, unfortunately, pushed them to chase supermarket sales even more intensely, which meant that the narrowing and discounting pressures have hardly eased.

The upshot of all this? A mainstream publisher today is nervous of acquiring or supporting a book unless they see the prospect of real retail support for it. Since that retail support has become harder to find, publishers have been cutting their lists – that is, publishing fewer titles. Since they're hardly going to turn away books by bestselling authors and their ilk, they've turned their hatchets to 'established' authors who have yet to cause a sensation at the tills, and they've reduced the number of debut novels purchased.

Is that helpful to you? It is not.

CONSEQUENCES

It would be nice to believe that, if fewer titles are being purchased, the average standard of those titles must therefore increase. Perhaps to some limited extent, there's truth in that, though I've seen no evidence for it myself. Rather, what's happened is that the market has become ever more conservative in its choices. Editors have come to believe that bravery doesn't pay, that safety matters.

I've experienced that caution myself – or almost. When I wrote *Talking to the Dead*, the first book in my Fiona Griffiths series, I knew I had created something that was zingily different from the police procedural mainstream. My character wasn't a hard-drinking, middle-aged, seen-it-all, male cop. She was a petite, junior, teetotal newbie in the world of crime detection. Also: she was Welsh. Also: she was nuts. She was in recovery from Cotard's Syndrome, a (genuine) psychiatric condition in which sufferers believe themselves to be dead.

She's a love-her or hate-her character. She is not standard issue.

Now, I knew my book was good. My agent thought so too. We quietly expected it to sell in a flash and … it didn't. It did sell, in fact, and sell well. In Britain, America, Germany, France and elsewhere, the book ended up being bought up by each country's leading crime publisher, and mostly for decent money. But whereas I'd been used to getting multiple offers from multiple publishers for my work, what I noticed here was that most publishers just weren't playing any more. In Britain, for example, I received just two offers: one from the leading crime publisher and one from Faber, a publisher primarily known for its literary work. The offer from Faber was enough to push my offer from Hachette towards very respectable levels, but where were the other dogs in this fight?

Well, to some extent, I know the answer. The comment back from HarperCollins was that they *loved* the book, editorially speaking, but they worried readers weren't going to bond with a character who could come across as rather negative. To decode that message: editors, who were smart, loved the book; readers, who weren't, couldn't be trusted to do the same. The comment back from Macmillan was they *loved* the book, editorially speaking, but they worried that readers wouldn't. From other publishers, similar responses. Publishers no longer trusted readers to buy and enjoy fiction outside a relatively narrow comfort zone.

Now, as I say, my book and my series flew anyway (though with a twist in the tale that I'll come to later). But the moral, for me, was that the world had got more conservative than the one I'd known ten years earlier. The risks of even good books failing had climbed. Additionally, Penguin Random House, who bought the book in the US, basically abandoned the series two books in. They loved me, editorially speaking (that phrase, always), but didn't have the guts or the patience to persist. That too was a change. There are any number of famous authors whose first books weren't these huge breakout hits. Those were people whose careers built incrementally, book by book, laying down a platform of excellence that ended up becoming too great to ignore.

That model has now gone. You need to get established with your first book or (possibly) two. After that, if success hasn't come, you will have to quit the game or reinvent yourself as a different kind of author.

Now, I don't want to pretend that the world of today is monolithic. Actually, the reverse is true. It's notable now how many literary prize-winning titles are launched by micro-publishers — the kind of publishers that truly don't give a damn what Walmart is buying. There's more vibrancy and invention at that micro level than ever there used to be. Likewise, although the industry has been painfully and inexcusably slow about opening up to more diverse voices, there is a progress and commitment there that is new and (my guess) irreversible. And self-publishing opens up an avenue to readers and income that never used to exist, or not on the current scale.

So I really don't want to say that things are all bad. Indeed, at Jericho Writers, we still help a ton of writers get published by really great publishers. And that age-old rule still mostly applies: great books always sell; good books may sell; mediocre ones never do.

A CARTON OF YOGURT

Since this chapter has hardly been a beacon of light and hope, I may as well add a little further to your pile of woes, while you have that nice bottle of Prozac so conveniently to hand.

Most writers, if asked to gauge the shelf life of their product, are confused by the question. If that Prozac is making you feel a little giddy, you might even find yourself winding up into a spot of oratory: 'Shelf life? Shelf life? Does Milton have a shelf life? Does Melville? Does Homer? The work of the pen is beyond compare, greater than kings, stronger than armies, broader than oceans, beyond time itself. Was it not the Bard himself who wrote, "So long as men can breathe or eyes can see,/So long lives this, and this gives life to thee"? Put that in your pedantic little shopkeeper's pipe and smoke it!'

Shakespeare, however, lived before the advent of the three-for-two promotion and the hurly-burly of modern publishing. Because retailers (online and physical) need to keep restocking their stores to look fresh, and because publishers won't spend marketing money unless they see positive returns on their investment, and because every month brings new titles out to compete with yours, it won't be long before your book leaves the golden lights of the front-of-store tables and the 'recommended for you' section on Amazon's home page.

I don't want to alarm you. Your novel will last longer than a pint of milk. It may even, just about, last as long as one of those pre-pack soft cheeses that need a month or so to ripen. But to be on the safe side, if you want to guesstimate the shelf life of your book, buy a carton of yogurt on publication day. When that carton has reached its best-before date, your book has probably also reached its. Your book will then slide from the front tables to the shelves around the side of the store. Your sales will slump by the regulation 5,000%. If your book was in a supermarket, it'll disappear altogether. Your time in the top ten thousand or top twenty thousand titles on the overall Amazon bestseller list has come to an end. Your book's life, is, for all practical purposes, over.

There'll be nothing you can do about any of this. The narrowing of the market has seen to that. Sorry.

But there are exceptions – lovely ones. There are the huge fiction and non-fiction bestsellers. Rare as hen's teeth, but still a dream you can dream.

There is also the small non-fiction book, such as this one, for instance. No sane retailer will want to pop it at the front of their bookstores. By its nature, it will only appeal to a small proportion of the store's potential customers – namely, the proportion wise and diligent enough to have written a manuscript of potentially publishable quality. Any retailer knows that these customers will be motivated enough to go and seek out specialist work, no matter where in the store it might be shelved. In practice, of course, books like this sell primarily online. (The earlier edition of this book was published by Bloomsbury, a large independent publisher. They had excellent distribution to bookstores in theory, but even so, 85% or more of sales took place online.) And online, because the book sits in the Writers' Reference section of Amazon's infinite shelving, readers know where to find it. The competition isn't too dense. And (because we at Jericho Writers know a fair bit about publishing, not just writing) we also make sure that the book is optimised for long-term, ongoing sales.

This kind of work doesn't provide a huge income, but it does provide an income. The first edition of this book came out in 2010. We republished it, completely revised, in 2020. We'll go on selling it for years to come. And every year, the darn book has made money. My original advance for this book was by far the lowest of any advance I've ever had. But the royalty cheques have been the greatest. And still they come.

The trick? To find your non-fiction niche, to title your book sensibly, to do the other bits and pieces on Amazon as intelligently as you can, and then to sit back and enjoy the royalties. You can do that via a publisher (who will take 75% of your royalties but save some of the hassle.) Or you can do it yourself and take all the royalties. But a pint of milk? A carton of yogurt? Nope. A book like this is like one of those old-school Arctic explorer ration packs, still good a hundred years later.

WORD OF MOUTH

I'm aware I'm entering dangerous territory here (Prozac is a wonderfully safe drug, but an overdose is still to be avoided), but I've not yet come to the end of my bad news.

Many newbie authors have a happy faith in 'word of mouth'. After all, J. K. Rowling's first book was turned down by one and all, no? And her publisher had hardly written 'world domination' into their budget projections. But kids started reading the books, and talking about them, and the books were firmly supported by librarians, and mums and dads started to get hooked as well, and they started talking about them too, and more and more kids in more and more countries were bitten by the bug, until the film industry took hold and made sure that everyone knew all about the heroic exploits of a certain bespectacled boy wizard.

All this is (more or less) true. It's also so rare that it's exceptionally hard to find examples of word of mouth lifting a book from obscurity to best-sellerdom. J. K. Rowling is a dazzling example, but I honestly can't think of any others. (And Bloomsbury marketed their heart out on that first JKR title; it wasn't just the magic of her pen.)

I'm not saying that word of mouth is unimportant – it is – but for that magical force to kick into action, you almost need (1) a strong position in store promotions and supermarket slots and/or a decent head start on Amazon, (2) a strong PR campaign behind you, and (3) press attention that gains a momentum all of its own. Without those things, word of mouth simply can't get traction. When you hear the phrase 'word-of-mouth bestseller' used about newly released titles, that bestseller will almost certainly have enjoyed heavy promotion and as much media campaigning as it was possible to secure *before* any word-of-mouth sales started to kick in.

The difficulty for modern authors in building reputation, sales and readership is compounded by the terrible swiftness with which publishers will desert their authors. Turning to literary fiction, let's suppose that your career followed the trajectory of William Faulkner. Lots of early rejections. Two novels, published, both for a puny advance and both commercial failures. That novelist today would be a busted flush. Much the same would be true of the British author, Graham Greene. Yet Greene and Faulkner went on to be amongst the most important voices in twentieth century literature. Those career trajectories just don't exist today. Publishers wouldn't have offered a new contract. Even if a smaller house had offered a book deal, the lack of promotional space and PR heft would have meant obscurity almost for sure.

The same oppressive logic applies to advances too. Suppliers of the most successful products have their advances bid upwards, thanks to competition among publishers. Suppliers of the least successful products have their advances reduced. Capitalism is a great and wonderful thing, but no one ever said that it was there to support literature.

THE TWENTY-FIRST-CENTURY READER

There's a further consequence of all this: namely, a shift in the reader's expectations of a bookshop. I remember as a teenager going to Mandarin Books, an independent bookshop near where I lived in London. The shop was tiny. It had no books out on tables at all. Mostly books were shelved spine out; every now and then books would be shelved with covers facing out. I used to browse in that bookshop seldom expecting to *recognise* a book. I didn't expect to find books about which I could say, 'Oh, that's [insert name of famous person]'s latest book,' or 'Yes, I heard about that on the radio,' or 'Oh, he's that bloke off the telly.' The delight of going to a bookshop was to discover the unknown. I relied to some extent on the extraordinary knowledge of the people who ran that lovely shop, but mostly I was just there to truffle up something new.

Contemporary marketing techniques have changed that expectation. Readers now enter a bookshop expecting something familiar. Names they've heard of, books they've heard mentioned. In a major bookstore recently, I saw a rack of shelves with a slogan that said something like 'Try Something New Today'. I cheered inwardly, because I thought that here was a chain bookseller doing its damnedest to bring wonderful but little-known works to a broader audience. I was so happy I was ready to kiss someone.

Then I got up close and saw that the shelves were dedicated to the works of one man: Michael Chabon. Now, I like Michael Chabon. He's a gifted, entertaining author of style and subtlety. But something *new*? The man leapt to literary celebrity with his very first book. He's camped out on *The New York Times* bestseller lists. He's won a Pulitzer Prize, a Hugo Prize, a Nebula Prize and more. His books receive countless positive reviews on both sides of the Atlantic. The idea that his work is unknown is simply ludicrous.

Bookshops, even relatively upmarket ones, have lost the confidence that they can introduce genuinely new work to their customers and expect them to buy it. Perhaps they're right. They have access to their sales data, after all. I suspect they aren't the real culprits here. We are.

THE NEWSPAPERS

Newspapers, too, have changed over the years. It was never the case that newspapers reviewed all books. Papers tended to ignore genre fiction, especially in paperback, no matter that it's the stuff that most people actually read, preferring instead to review hardback non-fiction of the sort that generates a decent book review. Many of those book reviews were never really intended to advise readers whether or not to buy a particular book. Most people, for example, would much sooner read a review of (let's say) a senior ambassador's memoirs than read the book itself. Even in the past, many books were widely reviewed and achieved meagre sales. Nevertheless, for professional writers, those reviews mattered. They gave some authority to the paperback edition; they supplied quotes for the next hardback to appear by the same author ('Praise for Jo Brown ...'). They also, even if in a limited way, gave authors a route to build from critical to commercial success.

These days, review pages are ever fewer. Some newspapers have eliminated their books pages altogether. Even the grander newspapers have less review coverage than before. What's more, much of the review space is effectively pre-allocated. If your book comes out at the same time as that of a big-name author, it will be the big name that has priority every time. It's the same with non-fiction. Newspapers have come to reflect the industry at large: narrowing the range of what gets attention, shining the light of attention on to ever fewer titles.

It's also very important to understand that quality alone achieves nothing. If your book has a bad cover and the PR effort flops, then it won't sell, no matter how fantastic the content. It won't matter, because no one will know. Newspapers will ignore it. The booksellers won't promote it. Readers won't buy it, because they won't even be able to find it in the bookshop or know to search for it on Amazon. Any nascent word-of-mouth campaign will die in its infancy.

Such things aren't rare events; they're commonplace. They're much commoner, in fact, than their opposite: a good book getting the recognition it deserves. Getting published is hard enough. Staying published is getting harder every year.

AMAZON

Oh, Amazon, Amazon.

Are we to love you or hate you? Or should we do both at once, with a good measure of fear baked into our mixed-emotion pie?

Well, for my part, I think that Amazon has done a vast amount of good. It's brought tech to a world that needed it. It's driven out the pirates. It's made all the books in the world available to all the readers in the world – and at prices that almost everyone can afford. If you simply look at Amazon in terms of the way it brings knowledge and art within the reach of almost everyone, you have to cheer it.

And it's not just that. It offers a route to publication for everyone. It'll take you five minutes to upload your work to Amazon. You will be charged nothing for the pleasure. Your work will be available worldwide and you'll be paid a huge royalty for every book you sell.

That royalty mathematics is worth knowing. If you sell a $4.99 e-book on Amazon, you'll get a 70% royalty, which puts $3.49 in your pocket. If you make the same sale via a traditional publisher, you will get one-quarter of that 70%, or $0.87. Except that the royalty will flow through the cash tills of your literary agent, so you only actually get 85% of that sum, or a total of $0.74. That is 21% of what the self-publishing author receives.

Amazon has made books cheaper for readers and more profitable for authors. That's quite a magic trick.

Now, the royalties alone aren't a reason to go hurtling off to the land of self-pub. Most adventures there end in disappointment. But Amazon *has* altered the options available to authors, and in a wonderful way. It has also altered the mechanisms by which books sell. So whereas a certain amount of traditional publicity was always seen as essential to achieving book sales through book stores, there are any number of Amazon-led authors who have achieved huge success without any PR whatsoever. (Or rather, they get the kind of PR which says, with some bafflement, 'Here's this author who has sold X million copies and seems to be fabulously well-known to his/her fans, but his/her book has never crossed our desks and we've never taken a phone call from his/her publicist, and it now turns out that he/she doesn't even have a publicist, so this whole thing is very confusing.')

This book is too long as it is, and certainly doesn't have space to delve into all the ways you can lead your own marketing on Amazon. But there is a chapter on how to build your own brand, and you need to read that chapter and actually do what it says. These things matter as they have never mattered before.

Oh, and if you do want to improve your author-led marketing savvy, then we at Jericho Writers have a brilliant course on self-publishing. Its advice is mostly relevant to trad authors too. Or you can buy books by David Gaughran, Tammi Labrecque, Robert Ryan and Nicholas Erik. Those people know what they're talking about. Because they too are mostly speaking to self-publishing authors, you'll have to chop and change some of the advice to apply it to your situation. But don't do *nothing*. Amazon lets authors take control of their own sales destiny. Don't let that opportunity pass you by.

AMAZON PUBLISHING

Amazon Publishing, or APub to its friends, is the biggest publisher you have never heard of. It is Amazon's own publishing arm, and it is an odd beast. Because Apple and the online e-tailers compete with Amazon in retail, they won't touch books published by APub. Because Barnes & Noble and other physical retailers (rightly) consider Amazon to be a mortal threat, they won't touch APub's books. So, and with some minor and temporary exceptions, Amazon Publishing is a publisher that publishes only via … Amazon.

Now, that feels like a strange and limiting position for a publisher, except that Amazon's vast retail reach and data-driven habits make it exceptionally good at what it does. It's generated dozens of million-selling authors. It's active in an increasingly wide set of genres and categories. And its authors love it. We once ran a 'Do You Love Your Publisher?' survey of 800+ traditionally published authors. Broadly speaking, the answers there were disappointing. (Authors did mostly love their agents but were much more doubtful when it came to their publishers.) Yet, anecdotally, the publisher that came out best was APub. One author who migrated to APub from a Big Five firm told me that 'the difference was night and day'. He's stuck with APub ever since and has sold a lot − a *lot* − of books.

Amazon's unusual willingness to engage with its authors is part of the clue to its success. A recent study (run by the Codex Group) looked at which book covers were the most successful at enticing readers to click a 'Read More' button located next to the cover. The books chosen represented fifty or sixty titles recently published by major publishers. Readers didn't know who was publishing the different books. They didn't care. Yet eight of the top ten titles in the study were published by APub. The group's creative director attributed their success in large part to a commitment to collaboration: a process of feedback and discussion in which the author was central. That is not, in my experience, the way it typically works at a Big Five publisher.

The purpose of this short section is to remind you that not all big publishers look alike or think alike. You probably first purchased this book dreaming of a contract with Penguin Random House, or HarperCollins, or one of their giant, traditional peers. If you get a contract with Amazon, your books will appear in print, but only of the online variety. If your mother walks into a bookshop to find your book, she won't find it. But don't be put off. Amazon works with literary agents, just like any other big publisher. It is relentless in its search for author quality. A contract from Amazon is, to my mind, at least as strong a mark of acclaim as a contract from anyone else.

And APub is a very, very good publisher. If you get an offer from it, you should consider it seriously. If APub is not on the list of publishers that your agent wants to submit your work to, you should certainly ask why. There may be good reasons, but it would be dumb not to ask. So ask.

THE GOOD NEWS

This section has been mostly pessimistic so far, although I honestly don't think that most authors, agents, publishers or booksellers would dispute its basic message.

But it's not all bad news. Book sales roll on. The English-speaking world is still full of avid book-buyers. Even in recession, the tills keep ringing away. So the first piece of good news is simply this: the market for books isn't vanishing any time soon.

And success is possible. New authors do sometimes manage to clamber over all the obstacles facing them and achieve success – and, when that success comes, it's likely to be on a larger scale than ever before. One agent, for example, was talking to me about one of his superstar clients. He said that, if her debut novel had been published fifteen or twenty years ago, and if absolutely everything had gone right for it, it might have sold 100,000 or even 150,000 copies. Any such achievement would have been hailed as a triumph – the best possible outcome. In fact, her debut novel was published just a few years back and has recently notched up its one millionth sale. The narrowing of the market is responsible for successes like this, as it drives ever more sales towards ever fewer titles. That may be bad news for all those authors who have seen their sales gobbled up by the million-selling blockbuster, but it's presumably rather nice for the blockbusting author herself.

Last of all – and this last point simply reiterates the single most important message of this book – the joy of creation remains the same as always. If you write mostly for pleasure, and only partly for money, a difficult publishing market can only ever have a limited effect on you. As long as your work is strong enough to find some kind of publisher, you'll still have a readership, no matter that it may be smaller than your work deserves.

You'll win not only joy, but honour too. In my dark past as an investment banker, I worked on some huge, landscape-altering deals. I worked hard, did well, was respected. And no one ever thanked me. No one ever wrote me a personal note saying that my work had moved them or touched them or meant a lot. I did my work. I got paid. And that, pretty much, was that. When it came to the launch of my first novel, however, people became effusive. Everyone *congratulated* me, as though I'd simultaneously passed an exam, got married and had my firstborn child. When people started to read my books, I became used to a little trickle of communications – emails, letters, online reviews, word-of-mouth comments from friends of friends of friends. Some of these communications were pedantic or silly, but most weren't. Most were expressions of thanks from people whom I'd never met. I could have spent a lifetime as an investment banker and never enjoyed any such gratitude from either clients or colleagues. This is still a good industry to be in – it's the best job in the world.

But enough of these things. You've learned about the market and have not much enjoyed the experience. Let's turn now to that book deal – the thing you've waited years to achieve.

Part Four

GETTING YOUR BOOK DEAL

A Publisher's Offer

Your agent has decided how to sell your work. For highly commercial work, that'll often be via an auction involving six or eight major houses. Other times, work will be carefully introduced to a more select shortlist. Still other times, an agent might choose to go direct to a single publisher to see if an appropriate deal can be struck without any kind of auction. The agent's rationale for choosing a particular sales process may well be opaque to you, but you don't need to worry. Some books just aren't suited to the mass-auction approach, and an agent won't get more money for them (let alone the right publisher for them) by trying to shove them down that road. So talk to your agent. Question them. Trust them. And let them do what they do.

HOW PUBLISHERS WILL APPROACH YOUR MS

A couple of decades back, your manuscript had to delight and dazzle your putative editor. If the editor was entranced, then he or she generally had the authority to acquire it whatever anyone else in the company may have thought. This editorial independence certainly allowed editors to follow their instincts. It also allowed them to take on manuscripts that were brimful of potential but which needed a significant degree of reworking. It also, however, marginalised the people in sales and marketing whose job it would be to sell the resultant book. It wasn't, in the end, the right way to do things.

These days, after corporate managements have professionalised every aspect of publishing, the acquisition process is thoroughly collaborative, just as it ought to be. Salespeople bring their intimate knowledge of retailers' likes and dislikes to bear.

Marketing people comment on how easy the book will be to market. The editor remains the fulcrum of this whole process. It'll be her job, if she believes in your manuscript, to whip up support for your book. She'll ensure that people across the firm are reading it. She'll do what she can to ensure that the acquisition committee meeting gives your book a thumbs-up. The more strongly she believes in your book, the more of her own authority she'll be willing to put on the line in support of it.

If and when your book is taken on, it'll be taken on with the support of the firm. When the book is a biggish acquisition and when an auction is hotly contested, it's perfectly common for the firm's chief executive to get involved in reading the manuscript.

All this is good news and bad. It's good news in the sense that a 'yes' from a publisher these days brings with it genuine consensus and a corporate commitment. It's bad news in the sense that your manuscript can't simply make an idiosyncratic connection with a single editor who happens to like what you do.

IF THE NEWS IS BAD ...

Even with a good book and a great agent, material sometimes doesn't sell.

As with many things in publishing, the harsh news may take a long time to become apparent. An editor may be interested – will need to talk to the sales and marketing team – may make positive comments – then end up saying no. A first batch of submissions may be rejected, but the feedback from the second batch may seem stronger. If that second batch ends up getting nowhere, then surely Desperation Press (motto: 'we print anything') will end up making an offer, however modest. As each successive round of submissions will last weeks and can last months, it can easily take a year to establish that, alas, there is no market for your book.

In such cases, you need to learn as much from the process as you can. Often enough, an editor will reject the manuscript by email to your agent. Those emails may be bland, but they will often be more substantive. In any event, an agent and editor will often chat, no matter how briefly, about your manuscript, and those chats will often contain vital clues about why your work is being rejected.

You will not, in all likelihood, have direct access to those exchanges, which are, after all, addressed to the agent, not to you. Nevertheless, even if these comments come filtered by your agent, they're well worth having. Very occasionally, the comments will effectively amount to nothing much more than, 'We liked this book and wish the author well, but it didn't quite blow us away.' If so, just write another book – but write it better. But maybe the feedback will be of more value. A children's author might be told that they need to ensure that their work has series potential. A thriller author might be told that he needs to bring more geopolitics into his mix. A literary author might be told that her style is too quiet for the market. Such things are always frustrating, but OK. So be frustrated. It's a foolish author who refuses to learn from feedback.

In an ideal world, your second project will enjoy your agent's careful supervision. I don't mean that your agent will be reading each chapter as it tumbles from your printer. But a good agent should want to know what your next project involves and to give you feedback once you have an outline and/or some sample material. Listen as carefully as you can to what your agent tells you. It's easy for authors to pick selectively from what they're being told, but you'll get the best results by listening hard and responding seriously.

Do also note that agents – like their kith and kin in publishing houses – can often be weirdly averse to putting things in writing. Anyone who has an ordinarily successful background in other industries will expect some kind of written follow-up to major business meetings. I don't mean that anyone these days would feel the need to keep minutes or write a formal business letter, but it would be normal to exchange an email which confirmed the salient points of any action plan. If such things aren't recorded, they can be forgotten. Given that you are new to this industry and will simply be ignorant of many of the market-related issues which a commercial publisher has to grapple with, you'd have thought that agents would be particularly concerned to ensure that their killer points were being accurately retained by their clients. In actual fact, such written communications are surprisingly rare.

You'd do well, therefore, to take on that task yourself. Write to your agent, saying something along the lines of: 'Dear Jon, many thanks for our very useful discussion yesterday. I believe that the major points we discussed were as follows ... If I've missed anything, do let me know – otherwise I look forward to getting stuck in. All the best, Jen.' If you have missed anything, your agent should pick it up and let you know. If not, you are setting forth with reasonable confidence that your course is a good one.

If you are trying to gear up for that second project and find that your agent has become increasingly unresponsive, it may well be that the agent wants to ditch you as a client. In a more businesslike profession, that ditching would be done properly. The agent would contact you to say that they were proud to have represented you, consider that they may have misjudged the market, and feel that they may not be the right person to represent you in the future. The communication – by email or phone – would be courteous, prompt and without judgement. Alas, such communications are all too rare. From my observation of the industry, it's almost more common for agents to allow a relationship to die of neglect than to end it properly.

If you think that you are being left to die of neglect, then you may as well take the matter into your own hands. Write a polite and businesslike email, saying that you've appreciated all the agent has done for you, but you want to be sure that this is the right ongoing relationship for you both. Say that you'd be delighted if the agent wanted to continue to represent you, but, if they felt it was right to terminate your relationship, you'd understand perfectly – you'd just like clarity. The point of the email is not to tip the agent over into declining you as a client, but to make it easy for them to separate themselves if that's what they want to do anyway. You haven't lost anything by becoming unagented again. Far better to have no agent than to pretend you have representation when, in all truth, you don't.

It's also worth saying that there is a small group of agents who would never opt for the 'die of neglect' strategy when the 'major emotional tantrum' one is so much more satisfying. The typical pattern with such agents is that a certain project is taken on with much enthusiasm. The news from the first and second round of submissions is less than positive. Email communications become slower and slower. Phone calls are not returned. The poor old client – who, in their regular life, is a normal human being with normal human expectations of ordinary business behaviour – nudges for a response on a particular point, only to be greeted with a sudden and wholly disproportionate outburst on some issue which the author had never even known was an issue at all. In such cases, just terminate the relationship and be pleased it's over.

GETTING AN OFFER

The foregoing paragraphs are important ones to have at the back of your mind, of course. An author needs to be prepared for all contingencies. Yet you know, and I know, that your book is something pretty special. No sane publisher will be turning it down any time soon. Even now, editors will be emerging excited from meetings with marketers and publicists, wide-eyed at the broad horizons of possibility. It is, in short, about time that one of them will be making an offer.

When they make an offer, they will make it direct to your agent. Their email will quite likely look something like the one below, which is an edited and abridged version of a real publisher's email, suitably altered to protect identities.

Dear Agent,

I'm thrilled to say that I'm now able to make an offer for Persephone's wonderful memoir. As you know, I've been really keen from day one, and happily my colleagues throughout the company have also fallen in love with this incredible story. We are all really keen to publish it, and believe we are best placed to make it a tremendous success.

I thought it might be nice for Persephone to see some of the fabulous feedback I've had [from other readers in-house], so let me present a small selection of quotes ...

'Really special ... just brilliant'

'Great voice, a very likeable character'

'Touching and affecting'

'I love it!'

'Let's hope that's a portent of what's to come!'

As you may know, we've had great success with similar titles here at XYZ Publishing Corp, such as the classic *My Life in Cross-Stitch* by Hermione Melville and the recent bestseller (24,000 copies since April) *Crochet Hooks and Buttonholes* by Charlotte Dickens. We would aim to position Persephone's memoir very squarely in this market, and believe we have the track record to make it a real success.

What we'd like to do is ensure that, through the title and cover, the focus is on Persephone and her remarkable story. One of the fantastic things about her writing is its lovely evocation of time and place – she conjures up the atmosphere of the age so brilliantly – and yet, for all its occasional darkness, somehow the story retains a charm and innocence that is incredibly touching. I'm sure you'll agree that this is what makes Persephone's story unique. We feel that the book will be most successful if we can present and edit it in a way that reflects this.

Our feeling is that we have an opportunity to shape the book a little more and also come up with a title that really positions the book squarely within the bestselling tradition of recent sewing-related titles. We suggest *It's Just Sew Me*, but this is something we'd be happy to discuss further with you in the context of a deal. We have some further, relatively minor, editorial issues which we'd like to discuss in due course.

I have attached a formal letter containing all the details of our offer, but I'll quickly summarise the basics here ...

Yours,

A. N. Editor

Several things are of interest about this communication. The first, and most important, is that the editor has read the work and genuinely loves it. The quotes from others in the publishing company will be genuine too. Publishing is an industry that does work on enthusiasm. If the editor weren't enthusiastic, she wouldn't make an offer.

The second point is how focused the editor is on the market. The author of this memoir (which, of course, had nothing to do with sewing) was a Jericho Writers client and, exceptionally, we acted for her as literary agents. I know for a fact that the author had no idea that she was deemed to be writing for a certain segment of the memoir market. It wouldn't have occurred to her that her book would be judged against the commercial success of various other titles, none of which dealt with the same subject as hers. Yet the editor would certainly have checked out the market with some care. She'd have worked out how retailers would bracket this title. She'd have checked sales figures for some of the leading titles in the genre. She'd have gauged as carefully as she could how this memoir was likely to fare, given the market context, and made her offer on that basis. Her comments about changing the title would have been made with a view to cementing this memoir's place in a specific commercial niche. If the author had been foolish enough to resist altering the title, the offer might have been withdrawn. The editor's market focus isn't foolish or narrow-minded. It's part and parcel of her job, which is to sell as many copies of a title as she ever possibly can. That means thinking as hard about the market as any decent author will about her prose style.

As for the outline terms of the offer itself, an editor will not, at this stage, seek to detail every last term of the contract. Publishing contracts are mostly pretty standard. Yes, from time to time, there will be circumstances which demand careful contractual elaboration, but for the most part one contract will look much the same as another – and, indeed, any established agency will have agreed a standard form or 'boilerplate' contract on behalf of their authors, which will form the basis of every agreement between those two firms. At this stage, therefore, an offer letter will confine itself to an outline of a few crucial terms – notably the size of the advance and the level of a few key royalties.

I'll discuss those royalties in much more detail when we come to look at the contract itself, but for now let me just reiterate that an agent negotiates this kind of thing for a living. His interests are exactly aligned with yours, so you don't need to worry too much about whether he's getting the best possible terms. He'll be doing his damnedest to do so. It's not just his duty calling him – it's his income.

THE AUCTION

In the best of all possible worlds, a flurry of opening bids will give way to one or two, or just possibly three, publishers duking it out for your book. I've been in that happy position several times in my career, and it's a curious place to be. Mostly, of course, it's delicious. Every day, another offer. You're richer today than you were yesterday; richer yesterday than the day before.

At the same time, it's a rather peculiar sensation. These publishers aren't fighting over *you* – they probably haven't met you yet. They're fighting over your work. What's more, their competition doesn't take the form you rather think it ought to. The various editors aren't vying with each other to demonstrate their understanding of your intellectual or literary project. They aren't anxious to discuss your next project, or how you see your career developing. Instead, they're just hurling bundles of cash at you and talking to your agent. Don't get me wrong. Anyone who would like to hurl cash at me should feel free to do so; they may do it all day long for all I care. I don't mind the sensation, but it is an odd one, for all that. I hope that one day you feel it too.

Because publishers are all looking at the same market, and because their methodologies for calculating advances are all essentially identical, it's surprisingly common for an auction to end with two publishers offering the exact same, or almost the exact same, amount. I've been in this position twice. On both occasions, major publishers of impeccable reputation were offering identical amounts to publish my work. At this dizzy point in your life, you are in the wonderful position of being able to choose your publisher. Even better, you get to *reject* someone: an author finally able to reject the rejecters. Life gets no sweeter than this – and a new chapter is called for, all the better to relish the moment.

Choosing Your Publisher

Your agent has sent your book out and been overwhelmed with offers. You are delighted with your agent but are happier still to have your self-belief so emphatically vindicated. The auction frenzy subsides, and you have two publishers offering the same, or very similar, amounts for your book. You need to choose one, knowing that your career may rest on the rightness of your decision.

The first point to make is that both publishers are probably fine. Publishing is not the kind of industry where to be first is everything, to be second nothing. I've been published by all of the top three global publishers. (I'm talking about trade publishers here; I'm ignoring the business and academic ones.) I've had offers from the next two on the list. I've either been published by or had offers from the three next-largest UK independents. I've had expressions of interest from a very large digital-first publisher. And honestly? One large publisher looks much like another. If any publisher tries something distinctive and successful, that innovation will be rapidly copied. If a particular publisher does well at attracting editorial or marketing talent to its four walls, the chances are that other companies will swoop in to lure it away. In my own almost twenty-book career, I've worked with at least ten different editors, and that's not counting a host of overseas ones. I've worked with more publicists than I am able to count. The marketing people and the rights people and the Smiley Beckys come and go in such a flood, you'll be hard put to remember their names.

In short, much as you may love the particular bunch of people who sign up you and your book, it's relatively unlikely that the same bunch will still be present as the second book in your (probable) two-book deal slithers its way towards the paperback shelves.

Nevertheless, you are presented with a choice, and you may as well make it as best you can – and that means choosing between what is put in front of you, not trying to guess what it might look like in the future. It's also worth saying that you should, if at all possible, *meet* the rival publishers. If you've already got a fair bit of industry know-how, perhaps it'd be OK just to talk to the competing editors by phone, but really, if you can, go and talk to them. It's a big decision.

Your agent should accompany you and talk things through with you beforehand, but most agents will be fairly passive when it comes to setting the agenda. Your potential publishers may be less passive, but their overwhelming concern is to come across as such wonderfully delightful people that you'll just tumble into their embrace. It's certainly not in their interest to bring up any potentially awkward topic of conversation that may nevertheless have a crucial bearing on how your book is published.

In short, you need to take control. You need to use the guidance in this chapter to develop your own agenda for that meeting, adjusting it as necessary to meet the demands of your particular book. You don't, by any means, need to come with a publishing strategy of your own. You aren't in a position to develop one, let alone execute it. But you should ask enough questions to ensure that you come away from the meeting knowing as much as you need to about how your publishers intend to publish your work and what they might be like to work with.

There's no set format for these meetings. I myself was once ushered into the publishers' boardroom and offered – rather oddly – a huge platter of cheese and celery sticks, which was energetically dished out by the company's CEO. More typically, you'll be shown into a functional-looking conference room and offered coffee and biscuits. You'll most certainly meet your putative editor. You will probably also meet that editor's boss (who probably calls herself a publisher). You will quite likely also meet a publicist. You may meet someone from the paperback side, if the publisher is the sort to separate out hardback and paperback publishing. You may just possibly meet others from management, sales and marketing. The whole meeting will probably last around an hour.

WHAT TO LOOK FOR

Crude as it sounds, the number of people who come to greet you means something. So too does the seniority of those pumping your hand and (in my case) offering me lumps of mature Stilton. If a company really wants your book, then it'll push the boat out. If a chief executive pops by to say how much they love your work, you can discount some of what they're saying: it's most unlikely that they'll have read more than a few dozen pages of it. Nevertheless, Great Personages don't make the trip down from the management suite for any old person, and it means something that they've come down for you.

Just as important, you should take stock of those little flattering comments that fall so sweetly on your ears. Your editor will certainly be saying nice things about your book. She couldn't possibly not. But what about the others – the PR person, the paperback person, the scrawny chap from marketing? If they nod and look sage as your editor is speaking, it's likely enough that they've read a hundred pages or so of your book – enough to thoroughly familiarise themselves with your genre, tone and style – but haven't gone much further. If, on the other hand, they weigh in with stories about how they were kept up late reading your book, how they cried at your ending, or anything else along those lines, you can take those comments at broadly face value.

Enthusiasm matters. One author recently made a high-profile move away from the publisher who had brought out her previous seven books to a smaller outfit which wasn't offering more money or better terms. The difference was enthusiasm. This author felt her publisher was now handling her in a flatly professional way. She calculated – correctly, in my view – that her interests would be better served by publishers who would bring both professionalism and passion to the game. Even if the financial outcomes ended up identical, and they might not, you'll have more fun with the enthusiasts.

YOUR EDITOR'S COMMENTS

Similarly, you should listen carefully to anything the editor says about her personal response to your work. Things may be said in passing that strike you as somehow missing a critical aspect of your writing, or as pigeonholing you in a way that you don't want to be pigeonholed. These remarks aren't casual, and you shouldn't dismiss them. Your editor is your interface between your manuscript and the market. You don't want her to present your work too crudely, yet you can't afford to have her be too timid either.

Much of the rest of this book will deal, in one way or another, with the knotty problem of approaching the market, so I won't expand on that subject here. Just be alert to the issue. You want your editor to understand your book. You also want her to have a sales strategy that is decisive, clear and forceful. If either needs to win, then it needs to be the latter every time, but in an ideal world both things will happily co-exist – and you will certainly be happier with an editor who never loses sight of the more subtle aspects of your manuscript. So note any comments: those you like, those you don't, those you aren't sure of. You can reflect on them at greater length in due course.

You should also, of course, ask about any editorial changes that the editor has in mind. At this point, you'll only get the broadest of broad-brush comments. They'll also be offered very tentatively, because the editor will worry that you're going to go off in some authorly huff if anyone suggests that your work is capable of further improvement. You, of course, aren't anything like that – and, as it happens, I think few authors are. Nevertheless, don't be fooled by that tentative approach. However gently your editor introduces something at this stage, as soon as the ink dries on the contract that gentleness will harden into iron. If you think your editor's comments are simply wrong, say so now. Get as far into the issue as you need to resolve it. If you think the comments are broadly right, so much the better. That's an excellent sign that you'll see eye to eye when it comes to the nitty-gritty.

HARDBACK VS PAPERBACK

Often enough, the publishers who are bidding for your book will have essentially the same publishing strategy in mind. That's not surprising, given that they're selling the same products into the same market. Yet it's remarkable how often strategies do vary, in particular when it comes to the big question of how to launch.

Traditionally, books were sold in hardback first. Hardback buyers got the pleasure of big awkward books that looked nice on a bookshelf, and they were for some strange reason happy to pay about twice the cost of a paperback for the privilege. (Libraries used to like hardbacks for the more logical reason that they needed books robust enough to withstand plenty of handling, but libraries are not the major buyers that they once were.) Because the simultaneous availability of a cheap paperback version would wreck the saleability of the hardback, paperbacks traditionally launched nine months or so after the hardback. For a typical book, paperback sales would be perhaps five times greater than hardback sales but, because hardbacks retailed at double the price of paperbacks and had a much juicier margin into the bargain, hardback publishing remained a crucial part of the ecosystem. Weirdly too, hardback publishing continued to be more prestigious, the pulp aura of the mass market having never quite left the paperback side of things. Back in the first decade of this century, that was how the world worked. It hadn't changed hugely since Allen Lane revolutionised publishing with the quality paperback in the 1930s.

Gradually, an alternative model began to evolve. For certain books – notably genre fiction – the vast bulk of potential sales lay in paperback. That wasn't just a question of price. It was also that paperbacks are for readers who really want to read: on the subway, on a beach, on a train, in a lunch hour – wherever and whenever the mood struck and the hour offered. Paperbacks weren't just for the unwashed mob. They were for people like you and me, with brains and money.

Now, the trouble with the old model of publishing for books whose sales potential lay in paperback was that all the launch costs and effort went into supporting the hardback. You couldn't launch a hardback without spending money on it, but that ate some of the paperback's marketing budget. More to the point, any PR effort would have to be concentrated on the launch of the hardback. (That's because newspapers are only interested in 'new' news and, by the time a paperback followed the hardback on to the bookshelves, its existence would have nothing newsworthy about it.) The old hardback/paperback model was therefore forcing some publishers into the paradoxical position of heavily promoting a product which *wasn't* expected to sell and cannibalising the sales effort behind the product which *was* expected to sell.

A new model therefore emerged. Quite simply, for some books, the hardback stage was eliminated. Books (particularly books by debut authors) were launched straight into paperback, with all the sales and marketing budget and all the PR effort focused hard on that single product. This change is bizarrely recent. My first novel was published in February 2000. When discussing that launch with the team at HarperCollins (who at that stage were still bidding against another large company for my novel), I found them oddly timid about their paperback-only strategy.

As it turned out, however, the paperback-first strategy was just a minor precursor to a much bigger and more existential question: what to do with the e-book?

PRINT VS E-BOOK

Unless you are with a digital-first, e-book-led publisher or imprint, your editor will almost certainly be thinking more about print than e-book, and more about physical retail than online. That's fine. By choosing traditional publishing, you are, for the most part, making the same choices yourself.

If your book does well with physical retail, you're sorted. A strong cover, plenty of retail exposure and a half-decent publicity campaign will ensure you sell well enough to get your career off with a spring in its step. I'd like to tell you that such happy starts are the result of your sparkling prose and ingenious plot twists, but they really aren't. When people buy your book, they haven't read it. When retail buyers agree to order your book, they haven't read it. They may know nothing more of it than a one-page entry in your publisher's semi-annual catalogue. It's true that, even to get into position for a strong start, your book has to have impressed an agent, an editor, and an acquisitions committee. It's also true that the larger your advance, the more earnestly your publisher will need to fight for those retail slots. But in the end, put bluntly, the difference between the golden lift-off of your dreams and the sodden one of common reality comes down, for the most part, to chance.

So let's just say that, on this occasion, you don't get the retail platform you wanted. Your first edition – hardback or trade paperback – may not shift many copies. Your paperback is already wounded, as retailers will look at your first edition and think, 'Why would I want to stock that?' So, yes, there is a conversation to be had about re-orienting the paperback for a second assault on the supermarket slots and the bookstore front tables. (And that conversation matters: the UK hardback edition of my own *Talking to the Dead* had a bland cover and fared only moderately. An utterly re-thought cover plus strong support from one chain bookstore utterly revived its fortunes in paperback.) But if physical retail looks like it's going to be infertile territory, any logical publisher should be thinking about online selling. Your strategy should, in tech-speak, pivot from print-led to e-book-led, and from physical to online retail.

That pivot is in principle easy to do. It is obviously logical. It is arguably an actual contractual obligation of the publisher. (Your publisher commits to publish your book – that is, to disseminate it commercially. If one route fails, that commitment doesn't or shouldn't lapse in any way.)

And yet ...

Yet most publishers never make that pivot. It's partly mindset: a continuing, baffling belief that some formats (hardback!) matter more than others (e-book). The mindset also prizes bookstore readers over Amazon readers. Ridiculously, it even prizes supermarket book-buyers, possibly the least committed readers of any group, over Amazon-buyers, many of whom will buy and read a book a week. It's also fear. In the good old days – as defined by publishers – they were the unquestioned monarchs of their industry. These days, Amazon is so dominant, and so little interested in the welfare of traditional publishing, that publishers are in fear of being squeezed to nothing. Jeff Bezos likes to repeat that, 'Your margin is my opportunity.' To a traditional publisher, that sounds pretty much like a mafia death threat. And, indeed, that's just what it is.

Any case, whether I'm right or wrong about causes, few publishers are willing or able to pivot effectively from a print-led campaign to an online-led one. There's not much you can do about the institutional inertia, but there are crucial things you can and must do at this early stage. (Remember that your leverage right now, before you sign that contract, is higher than it ever will be again.) The key thing you can do is *ask the question*. You need to say something like: 'Thanks so much for outlining your thoughts on sales and marketing. I'd just like to ask what happens if we don't get the retail uptake we want. If bricks-and-mortar retail outlets don't come through, what will be done to generate online sales?'

That will be a remarkably astute question for any newbie author to ask, and it will get a proper response of some sort. The response is likely to be so heavily hedged around with ifs and maybes that you can't really hope to cash it in at a later date, but the fact you are already alert to the issue is a brilliant signal to send. And also, you are now in a position to ask your crucial follow-up. And please, you must ask this question, even if you are the timidest, least assertive author in the world. Your career may well come to hinge on it.

Your follow-up question is, 'OK, and if things don't go well in bricks-and-mortar stores, how would you price the e-book to help it sell?'

Calling that the million-dollar question is maybe slightly inflating your likely sales. But the question still has enough dollars behind it that you must ask it. If your physical sales disappoint, and your e-book is being sold at $11.99 or $12.99, your e-book will fail too, and your career is highly likely to die. The most obvious route to finding readers and resuscitating your career is simply to price the e-book at a level which will entice readers to take the risk on a new author. A low price alone will not cause a tidal wave of sales, but there are author-led approaches which will help you build a platform for future sales. (More on this later.)

But there is no author-led approach which will help you sell a meaningful number of e-books at a price in excess of $10.00 (or £7.00, if you are a subject of HM the Queen). Really – and again, I'm only talking about a situation where bricks-and-mortar strategies haven't really worked – you need your book to be priced at a maximum of $5.99 or £3.99. Less than that is good. If your e-book is priced above those thresholds, your beloved publisher's pricing strategy is choking off readers and sales in the only market left to you. You can't stop that happening, but your best strategy is to ask now, push for a real dollars-and-cents answer, and note the answer in an email to your agent/editor after the meeting.

And yes: I know you're nice and polite and well brought up and you don't want to look pushy in your very first meeting with your potential new publisher. But ask anyway. Get an answer. Don't leave this matter for the future. By then it may be too late.

LAUNCH DATES

Another huge decision to be made concerns the timing of any launch. The two major sales seasons in publishing are Christmas and the summer holiday reading season. The 'Christmas' season starts in about September. Indeed, if there's a huge title being launched in September, the Christmas selling season may even edge into August (and, yes, I share your distaste at that particular thought). The Christmas season is the traditional period for launching hardback books by big names, both popular and serious. It's also the major season for gift books, for cookery books and for celebrity-led titles. From the debut author's point of view, Christmas is both tempting and dangerous. It's tempting, because a Christmas bestseller may well sell more copies than a bestseller at any other time of year. It's dangerous, because perfectly good books can tumble beneath the celebrity and big-name steamroller and be splatted from sight.

Summer, on the other hand, is the season of paperbacks, of beach reads, of popular fiction. Because sales are strong in summer, that's also the period when big-name authors are most likely to release their paperbacks, thereby potentially crowding out lesser names.

It's common, therefore, for debut authors to be launched at a time when competition is thinnest, anywhere from January to April, for example. Again, however, different publishers will have different approaches. That may partly be down to different sales strategies. It may also be because of varying access to retail space. If, for example, a publisher is confident that they can get you on to the shelves of a major supermarket in August, that would be a strong incentive for them to launch you then. A publisher with a different publishing schedule and a different set of retail relationships may want to launch at some other point.

The more you understand about what your publisher is doing and why they're doing it, the more you'll be in a position to assess which of two rival strategies makes more sense. Yours is never going to be an expert verdict, but it will be *your* verdict and therefore one that you'll be able to live with more comfortably, come what may.

Do also note that lead-times in publishing can be weirdly long. A publisher will want at least six months in which to sell the book into the trade. So, if you strike a deal today, then the absolute earliest you'll see a book on the shelves is in six months' time. If your book is red-hot topical – let's say it's a biography of a major celebrity who has just (and, I hope, coincidentally) died – then perhaps a publisher will rush it out sooner. But red-hot topical does mean just that. If Iran happens to be in the news, and your book is a memoir of your Iranian childhood, that is not red-hot, nor even close. For nearly all books, that six-month lead-time will be sacrosanct.

What's more, six months is the absolute shortest time that it takes to launch a book. I sold my first novel one October. The publisher wanted an early spring launch, in order to ensure maximum paperback sales potential. Since we'd already missed the catalogue for the spring coming, we had to wait another full year – that is, a full seventeen months from striking an agreement. That's on the longer end of things, but it's not extreme.

TITLE AND DESIGNS

I've talked a little about titles in an earlier section, stressing that titles can change rapidly and randomly. All the same, you want to know what your potential publisher's thoughts on titles are. If they like your title, all well and good. If they want to change it, what they want to change it to may tell you a lot about how they're thinking of packaging and selling your book.

I once worked with a client whose memoir told the story of his life as a teenager in a British reform school of the late 1950s. Reform schools were for criminal youths. They were tough, aggressive places, and my client (who had, in fact, done nothing criminal) was forced to become tough and aggressive himself in order to survive. The book was hard, masculine and full of fighting and swearing. Its original title was *Dead Before Christmas*, the phrase deriving from a threat made to the author when he arrived at the school.

However, the publisher who bought his work decided that they would sell his work as a misery memoir. Since those memoirs have a basically universal cover design – soft pastel images of sweet children with large, appealing eyes – the publisher decided against doing anything radical with this one. Since *Dead Before Christmas* sounded too tough, the publisher altered the title to the pleading *Please Don't Make Me Go*. The cover image showed a small boy – much younger than the author was in the period covered by the memoir – staring out with the compulsory large, appealing eyes. The new title and cover design made an absolute nonsense of the book's content.

I don't tell this story as a warning. The book leapt onto the non-fiction bestseller charts and stayed there for weeks. But knowing the kind of titles your publisher is thinking about will tell you a huge amount about how they are thinking of marketing your book. If you're talking to two different publishers and they have different approaches to the title, be alert to those differences. They won't be casual.

The issues are similar when it comes to cover design. At this stage, there won't be a cover design developed for your book, so it doesn't make sense to ask to see one. But you can and should ask to see any comparable titles that the publisher has produced. The books that they pull out to show you will almost certainly tell you a lot about how they see your own title. Even if they can't show you a precise cover image, they probably will be able to say something about the kind of design they have in mind. Those ideas will always be presented as the very sketchiest of all sketchy thoughts, but those sketchy initial ideas have a habit of turning into fact, so again, if you don't like what you hear, now's the time to find out.

MARKETING AND PR

You may also want to raise the subject of marketing and PR, but, if you do, then do so with low expectations. As we'll see further in a later section, marketing budgets have largely been eaten by retailers, who in turn have largely given away their extra revenues in the form of discounts to their customers. The result is that publishers these days have almost no cash left with which to market a book. If your potential publishers do sketch out any significant marketing plans, take note. If they say nothing much, feel free to ask, but do so gently. Most likely you'll be told (truthfully enough) that somebody just ate their wallet.

Another reason for not hammering away at the marketing issue is that publishers simply won't know. Their sales team will try hard to get your book into stores. If they do well, there'll be a big marketing budget to support that retail platform. If they do badly, your marketing budget will be drained into other pockets. (Not that anyone will tell you this is happening.) While the size of your advance will affect the way publishers view your book at the outset of a campaign, the size of orders from stores will shape their actions when it most matters.

On the PR front, things are different. A good publicity campaign can achieve widespread coverage of your book at a relatively low cost. But though you should certainly feel free to talk about PR (and you will probably be introduced to your future publicist at this initial meeting), there won't yet be much to say. The publisher will rustle up as much publicity for you as they can. At the same time, they are months away from launching that campaign and will have little or nothing to say in detail now. So by all means try to get some feel for your publicist, but don't expect a detailed plan of action. It's way too early for that.

CHEMISTRY

So far, this section has been all coldly rational. That's all well and good, but rationality alone misses the crucial element of chemistry.

Do you get on with your editor? Do you like your publicist? Do you feel they liked your work and understood it and genuinely meshed with some of its deeper themes?

If you meet two different groups of publishers and you come away entranced by one bunch and feeling solidly businesslike but unelated about the second, then you will almost certainly go with the first. Both with my own work, and when helping our clients at Jericho Writers, I've observed that chemistry trumps rationality every time. Or, perhaps more accurately, I've noticed that chemistry just gets to the right answer quicker than rationality can.

It is worth ploughing through all the previous headings in this section – if only because you need to have something to talk about at your meeting and you may as well be talking about stuff that matters. Also, if you get on well while talking seriously about the publication of your book, then that's a much more significant omen of success than it would be if you were just chatting and wondering how much Stilton you're expected to eat.

DECISIONS

Once you've met your two possible publishers, sit down with your agent, talk it over and make a decision. You don't absolutely have to make a decision that same day or the next one, but the truth is that you've probably made up your mind already. Take a deep breath and say yes to the publisher you liked the best. It's now time to sort out money and sort out a contract.

ADVANCES, RIGHTS AND ROYALTIES

In a way, you don't need to worry too much about advances, rights and royalties. If you have an agent, your agent will negotiate these things. They know what they're doing. Their interest is in line with yours. Just let them go at it. Quite apart from anything else, if you've achieved competitive bidding, the auction will have flushed out the best price the market is willing to pay for your work. If no auction was achieved, you are not in a brilliant negotiating position, so you'll just need to take the best your agent can manage to achieve.

If your book is a smaller title and you don't have an agent, the sums of money involved are likely to be small enough that you can, in a way, afford to be relaxed. Perhaps you might be offered an advance of $1,500 when you might, if you were pushy, be able to force that to $2,000 – in which case, negotiate as hard as you feel you want to. For the majority of authors at this end of the market, the issue isn't the money, but getting your work into print. If that's the case, then don't get hung up on details. What matters most is working effectively with your publisher to maximise sales. Indeed, with smaller publishers, you may not be offered an advance at all. A book deal struck on the basis of a zero advance and an acceptable level of royalties may well represent a fair balance.

(Just to be clear, however, a zero advance is very different from a negative advance. If you are asked for money upfront – by way of 'author contribution', 'subsidy publishing', to defray 'production costs' or anything else – then you are not being offered a commercial deal. What you have in front of you is just one more variant of vanity publishing, and you should avoid it.)

Overall, therefore, few authors will really need to stress about royalties and all that. Big book deals should be handled via agents, who will look after your interests. In smaller book deals, the sums of money are often small enough that you just don't need to worry.

Having said all that, however, this section will guide you through the main financial elements that make up a book deal. That way, when your agent starts talking about serial rights, you won't be tempted to say, 'er ... Kelloggs?'

THE ADVANCE

Authors' advances are the bit of a book deal that get the most media coverage. It's the only element which is guaranteed. I've made a good living as an author, because I've always achieved high advances for my books. The subsequent sales of those books have often been disappointing, sometimes because of sloppy publishing, sometimes because of outrageous bad luck – and once or twice, perhaps, because my books weren't as good as they should have been. Nevertheless, if I'd been forced to subsist on royalties only, I'd have had some fat and happy years, but other years when I'd have been reduced to eating the bark off trees. If you want to avoid a year or two of grazing bark, you need to achieve a good offer. That's your agent's job, not yours, but it's worth knowing a little about what he is up to.

First, you need to understand what an advance is. Crucially, it's yours. It's not refundable. It's your money to keep even if the book sinks like a stone. (Assuming that you've delivered the manuscript, of course. If you are commissioned to write a book and then never deliver it, you will be asked to refund any advance you've received, and quite right too.)

On the other hand, you don't get the advance *as well as* royalties; you get it by way of an advance *against* royalties. We'll deal with this subject in plenty of detail in just a moment, but for now think of them as a payment made for each book sold. Let's say, for example, you get $0.70 per paperback copy sold. Let's also say that your advance is a healthy $20,000. In order to receive one single penny in royalties over and above that advance, you have to sell enough books to completely cover the $20,000. In this example, you'd need to sell about 28,500 copies of your paperback, earning $0.70 on each one, before you had cleared your advance. If you go on to sell even more copies, you are said to have 'earned out' your advance. Royalties will start tinkling happily into your bank account – and you will have a very cheerful publisher.

But earning out isn't everything. Back in the good old days of publishing, when lunches were long and very liquid, authors were paid less by advance and more by royalty. As literary agents came on the scene, they drove advances up, to the point now where it is perfectly common for a decently successful author never to see a royalty cheque at all. One agent once told me that, if ever a royalty cheque crossed her desk, she regarded it almost as a sign of failure: an indication that she hadn't forced the bidding high enough in the first place. That's rhetorical overstatement, but the point remains sound.

You won't, however, get the advance all at once. It's generally sliced into chunks and fed to you piece by piece. The normal pattern is roughly as follows:

25% payable on signature of the contract;

25% payable on delivery and acceptance of the manuscript;

25% payable on 'first' publication (typically the hardback version);

25% payable on 'second' publication (typically the paperback).

Some of the time, these events coincide. If you are selling a novel, for example, you won't get an agent or a book deal until your manuscript is complete and polished. The signature of the contract will therefore take place simultaneously with the acceptance of the manuscript, so you'll get both chunks of money at the same time (or the contract will dole out the money in equal thirds, instead). Equally, if you are being launched straight into paperback, the first and second publication will take place at the same time, so the last two payments will also come simultaneously. The payment pattern does vary, so check your contract.

Occasionally publication schedules will vary for reasons that have nothing to do with you. If that does happen to you, and you find yourself short of cash that you had legitimately expected to receive, talk to your agent or your editor. Your publisher may well be happy to make the payment early.

It's also worth noting that the above delivery schedule will apply to most novels and to most non-fiction aimed at a broad audience. If you are writing a much narrower type of non-fiction – like this book, for example – you are quite likely to receive your money in just two chunks, the first on signature, the second on delivery. This rather simpler arrangement has the happy effect that, once you have done your work, you get paid. Because of the delays between delivery and hardback/paperback publication, it's not uncommon for authors of more popular work to wait two years or more to receive their advance in full.

ROYALTIES – THE DUMMIES' VERSION

The whole business of royalties can get complex, so I'll offer a simple version that tells you at least 90% of what you need to know. So:

Royalties are either paid as a percentage of the published price, or a percentage of the price received by the publishers from the retailers, termed 'net receipts'. For certain areas of publishing, such as specialist non-fiction and academic publishing, net receipts are the norm.

In this simplified explanation, there are only a handful of royalty rates that matter: those for hardbacks, those for paperbacks, those for e-books, and those for audio. In the case of print royalties, the going rate may step up the more books you sell. A reasonably typical schedule might be something like this:

Hardback royalties
10% of published price for first 5,000 copies sold

12.5% of published price for next 5,000 copies sold

15% of published price for all copies after the first 10,000

Paperback royalties

7.5% of published price for first 30,000 copies sold

10% of published price thereafter

E-book royalties

Normally 25% of net receipts

Audiobook royalties

20% of net receipts

The more your book sells for, the more an agent is likely to be able to push for better royalties. Even then, however, it's more likely that you'll see a stepping down in the thresholds than an increase in the percentage rates offered. Thus, for example, an agent might be able to get that 10% paperback royalty rate to kick in from 15,000 copies rather than 30,000.

If you are selling a niche manuscript to a niche publisher, you shouldn't necessarily expect to see those higher royalty rates featured in your contract at all. That's not because the small publisher is making a fortune by ripping you off, it's more likely because nobody involved is going to make any real money. And if your book (for example) is heavily illustrated, your royalties are likely to be lower and without any escalator element (that is, no additional percentages once certain thresholds have been met). Again, that's not because you're being ripped off, it's because the economic arithmetic is different.

Calculating what is due to you is complicated, but you will never need to perform these calculations for yourself. They'll be made by your publisher, who will send you twice-yearly statements. Your agent, in principle, will check these things, though independent checks have shown that publishers nearly always get them right anyway. In short, if you don't want to do the arithmetic, then you won't need to. It's also worth noting that publishers have evolved a weirdly inscrutable form of royalty statements. If you want to ask your agent or editor about the detail, then do. They're often baffled as well.

ROYALTIES FOR ROCKET SCIENTISTS

If you don't want to know any more about royalties – well, you may not need to. Many authors never see a royalty cheque anyway (because, in more mainstream consumer markets, advances are often not earned out) and calculating these things is never going to be your task. Nevertheless, some people just like to know about these things, so here goes with a bit more detail.

Export sales

All the calculations above assume that your sales are 'home' sales: that is, sales made in the publisher's home market. Your publisher may, however, also be selling your book abroad, in which case your royalty will be payable not on the published price of your book, but on the price received or 'net receipts' by your publisher.

That might sound sensible, if MegaCorp Inc. were selling to the independent Kiwis'R'Us Publishing (NZ) Ltd; but the larger publishers are highly international concerns, so mostly you'll find that MegaCorp Inc. has just sold your book to MegaCorp (NZ) Ltd. So by transferring rights from one corporate pocket to another, your publisher's obligation to you has just halved. If you think that's fair, I'm going to guess you are a tax lawyer.

Deep discounts

The good news about supermarkets and 'pile-'em-high' booksellers is that they sell a lot of books. The bad news is that they drive a hard bargain.

The system operates via a set of 'deep discount' royalty reductions. Thus, if your publisher sells a book to an independent family-run bookshop, they might be selling a $15 paperback at a price of $7.50. The bookshop makes a profit of $7.50 when they sell the book. The publisher has also made money. Everyone's happy. But a supermarket, for example, might refuse to stock the book unless they can buy it at just $6.00, or a 60% discount to the published price. That's still a good deal for you – you want supermarket sales – but publishers will be quick to pass their margin reduction on to you. These reductions look like they eat a long way into your royalty payments ... but you want the sales anyway. Sales are precious.

The weird and wonderful

Although I've mostly spoken as though there are only a few different formats (hardback, paperback, e-book, audio), there are actually many more than this. Large-print books for libraries? Books for the blind? Special editions for newspapers or book clubs? Those things will have their own sweet royalty arrangements. Don't fuss too much over them. They'll never amount to much.

RIGHTS

We've dealt thus far with advances and royalties. There is a third ingredient of your income as a writer which deserves mention, namely sales of rights. Though technically in a different category, rights sales operate rather similarly to royalties. As before, the main point to remember is that any 'income' you achieve by rights sales will be set against your advance. Since plenty of advances are never earned out, what follows may well be somewhat theoretical.

The rights that are most commonly sold are 'serial' rights. Typically, for example, a newspaper might pay $2,000 or $3,000 for the exclusive right to print a chunk of an upcoming non-fiction work, normally around two or three weeks in advance of publication. If you are a Trump-insider with something gob-smacking to say about the Trump White House, the sums involved will have another couple of zeros attached. An author would typically expect to earn 90% of the proceeds of that 'first serial rights' sale. If a second serialisation deal happens (which is much less common), the author's share typically falls to more like 75%.

If a publisher has bought world rights to your MS, you would also expect the lion's share of any proceeds derived from its sale overseas – typically 80%. In effect, your publisher is acting as your agent, and you are paying an agent-style commission for the service provided.

For most other rights sales – radio reading and other audio, anthology and quotation, large-print, educational and a whole host of other curios – you should expect to divide proceeds about 50/50 with your publisher. You should not give your publisher the right to sell your MS to the film and TV industries – that's a right you want to retain for yourself – but, if for any reason you do yield those rights, you would normally expect about 75% of any net proceeds. More of all that later.

IF YOU DON'T HAVE AN AGENT

If you don't have an agent, then the advice given at the start of this section – don't worry about any of this; your agent will handle it for you – may strike you as somewhat less than satisfactory. As a rule of thumb, however, if you are offered terms broadly in line with the terms outlined in this section, then your publisher is offering you a perfectly fair deal. If you can squeeze things higher, then do. If you can't, at least you tried. Some small publishers operate on budgets so minuscule, and are driven so much more by passion than by money, that it would hardly be reasonable to mind if they do end up offering terms worse than these. And, if you're worried, sign up for the Authors Guild (US) or the Society of Authors (UK). Those guys will examine your contract and alert you to anything that shouldn't be there.

VARIANTS

This section conveys the state of rough play in the market at the time of writing for a typical deal with a mainstream consumer publisher. But every book deal is different. The market changes. If you are being offered terms worse than those laid out in this section, you should certainly feel free to talk to your agent or publisher. But don't do so with the conviction that you are being treated in bad faith. You most likely aren't.

YOUR PUBLISHING CONTRACT

When I first received a publishing contract, I read it through and asked my agent about anything I didn't understand. She was surprised, telling me that as far as she knew no authors bothered to read a word of the document before signing.

I don't advocate such a laid-back attitude. You are entering into a long-term relationship. The contract may look about as appealing to read as an insurance document cross-bred with a tax return, but it's still only a few pages of ordinary English sentences and you are a writer, after all. You're allowed to be terrified of numbers, but these are words. Furthermore, by entering into a contract with a publisher, you aren't just agreeing to sell your manuscript, you are also making a number of undertakings that you need to abide by. It's easier to do that if you know what they are.

ANATOMY OF A CONTRACT

Fortunately, it's not that hard to predict what your contract will look like. It'll look rather like the one set out in the rest of this section. That's partly because each contract deals with broadly the same set of rights, obligations and contingencies, and partly because publishers have, over the decades, come to adopt a largely common approach to dealing with them. If you have an agent, then it's likely that your agent will have negotiated a template or 'boilerplate' contract with your publisher to cover all relationships between the two firms. That template will then simply be modified to reflect the particular terms and needs of your deal. The potential list of variations is too long to go into here. There are some linguistic differences between American and British

185

contracts. But don't fuss too much over the details. The bones of all publishing contracts are broadly similar.

We'll look at a typical contract in a moment. Just a few comments first.

For many readers, the typical first contract will comprise a two-book deal. If you are selling a novel, or a certain type of mainstream non-fiction, publishers usually offer for two books rather than one. In a standard two-book deal, you'll sell (let's say) the novel that you've already written and will agree to write a further manuscript under the same terms and conditions. You'll have plenty of time to write that second manuscript, though the days of infinitely elastic deadlines are now over. Check to see what deadline your publisher is proposing for delivery of the second manuscript and be sure that you're comfortable meeting it. If in doubt, talk to your publisher. They are apt to be snappish if you miss your deadline.

(Oh, and on the subject of two-book deals, I have to tell you this story. At a festival once, I was on a panel with a novelist who had no idea that she should expect to get a two-book deal. When her agent secured just that, she was terrified. She was due to meet her publisher in two weeks' time and she had written just the one novel. She felt like a naughty schoolchild, who'd failed to do her homework. So she took a fortnight off work and wrote fourteen hours a day, so that, when she met her publishers, she was able to deliver not one manuscript but two. The publisher was astonished.)

Your second manuscript, of course, needs to be something like the first. If you sell a wonderful, upbeat chick-litty romance to a publisher, your second book can't be a literary novella about suicidal Frenchmen. They will hurl it back at you if do.

Two final comments.

The first is that, despite the essential sameness of nearly all publishing contracts, it can take an uncannily long time to produce them. It's not uncommon for it to take three months from agreeing a deal to signing the contract for it. Given that the principal terms of the deal have already been agreed, and given that standard form ('boilerplate') contracts already exist, I think it's absurd that they take as long as they do. If you want to chase, then chase.

Finally, let me repeat the advice with which I closed the previous chapter. If you want a career as a professional author, I do advise you to become a member of the Authors Guild (if you're American) or the Society of Authors (if you're British). Your agent is your first line of defence, but agents can die, move, retire, go mad, get drunk, fall ill, lose their wits, find God, go gaga, have visions – or, in short, be afflicted with any or all of the disorders which routinely affect agent-kind. Your only certain refuge in this vale of tears is the support of the major author organisations. Join one.

A SAMPLE CONTRACT

While every contract is different, they have a lot of similarities. This one is for a sale of world rights. The contract text is in Roman lettering below. My comments are italicised and follow each paragraph. I've avoided a host of minor complexities in what follows, so don't be surprised if the contract placed in front of you has a few wrinkles over and above what follows.

Also, just to be clear, this contract is composed of real contracts, sourced from different publishers and from different territories. Your contract will not replicate this in detail, though in substance it broadly should.

MEMORANDUM OF AGREEMENT

made this – day of 20– between William Shakespeare, c/o A Literary Agency (hereinafter called the 'Author' which expression shall where the context admits include the Author's executors administration and assigns) and Mega-Corp Publishing Inc. of MegaCorp Plaza (hereinafter called the 'Publishers' which expression shall where the context admits include the Publishers' successors in business and assigns and any imprint of MegaCorp Publishing whether under its present or future style) whereby it is mutually agreed as follows respecting a work by the Author at present entitled *Romeo and Juliet* (hereinafter called 'the said work').

The preamble identifies the two contractual counterparties, namely you and the publisher. Although you will (assuming you have an agent) always be 'care of' your agency; your agent is not a party to this transaction. The date of the contract will only appear once it's been signed by all parties. The bit about executors and assigns (in the clause that relates to you) means that your heirs will continue to benefit from the contract, even if you are knocked over by a car. The bit about successors in business means that, if your publisher is bought up by someone else, or changes their legal structure in some other way, the resultant entity will still be bound.

1. The Author hereby grants to the Publishers during the legal term of copyright the sole and exclusive licence to publish the said work in volume form in all languages throughout the World subject to the conditions following. [The Author has delivered the said work to the Publisher and the Publisher has accepted it.]

This is it! You are selling your book. This is the clause that hands over the rights in your manuscript to the Publisher. Copyright protection lasts for the duration of the author's life plus the first seventy years thereafter. The bit in square brackets will only be there if the Publisher has formally accepted your manuscript. Quite often there'll be a bit of editorial stuff which precedes formal acceptance, which means you can sell your work before it's accepted. If you haven't yet supplied a full manuscript, which will often be the case for non-fiction writers, then there will be a deadline for you to do so.

2. The Author hereby warrants to the Publishers:
    i. that he has full power to make this Agreement,
    ii. that he is the sole author of the said work and is the owner of the rights herein granted,

iii. that the said work is original to him and has not previously been published in volume form in the exclusive territories covered by this Agreement,

iv. that the said work is in no way whatever a violation or infringement of any copyright or licence,

v. that all necessary permissions for the use in volume or serial form of all copyright material quoted in the said work have been granted and any fees payable to copyright owners have been or will be paid by the Author,

vi. that the said work contains nothing obscene, blasphemous, unlawful, defamatory or libellous,

vii. that the said work contains nothing which has been obtained in violation of [local laws],

viii. that all statements contained therein as purported facts are true,

ix. that any recipe, formulae or instructions in the work, if followed accurately, will not injure the user or any other person, and

x. that the work does not breach any right of privacy nor any duty of confidence.

Your excitement at para 1 is likely to dissipate rapidly on encountering para 2 (which can appear much later in the contract). Sections i to v above are saying that you are the author of the book (you haven't stolen it from anyone else and have secured whatever permissions are required). You also need to confirm sections vi to x above that the material is lawful in various other respects. Most authors will find it easy to make the warranties listed above. Some will need to pause for rather deeper consideration — and may need to peruse the section on libel in this book with some care. You do need to read the above paragraph, and, if you have any hesitations about any part of it, ask.

Do also note that (in books that make extensive use of quotations from copyright material) most authors will not have solicited all the permissions required before signing this contract. Indeed, it's hard to obtain a permission without a book deal in your pocket, because those whose job it is to hand out permissions always ask about publishers, publication dates, print runs and the like. Nevertheless, as long as you obtain all permissions in good time, it doesn't really matter to anyone whether you have them at this point or not. If your work is an illustrated one, it may be that the publisher will pick up the costs for clearing permissions. A publisher also often picks up the costs of indexing the work, should this be required.

Likewise, the requirement in the contract that 'all statements contained [in the book] as purported facts are true' *needn't bother you too much either. It is, in fact, extremely difficult to produce a book-length work of non-fiction and to make no factual errors whatsoever. But if you get the big things right – and especially the things that may verge on the defamatory – then you should be OK. The publishers are highly unlikely to suffer any financial loss from a few minor errors of fact, which means that any liability would be highly theoretical.*

3. The Author hereby agrees to indemnify the Publishers against all actions, proceedings, claims, demands, losses, damages and costs (including any legal costs or expenses and taxes attributable thereto) properly incurred and any compensation, cost disbursements, and taxes paid by the Publishers on the advice of their legal advisers to comprise or settle any claim (provided that the Author has been consulted by the Publishers) in consequence of any breach (or alleged breach) of this warranty or of any negligence on the part of the Author in the preparation of the said work. The Publishers reserve the right to insist that the Author alter the text of the said work in such a way as shall appear to the Publishers appropriate for the purpose of removing anything which on the advice of the Publishers' legal advisers is considered objectionable or likely to be actionable at law but any such alterations or removal shall not affect the Author's liability under this warranty and indemnity herein contained. Should the said work become the subject of a complaint alleging libel, the decision of the Publishers as to whether or not to repudiate liability to contest an action if proceedings ensue or to settle the claim upon such terms as

they may be advised shall be final and the Author shall have no grounds for action against the Publishers in respect of its implementation provided that the Author has been consulted.

The warranties and indemnities stated above shall survive the termination of this Agreement.

This is the scariest clause in the contract, and by far the most unfair. You – little old you – get to indemnify MegaCorp against any costs that it may incur as a result of libel action, or any other actual or putative breach of your undertakings in the first chunk of this paragraph. It doesn't matter whether the claim for libel (or anything else) is upheld in a court or not. Indeed, your publisher may choose to settle any claim, whether or not you want them to. The publisher's obligation is merely to consult with you before they take action – they don't have to take any notice of what you say. Your publisher can then require you to pick up every single one of the costs, legal and other, that they've incurred in the process.

Under these conditions, you could easily go bankrupt, even if you are blameless. Nevertheless, I've never heard of these risks actually materialising. You need not to have stolen your material from anyone else. You need to avoid libelling anyone. You need to avoid doing anything else that's stupid or wrong. And if you manage to do those things all right, you'll be just fine.

4. The Publishers shall publish the said work within eighteen (18) months of the date of this Agreement unless prevented by circumstances over which they have no control or unless mutually agreed, and subject always to Clause 2.

Publishers can't not publish your book. The contract doesn't simply require that they pay you the agreed sums, but that they do in fact publish your book. It would be normal to see a deadline in the contract that allows for some slippage. So, if, for example, everyone is intending to see you published within twelve months, then the contract might use an eighteen-month deadline. It would be highly unusual for this deadline to be breached and never without your consent.

5. The Publishers shall pay to the Author

That is a beautiful word, is it not? The fourth one, I mean. Simple, precise and so sweet on the ear.

(a) The following royalties:

   (i)   on a hardcover edition published under the Publishers' own imprint:

   Home sales: Ten per cent (10%) of the published price on the first three thousand (3,000) copies sold; twelve and a half per cent (12.5%) of the published price on the next three thousand (3,000) copies sold and fifteen per cent (15%) of the published price on all copies sold thereafter.

   High discount sales: On home sales where the discount is fifty-two and a half per cent (52.5%) or more, the royalty payable shall be four-fifths of the prevailing royalty. On all hardcover home sales at a discount of sixty per cent (60%) or more, the above royalties shall be paid at a rate of three-fifths of the prevailing royalty.

   Export sales: Ten per cent (10%) of the price received by the Publishers on the first three thousand (3,000) copies sold; twelve and a half per cent (12.5%) of the price received by the Publishers on the next three thousand (3,000) copies sold and fifteen per cent (15%) of the price received by the Publishers on all copies sold thereafter.

   (ii)   On mass-market paperback editions published under the Publishers' own imprint:

   Home sales: Seven and a half per cent (7.5%) of the published price on the first twenty thousand (20,000) copies sold and ten per cent (10%) of the published price on all copies sold thereafter.

   High discount sales: At a discount of fifty-two and a half per cent (52.5%) or more, the royalty shall be four-fifths of the prevailing royalty. On all paperback home sales at a discount of sixty per cent (60%) or more the above royalties shall be paid at a rate of three-fifths of the prevailing royalty.

Export sales: Twelve and a half per cent (12.5%) of the price received on all copies sold.

(iii) On trade paperback editions published under the Publishers' own imprint:

Home sales: If the Publishers' first edition, ten per cent (10%) of the published price on all copies sold. If not the Publishers' first edition, seven and a half per cent (7.5%) of the published price to ten thousand (10,000) copies sold, ten per cent (10%) of the published price thereafter.

High discount sales: At a discount of fifty-two and a half per cent (52.5%) or more, the royalty shall be four-fifths of the prevailing royalty. On all trade paperback home sales at a discount of sixty per cent (60%) or more, the above royalties shall be paid at a rate of three-fifths of the prevailing royalty.

Export sales: Ten per cent (10%) of the price received to ten thousand (10,000) copies, twelve and a half per cent (12.5%) of the price received thereafter.

(iv) On remainder sales: ten per cent (10%) of the sum received from the sale of any copies sold as a remainder, i.e. at less than two-fifths of the published price and above cost. The Publishers shall give the Author an opportunity of purchasing some or all of the remainder copies at the remainder price such option to be exercised if at all within twenty-eight (28) days of notice being given to the Author of the Publishers' intention to remainder the said work. It is agreed that no remainder sales shall be made within twelve (12) months of first home publication. No royalty shall be paid on copies remaindered at or below cost.

(v)   On Publishers' e-book – twenty-five per cent (25%) of the price received by the Publishers.

An e-book will be the text of and any illustrations in the work in whole or in part in digitally accessible and/or electronic form for the purposes of reading/viewing. No enrichments shall be added without Author's consent. All terms to be reviewed two (2) years from first publication of the work.

(vi)   On Publishers' own Audio exploitation: use by the Publishers of the work in abridged audio form, physical version, a royalty of seven and a half per cent (7.5%) net receipts to 7,500 copies and ten per cent (10%) thereafter. On Audio Download, a royalty of 15% net receipts.

(vii) On the Publishers' large-print editions: ten per cent (10%) of the price received.

(viii) On the Publishers' educational editions: ten per cent (10%) of the price received.

(ix)   On all sales of unbound sheets: ten per cent (10%) of the price received.

(x)   On Sales Outside Normal Sales Channels: ten per cent (10%) of the price received.

Phew! You can see what I mean about this royalty stuff being tediously complicated. Since most of the line items ('All sales of unbound sheets' – what?) are minor or minor-approaching-totally-made-up, you don't have to worry about them. Have a quick chat with your agent on the major elements, and that's really all you need. As far as I know, I've never earned a single bent penny from sale of unbound sheets.

(b) An advance on account of all payments due to the Author under the terms of this Agreement of:

$40,000 TO BE PAID AS FOLLOWS:

$10,000 on signature of this Agreement by both parties.

$10,000 on delivery and acceptance of the said work.

$10,000 on first publication of the said work.

$10,000 on second publication of the said work.

This is your advance —$40,000 in this example. Note that you don't get the advance plus royalties. You get the advance as an advance against royalties. So, if your book never accumulates enough sales to pay off your advance — and many books never do —you won't ever see a royalty cheque.

6. The Publishers shall render statements showing royalties and all other monies due to 30th June and 31st December in each year after home country publication within three (3) months of such dates and shall then pay all monies due to the Author, except that if the sum is less than fifty dollars ($50.00) they may hold it over until the following royalty period.

I'd love to know how long this clause has been standard in the industry. Amazon reports sales to self-published authors in something very close to real-time. It pays the royalties accrued in one month by the end of the month following — so June's royalties are paid at the end of July, for example. The 'wait six months, then another three' model of the big trad publishers can't possibly be justified by anything except MegaCorp Inc.'s desire to protect its cashflows at the expense of yours. In effect, you are providing zero-interest loans to a multi-billion-dollar enterprise. That said, you can't do anything about it, so just suck it up. The royalty you earned on 1st July will clink into your bank account on 31st March in the year following ... except that it'll clink into your agent's pocket at that point, so you'll still have to wait for a few days for the pennies to arrive.

More importantly, publishers have historically been appalling at releasing timely information to authors. Worse, I can think of several occasions when publishers lied or wildly misled me about sales — a stupid tactic when everything emerges into the open eventually. These days, bigger publishers do have online author dashboard systems which deliver reasonably timely data in a somewhat useful way. I've never yet encountered a system as rich and easy to configure as Amazon's, but at least you get the basic data. I do recommend that you download and store the data received. I know of at least one big publisher's system which makes it impossible to usefully extract data that is more than a year old. Since you may well want to compare the trajectory of your book #3, versus book #2, versus book #1, you do need that historic data. So download it and keep it safe.

7. The books of account of the Publishers so far as they relate to any matter arising out of this Agreement shall be open to inspection by the Author or the Author's duly authorised representatives by appointment at any reasonable time, and at the Author's expense. In the event that errors are found in excess of one hundred dollars ($100) in the Publishers' favour, the cost of that investigation will be borne by the Publishers.

You have the right to audit your publisher's royalty accounting, but you probably won't. The major author organisations make regular random checks of publishers' accounting systems and errors are in fact very rare. When errors do arise, however, they are more often than not in favour of the publisher; which suggests that there's still room for improvement.

8. The Publishers shall have the right to set aside as a reserve against returns twenty per cent (20%) of any royalties earned on the Publishers' hardback edition of the said work and twenty-five per cent (25%) on a paperback edition of the said work, as shown on the first royalty statement after publication or reissue and to withhold this sum up to the third royalty account thereafter, following which all monies due shall be credited to the Author's account at the time of the next royalty statement.

Publishers sell books to retailers on a sale or return basis. (Or rather, nearly all of them do. There are moves afoot to try to change that, but the system is so far resisting change.) As a result, selling books to a retailer doesn't necessarily mean that you've made a sale. It's perfectly possible for your publisher to get out (say) 10,000 books to retailers, then find that 3,000 of them come back again in due course. To handle this problem, publishers can make an allowance for possible returns against any royalty payments that would otherwise be due. That won't reduce the total amount of money that you receive in total, but it does alter the timing.

9. [The Publishers shall receive no shares of any monies received from the performance on sound radio or television of a play based on the said work either for a single performance or in instalments and it is further agreed that in the event of a motion picture or television film sale being made of the said work and on notification of such to the Publishers interest in any broadcasting or television rights in the said work shall automatically cease.]

You wouldn't normally sell film and TV rights to a publisher in the first instance, and this clause is just making that clear. The clause is in square brackets, however, as it's not really needed and often doesn't appear. It's not needed because the contract makes clear what rights are being sold. If you haven't sold a particular right – such as the TV and film rights – then the contract doesn't strictly speaking need to say anything additional, though it's common to see words to the effect that 'rights not explicitly granted under this contract are reserved for the author'.

10. The Author shall receive on publication five (5) copies of the Publishers' hardback edition of the said work and ten (10) copies of any paperback edition published by the Publishers and shall be entitled to purchase further copies for personal use (but not for resale) at thirty-five per cent (35%) trade discount, such copies to be paid for on presentation of the Publishers' invoice. The Publishers shall send to the Author at least two (2) copies of any other edition of the work published by or under licence from the Publishers. The Publishers shall supply the Agent with two (2) presentation copies of the Publishers' hardback edition and five (5) copies of any paperback edition published by the publisher and two (2) presentation copies of

any other edition of the work published by or under licence from the Publishers. The Author's copies shall be sent direct to his agent at: A Literary Agency.

You get some free copies of your book when it comes out. You can buy more at a discount if you want. Don't forget to give one to your mother. She gave birth to you, you selfish brute.

11. The Publishers shall consult the Author and obtain his approval over jacket copy and design, such approval not to be unreasonably withheld or delayed. The Author shall be shown proofs of the jacket and consulted thereon, but the final decision shall be the Publishers'. No changes in the title or text of the said work shall be made without the Author's consent, such consent not to be unreasonably withheld or delayed. The Publishers shall inform the Author of the number of copies in the first and subsequent printings, if so requested.

OK, first the good news. 'No changes in the title or text' of your work can be made without your consent. In other words, when it comes to content, the Publishers can't so much as change a comma unless you're happy for them to do so. This is the one area of the whole publishing process where you truly are king or queen. Enjoy it.

The less good news is that your rights are vastly more restricted when it comes to other aspects of your work. The language in the first sentence above actually yields the author more power than is awarded by some contracts – that is, it gives you a veto right over jacket copy and design, so long as your veto is not 'unreasonably withheld or delayed'. Other times, you'll see language which gives you the right to be consulted but does not oblige the publisher to take the tiniest bit of notice of your opinions. As a practical matter, publishers will want you to like their jacket design, and neither you nor your editor will want to get all legalistic about the matter. But this is an area where the balance of power lies with the publisher, so you can't behave like a diva and expect to get away with it.

Finally, do note that the clause above does oblige your publishers to tell you how many copies they're printing, if you ask them. As it happens, there is a lot more information that they could and really should give you. These days, after all, print runs are short and rapid, so print runs just don't tell you much. Much more to the point are questions like: 'What chain bookstores are entering my book into their promotions?', 'What is the uptake like from the supermarkets?', 'What have you sold online so far?', 'How is the book performing against target?', 'How is my book going to be positioned in the travel sector?', 'Are there [a few weeks after publication] any indications about the level of returns?' If you know to ask these questions of your editor, she'll do her best to tell you, but publishers seldom volunteer this crucial information of their own accord, and what they do tell you is not always to be relied upon. The sad truth is that you will most likely be left mostly in the dark or left to pore (endlessly) over your Amazon sales rank and your author dashboard. If you ask me, publishers should communicate much better than this.

12. In ample time prior to Publication, the Author shall be sent a questionnaire inviting him to supply personal information relevant to publicity and marketing and to suggest who should receive review/free copies.

Self-explanatory, but not something found in every contract. After all, both parties have every incentive to collaborate actively.

13. If any alterations from the copy as delivered to the Publishers be made in the proofs by the Author the expenses incurred by the Publishers in making such alterations over and above the sum of ten per cent (10%) of the cost of setting the said copy shall be borne by the Author. The Author shall be notified if his corrections are likely to exceed ten per cent (10%) of the setting costs. The Publishers may deduct these costs from any monies payable to the Author under the terms of this Agreement or may present the Author with an invoice for payment, which the Author will settle within sixty (60) days of receipt.

It's kind of amazing that you still see this kind of language; it's another relic from the time of Melville. This clause dates from the time when books were set by men in brown coats bending over trays of metal type. If an author made changes to the text after it was set, then the author was creating cost and expense for the publisher, for which the author, quite rightly, would be liable. I'd always assumed that this clause was just a relic of the old days – I didn't see how it could work now that the whole process is electronic. But my copyeditor assures me that it works just fine, and if a careless author messes around with the text at a late stage, the result is likely to be a couple of hefty invoices. So take care.

14. If at any time the Publishers allow the said work to go out of print or off the market in all trade editions and shall not have reprinted and placed on the market a new edition or impression within six (6) months of receiving written notice from the Author then all rights in the said work shall revert to the Author forthwith, except for any existing licence agreement or contract entered into by the Publishers prior to the date of such reversion.

OK. This is a bit of a bugbear of mine, and it may one day become a bugbear of yours. Here's the issue. In the old days, before e-books and print-on-demand, books were printed in print runs of, let's say, not less than 500 books. If a publisher thought a print run of that scale was going to be unprofitable, they'd let the book go out of print. If it stayed out of print, the author could reclaim the rights, as outlined in this clause. All good, right?

Trouble is, since e-books are never out of print and print-on-demand means that any book can stay in book for an eternity, the clause as presented here, in its traditional form, basically offers zero help to the author. Reading between the lines, it's saying, 'you can never ever have your rights back, ha-ha-ha-ha ha!'

But suppose that in a few years' time, your book is to all intents and purposes dead. It is #467,067 on the Amazon bestseller list. No bookshop in the world holds a copy of your book. The publishers aren't marketing it. You don't even, meaningfully, have an editor or marketer responsible for thinking about that book. And you want it back. Perhaps just for sentimental reasons, or perhaps because you want to self-publish it, or bring out a new edition, or for some other reason. Now, that should be an easy deal to do. Your publisher has no particular reason to hold onto these rights. They're not earning anything. So they should just be willing to give them to you or (more sensibly) sell them according to a simple formula. One big international group values intra-group rights sales at five times last twelve month sales. (So if your book brought in $500 to the publisher over the last twelve months, you'd have to pay $2,500 to get the rights back.) Simple, right?

Except that publishers are wildly, crazily resistant to releasing rights. I once tried to get a package of seven books back from HarperCollins. It wasn't that I had some big secret film deal up my sleeve and was about to pull a fast one. It was just that they were doing nothing with the books, and I thought there were good things I could do, and I wanted to try. Also, I just cared about the books.

But oh my gosh and oh my golly, it was hard to have a sane conversation with HarperCollins. The editors once responsible for them had long since left. I was reduced to having a conversation with a guy in the general counsel's office, who kept on emailing the two different imprints concerned for input. They mostly didn't answer him. (Why should they? They had nothing to gain.) When they did, because of my annoying persistence, they came back with insanely high valuations, with add-on payments to be made for all kind of future eventualities. As a commercial conversation, this was barmy. But if you're a gopher at one of MegaCorp's imprints, you have two choices: (i) sell the book at a sane but modest valuation, (ii) not sell it at all. There is zero upside in taking the first of these routes. Your boss will not say, 'Wow! You just earned us $2,500 when we were only expecting $500. Well done you! Have the rest of the day off and feel free to borrow my yacht.' But there is a downside. What if some sneaky author does have a massive film contract in his pocket when he repurchases the rights? Sure, the film rights are his in any event, but the books could really sell big off the back of a successful movie. In that case, your boss is going to go roaring round the office yelling, 'What IDIOT sold these books for $2,500? When I find that moron, I'm going to sail out into Chesapeake Bay and drop her off my yacht.'

So sane commercial conversations are virtually impossible. Really, the industry needs to smarten up and understand that it needs to find an efficient, largely automatic way to revert rights to writers once books have *stopped selling in any meaningful quantity. For present purposes, you should talk to your agent about including a reversions clause and push for the most robust language you can get. You probably won't get much (neither your agent nor your publisher will be particularly minded to help), but you'll get nothing if you don't ask. The sort of language you should look for is something like this: 'For the avoidance of doubt, the said work shall be considered to be out of print if sales of the work total less than two hundred and fifty (250) copies over two (2) consecutive accounting periods.' Your aim is to get that 250 number as high as you can.*

15. If the Publishers fail to fulfil or comply with any of the provisions of this Agreement and shall not within one (1) month after written notification from the Author rectify such failure or if they go into liquidation otherwise than for the purpose of reconstruction or when a receiver is appointed this Agreement shall thereupon terminate and all rights in the said work forthwith revert to the Author who shall be free to license any other person to publish the said work notwith-standing anything to the contrary contained or implied in any part of this Agreement and without prejudice to any claim which the Author may have either for monies due and/or damages and/or otherwise.

If the publisher goes bust — most likely as a consequence of their fail-ure to turn you into the global bestseller you surely ought to be — the rights in your work revert to you. If your publisher breaches this contract and doesn't promptly remedy that breach, again the rights revert. Many contracts won't contain a clause quite as beefy as this one — very often, for example, a publisher would need to default on their payment obligations to you before you can demand a reversion of rights. Disputes over relatively minor matters (e.g. has anyone sent you your free copies or not?) are obviously unlikely to trigger this clause, no matter what the contract says.

16. This Agreement expresses the entire understanding of the parties to this Agreement and no rights, licences or other in-

terests are granted to the Publishers other than those specifically set out in this Agreement.

*Belt and braces stuff. It's worth being clear about who's selling what
to whom. This clause simply makes it clear that, if you aren't explicitly
selling a particular right in your work, the publisher is not entitled to
exploit it.*

17. The Publishers undertake that the name of the Author shall
    appear in its customary form with due prominence on the title
    page, binding and jacket of every copy of the work issued by
    the Publishers and shall include in all copies of the work a
    complete and correct copyright notice as follows:
    © William Shakespeare 20– (20– being the year of first publi-
    cation)

*Mostly self-explanatory. 'Customary form' means that your name
appears the way you normally write it. Thus, my name appears as 'Harry
Bingham' on my books, no matter that my full legal name is Thomas
Henry Bingham. If you happen to be called, let's say, Daniel Brown but
always call yourself Dan, then you will simply have to discuss with your
publishers how to present your name so that you are properly identified
but in a way that doesn't confuse or mislead readers who might be looking
for the next book about shenanigans in the Vatican. Publishers generally
prefer to avoid pseudonyms – because it is hard to achieve maximum
impact from publicity activities if you and your book go by different
names – but the preference is not very marked.*

*I was once asked to change my name to a woman's name (for a Ger-
man edition of one of my novels) and I know a woman who became a
man for the purposes of publication.*

18. The Author hereby asserts his moral right to be identified as
    the author of the said work, and the Publishers undertake: to
    print with due prominence on every edition of the said work
    published by themselves the words 'The right of William
    Shakespeare to be identified as author of this work has been
    asserted by him'; to make a condition of contract with any

Licensee concerning any edition of the said work to be published that a similar notice of assertion shall be printed with due prominence in every edition published by or further licensed by such Licensee.

All this simply requires your publishers and any parties who buy the right to sub-license your work (e.g. for those large-print books for the visually impaired), to assert your moral rights to be identified as author of that work. If you don't know what moral rights are all about, you probably don't need to know. The assertion of authorship which matters most is your name in big letters across the front of your book. That's the one that's going to make your mum happy.

19. This Agreement shall in all respects be governed by and interpreted in accordance with the laws of New York/England/The People's Republic of Ruritania

Self-explanatory, except that they are the laws of England and Wales, are they not?

20. If at any time the Publishers consider that the copyright in the said work has been infringed and the Author after receiving written notice of such infringement from the Publishers refuses or neglects to take proceedings in respect of the infringement, the Publishers shall be entitled to take proceedings in the joint names of the Publishers and the Author upon giving the Author a sufficient and reasonable security to indemnify the Author against any liability for costs; and in this event any sum received by way of damages shall belong to the Publishers. If the Author is willing to take proceedings and the Publishers desire to be joined with the Author thereto and agree to share the costs, then any sum received by way of damages shall be applied in payment to the costs incurred and the balance shall be divided equally between the Author and the Publishers. The provisions of the clause are intended to apply only in the case of an infringement of the copyright in

the said work affecting the interest in the same granted to the Publishers under this Agreement.

Not a clause that's likely to trouble you much. If someone infringes your copyright, and your publisher wants to take legal action, then you can (i) agree to share the costs of the lawsuit and divvy up any proceeds 50/50, or (ii) choose not to incur any costs of the lawsuit but also give up any right to any proceeds that may arise. Either way, however, you agree that the publisher can sue in their name and yours, so long as (if you have chosen not to incur any costs) they give you a legally binding indemnity against any such costs. The chance of you wanting to sue (or murder) a copyright pirate is high. The chance of you doing so is vanishingly small.

21. The Author shall not during the currency of the Agreement without the consent of the Publishers prepare or cause to allow to be published other than by the Publishers any written material which shall be an expansion or abridgement of the said work or of a nature likely to prevent the sales of either copies or of rights in the said work.

If you sell your work, you sell it. You can't sell The Complete Encyclopaedia of Trilobite Fossils *to publisher A, then seek to sell* An Expanded Encyclopaedia of Trilobite Fossils *to publisher B. These issues are of much more concern to non-fiction authors than to novelists. I can't imagine a situation where my selling novel B to a publisher could impair the sales of my novel A.*

22. The Author agrees that before publication he will undertake not to publish or broadcast the said work or cause to be broadcast or published any material about the said work in the exclusive territory without prior consultation with the Publishers.

You can't engage in PR activities relating to the book without talking to your publisher in advance. You shouldn't want to, either.

23. Advertisements may not be inserted or printed in any edition of the said work, whether issued by the Publishers or their licensee, without the Author s written consent, except for listings of the Publishers' or their licensee's own works of a similar nature where there would otherwise be blank pages at the end of a paperback edition of the said work.

You won't suddenly find yourself endorsing products without your consent, the one exception being that publishers can advertise comparable books on their list in those blank pages at the back of the book.

24. This Agreement and the rights and licence hereby granted may not be assigned or transmitted by the Publishers without the prior written consent of the Author, such consent not to be unreasonably withheld save as herein expressly provided.

In the mortgage industry pre-2008, you never really knew who owned your mortgage, because everyone was flogging their rights to everyone else. It's not like that in publishing, where publishers aren't allowed simply to sell their rights in a work to some other party. If they want to do that — and they're unlikely to — they need your permission.

25. All statements of accounts and all monies shown thereon to be due under this agreement shall be paid to the Author's agents, A Literary Agency, who are hereby irrevocably au-thorised to collect and receive such monies and to charge the Author their agreed commission on all sums payable by the Publishers to the Author during the validity of this contract and any extensions and renewals of it and the Author declares that the receipt of the said A Literary Agency shall be a good and valid discharge in respect thereof and the said A Literary Agency are hereby authorised to negotiate as agents for the Author in all matters arising out of this agreement.

All the money coming your way as a result of this agreement will go to your agent in the first instance. Your agent will help themselves to your commission, plus any sales tax on that commission, and may also charge a few minor fees relating to any expenses incurred. You are also agreeing that your agent is authorised to negotiate matters arising from this agreement on your behalf.

26.

    (a) The Publishers may use or permit others to use the Author's name and likeness, the title of the said work and selections from the said work in advertising, catalogues, promotion and publicity related to the publication and/or licensing of the said work including (but not limited to) broadcast (without charge) by radio, television or cable or distribution via any form of electronic transmission including online or satellite-based data transmission.

You agree to let the publisher use your name and mugshot, plus chunks from the book itself, in publicising your work.

    (b) The Author will make himself available to promote and publicise the said work as the Publishers shall reasonably require particularly during the two (2) weeks at the time of publication, the Author's agreed costs in such promotion to be borne by the Publishers.

Self-explanatory – and, of course, it's very much in your interest to be as co-operative here as you possibly can be. To be prudent, I wouldn't go on any long holiday in the four to six weeks around publication. It's rare that all PR activity takes place within a single fortnight.

27. It is hereby agreed that the Publishers shall have first refusal of (including the first opportunity to read and consider for publication on fair and reasonable terms) the next work of adult fiction by the Author suitable for publication in volume form, such work shall be the subject of a new agreement between the Author and Publishers on terms to be agreed between the parties hereto, such terms to be fair and reasonable. The Publishers shall give their decision on the said option work within

one (1) month of their receipt of synopsis, outline or complete typescript copy of the option work.

This clause – or versions of it – will appear in most contracts that are placed in front of you. This is a delicate area and one well worth understanding. The issues are these.

On the one hand, your publisher is making an investment not simply in this book, but in you and your future career. So they deserve first dibs on your next work ... if for example, it's a work of fiction, or the kind of mainstream non-fiction work which aims to appeal to a broad audience. If the work is a narrowly subject-led manuscript, you probably shouldn't offer first refusal rights on further work. If you are contemplating a series of further works on the same or closely related subject areas, you should discuss all that upfront.

On the other hand, don't think that those rights of first refusal don't cost you anything, because they do. If publisher B would, in principle, be interested in acquiring rights to your next novel, but they know that publisher A already has first refusal rights, publisher B is much less likely to go to all the effort of bidding assertively for the book, because they (rightly) fear that the effort may be wasted.

For novels and broad-spectrum non-fiction, the above clause represents a normal way to resolve this tension. And, of course, when it comes to selling your next MS, your agent will be able to guide you through all the thickets that will arise at the time.

Signed by

Publishers ....

Author ....

You'll normally receive two or three copies of the contract and will be asked to sign and return them all, without dating any of them. As soon as you do that, the publisher will sign and date each copy. You'll get one, your agent will (probably) get one, and your publisher will have one. All this is normally handled electronically now.

CONCLUSION

That's it, really. The contract will be quite long, but the anxiety-inducing passages are few. You should read the document and raise any questions with your agent or your editor. And one little plea from me. Right now, in the thrill of a new book deal, you won't care about reversion clauses, but you may very well do in time. So ask. Your future self will thank you.

Libel and Other Routes to Bankruptcy

Everything in your contract matters and you will, naturally, read it attentively from cover to cover before signing it, but there are, for most authors, only a few areas with the potential to render you bankrupt, destroy your marriage and leave you begging for coppers outside your local supermarket.

Those areas are anything that could bring you within reach of the law courts. It's not likely that anything you write will expose you to legal threat, but if you are even a little concerned, you *must* be sure of handling it correctly, as you may pay dearly if you don't. Authors who need to worry about these things include the authors of 'misery memoirs', where the wrongdoers are still alive. They may also include the authors of current affairs or investiga-tive-type books that make serious allegations about individuals or corporations. It is, however, rare for a novelist to have to worry, and most non-fiction simply doesn't go into the sorts of areas from which legal claims are likely to arise.

Oh yes, and I'm not a lawyer, and this book has a global audi-ence, and no lawyer on earth knows the law in every jurisdiction, and I absolutely and certainly don't. If in doubt, talk to a pro.

With that disclaimer neatly in place (short summary: 'Don't sue me'), let's proceed to consider the major hazards.

LIBEL

In law, and depending on the jurisdiction, you are likely to have defamed a person if you make written statements which (i) expose him to hatred or ridicule, (ii) cause him to be shunned, (iii) lower him in the estimation of 'right-thinking' members of the public, and/or (iv) disparage his work. If you make such a statement about someone, that person can go to court to seek compensation for the harm done to their reputation. The object of the law is to balance the rights of free speech against protection for the reputation of individuals. (For historical reasons, British libel law is more favourable to the libelled than elsewhere, so authors publishing in the UK need to be extra-careful.)

There are, however, some important restrictions to the scope of the law and some valid defences. In terms of scope, it can be helpful to know that you can't defame the dead, so (as far as libel goes, at least) you can say whatever you like about them. You can only defame individuals; you cannot defame an entire class. So you're welcome to say horrible things about (ooh, I don't know) all psychiatrists, but you can't defame one psychiatrist in particular. And if you are determined to say something defamatory about a specific individual, changing their name or altering their identity in other relatively modest ways will not help you. If the individual's identity would be clear to those who know them, you may still be committing libel.

You should also be clear that *any* published statement can give rise to libel. It doesn't matter if you have chosen to self-publish your book. If you distribute a significant number of copies of your book, you are spreading allegations about someone and the question of libel does arise. It's true that if your sales are meagre the level of any damages will also be lower (because damage to reputation will be less, the fewer the people who are aware of the allegations), but that may not be a great comfort to you when the libel writ pops through your letterbox. Comments made online can also, obviously, be libellous.

There are, however, defences against such a claim. The first and best is that what you say is true, but *you must be able to prove its truth*. It's not enough for you to show that what you say is probably or quite likely true. You must be able to provide a courtroom quality of proof for your allegations. That can be a big ask and in many cases what it really boils down to for an author is that your allegation has already been tested in court and upheld.

First-time writers most often encounter concerns about libel when they are writing about difficult periods in their own lives. Let's say, for example, that you are writing a memoir in which you state that your stepfather used to physically abuse you. Clearly, that allegation is defamatory. You can't protect yourself by changing the individual's name, as you probably have only one stepfather, so the person's identity is clear. You can't simply change a few facts and call the memoir a 'novel', unless you change things so extensively that you are no longer writing a memoir at all.

For most authors in this position, the only way to be sure that you're safe from libel is if your stepfather's abuse was ever exposed in court and resulted in his criminal conviction. If he has been convicted, then you are safe to expose the full detail of what he was convicted for. Naturally, you will make many statements in your book that you can't prove individually, but you probably don't have to. If the thrust of your book is to describe your stepfather's abusive habits and the man has already been convicted of the physical abuse of children, then you are very likely in the clear ... though do read on for some important further comments.

Other valid defences to a libel claim are that your statements are fair comment – a test which requires that your statements are statements of opinion, that they are based on true facts, that you genuinely believe what you say, and that you are not inspired by malice. This defence lacks the clarity of the previous one and, if you believe that you are covered by it, you will certainly want to take proper legal advice before proceeding.

There are other defences too, but this is a broad overview, not a detailed guide, so I won't get into them. Instead, three final comments.

First, you never want to get anywhere near a libel court. Whether you win or lose, the case will rip your life apart. Take care.

Secondly, plaintiffs in a libel case generally name both the publisher and the author. Your publisher is unlikely to know all the facts connected with the putative libel, so the author/publisher contract generally places quite a heavy burden on the author. As a rule, your contract will almost certainly make you extensively liable for bearing the costs of any libel claim, whether or not that claim is upheld. That's not fair, but again: take care.

Thirdly, don't paralyse yourself. None of these issues arise until you get into print. If you are writing a memoir about a troubled childhood, then just let rip. Say what you want to say. Express yourself with freedom. Don't worry about what a libel lawyer might think, because if you do that you will find yourself barely able to construct a single sentence. When you have completed your memoir and made any revisions that you want to make, you should start taking the libel issue seriously. But let the work come first.

Then, when you get as far as a book deal, talk openly to your publishers and agent. Be honest. Raise any concerns. You should do as much as you can at this stage to ensure that the book which heads for the printing press is as safe as possible from attack. If you skimp on effort or openness at this stage, you may come to regret it very much down the road.

PRIVACY LAW

Many jurisdictions, and all European ones, have enshrined privacy protection in law. Again, write what you want to write, then pause for thought prior to publication.

At Jericho Writers, we once worked on a brilliant memoir about a woman trapped in an abusive marriage. The husband was eventually brought to trial and convicted of multiple charges. It looked to me like the book was cleared for publication. No libel issue would arise, because the man's guilt had already been proved. Alas, alas, although we found that (brilliant, brave, amazing) client an agent, no publisher would take the book because of the woman's mother-in-law. The mother-in-law had been an accomplice – a more-than-willing accomplice – to all that had gone on, but she had never been convicted of a crime and she had a legal entitlement to privacy. So her possible claim against the book put an end to its publication.

Personally, I was shocked at the industry's feebleness. If it can't publish books like that, what moral authority can it claim? The chance of a sole individual choosing to sue a multi-billion-dollar publisher over privacy issues was always small, and the multi-billion-dollar company was hardly going to be much injured by the result. I think publishers should have the boldness to take those risks. That's what they're there for.

PLAGIARISM

If you want to ruin your life, I'd recommend libel as your optimal strategy, but other options do exist, and the prudent self-destructive author will want to review them all.

Plagiarism occurs when you use or closely imitate the language or thoughts of another author and pass them off as your own. Thus, if you were to take the above section on libel and paste that into your own work, representing it as your own wise thoughts on the subject, you would be guilty of plagiarism. Such acts are, however, relatively rare. It's also hard to believe that they happen by accident, which means that it's simple enough to avoid plagiarism risk: just don't nick other people's work.

There is a rather more subtle point lurking here. What precisely constitutes the close imitation of another person's thoughts? Shakespeare took material for *Macbeth* from Holinshed's *Chronicles*. Was he guilty of close imitation? How close is close? (The chapter on copyright goes into this in more detail.)

Because all literature exists in constant imaginative reverberation with itself, courts tend to construe the 'close imitation of thought' test very narrowly. It's fine to be influenced by something, even over-influenced. What you can't do is cleave to someone else's storyline and characters in a way that takes their work, changes the language and then represents it on the page as your own. If in doubt, you would do well to make full and generous acknowledgement of those sources that have most inspired you. If in serious doubt, you would do well to have someone proficient to read both texts and advise you on whether there is a case to be made against you. As I say, though, it's hard to believe that real plagiarism ever happens by accident, so the simple rule is just don't plagiarise others and you're highly unlikely to get into trouble.

COPYRIGHT INFRINGEMENT

Copyright infringement occurs when you reproduce a substantial part of other people's work by copying their words, whether you acknowledge it or otherwise, but you don't seek permission in the appropriate way. (Except under limited circumstances, an acknowledgement will be irrelevant when it comes to determining whether copyright has been infringed.) And permissions may have to be paid for.

There is no hard and fast rule for what qualifies as substantial, so, depending on the material, even a sentence or two might be considered substantial copying. Again, it's simple to get these things right. If you are quoting copyright work, ask permission from the copyright holder, usually the publisher. Often that permission will be granted for free. Sometimes you will need to pay something. Often enough, if I've had to seek permission for something (some of my non-fiction work), I've asked the question and just never heard back. (I took that to be an invitation to quote for free. No one has ever argued otherwise.) So be diligent, make your requests, and you won't get into any trouble.

NIGHTSHADE WINE AND YEW BERRY COMPOTE

The last excitingly novel way of ruining your life is to incorporate a recipe or instructions in your manuscript liable to cause death or injury to anyone attempting to follow them. Thus, if a famous TV chef happened to include in their cookbook a recipe for wine made from deadly nightshade, or a fruit compote brewed from poisonous yew berries, then they'd likely face a spate of claims. Again, few authors will find themselves in this position, but, if you are contemplating a book of toxic recipes or home experiments that may, if they go a tad wrong, blow readers' houses sky high, you may wish to adjust course before it's too late.

IF IN DOUBT ...

Finally, while these guidelines will be sufficient for the great majority of authors, they will not be sufficient for everyone. The final and most important rule is this: *if you are in any doubt whatsoever about your legal position, take professional advice prior to publication.* If you don't, you may regret it.

But also – don't be too scaredy-cat. I once collaborated with an author on a genuinely excellent book, *Planet Ponzi*. The author was a Wall Streeter with a lot to say about the scams pulled by Wall Street and the government. He wanted me to assist with an editorial wash-and-brush-up. And his book did not go gentle on its targets. The publisher knew what kind of book this was going to be and ordered a full legal review of the text. (That wasn't a black mark against the book, by the way. The publisher wanted something hard-hitting. I'd guess a legal review was in the budget from the start.) The lawyer involved raised a fair number of queries. In some instances, we altered the text a little. In some cases, the publisher was fine with the text as it stood. In still others, we wrote direct to the companies involved for comment.

I remember writing to the SVP Investor Relations at one very big, very rich, very well-known Fortune 500 company. We said, 'We have written the following in our forthcoming book and would invite you to comment.' We then quoted our passage which accused the company (bluntly and colourfully) of outrageous tax-dodging. The SVP wrote back telling us that we were completely wrong and that he utterly rejected the statements being made. We wrote back, pointing out that our claims were drawn from the firm's very own annual report (we quoted the exact text and footnote) and the SVP withdrew his objections. He asked us, I think, to say something about the firm's extensive work in the community, blah, blah, but I don't think we did. We didn't alter our comments about the tax-dodging, except to make them a little more forceful. We ran the final text back past our lawyer (who was paid by the publisher, not us) and the book went out without a problem.

And on that happy note, we can leap forward to things altogether more appealing. It's time to talk about world domination.

Towards World Domination

Chronologically speaking, your agent is unlikely to start selling your work overseas until you've got a settled manuscript. That means working through editorial issues with your domestic publisher. It may even mean waiting for bound proofs or actual hardback copies of the book itself. Nevertheless, since this part of the book deals with rights and contracts, we'll complete that discussion here, before moving forward to talk about publication itself.

ENGLISH-LANGUAGE SALES, OR: WHO SELLS WHAT TO WHOM?

For most British or American writers, the largest slice of their income will come from home sales to their home publishers. There's something counterintuitive in this. No matter where your home market is, there are a lot more book-buyers and book sales outside it than within it. I'm British, but I've sold books to every major country under the sun, including the US. In total, that has given me exposure to a vastly larger number of buyers – billions of them – than I've had via my home market alone. For all that, however, those territories have done not much more than substantially supplement my total income from writing. For most writers (except those already based in tiny markets), those overseas billions will constitute a side order of fries, not the main course itself. The reason is that most publishing markets are still more domestic than international.

Furthermore, when it comes to selling books into non-English-language territories, publishers are having to adjust their sums to take account of translation costs. Since those costs are effectively coming out of your advance, the value to you of unit sales overseas is likely to be less than that of home sales. There are exceptions to these rules – the handful of genuinely global mega-authors who sell as well in Tokyo and Berlin as they do in New York and London. But for the rest of us, the following rules are likely to apply:

If you are American

Your home publisher is likely to acquire English-language rights to US, Canada and the Philippines, plus a range of other territories too. The pattern of these rights blocs all feels a bit post-colonial, but then again it *is* a bit post-colonial. That's how the publishing world likes it.

If you are Canadian

A Canada-based publisher selling Canadian authors to the Canadian market may acquire rights only for Canada. You will, therefore, be looking to find a US publisher (to cover the US, the Philippines and other ancillary territories) plus a UK publisher to handle Britain, Europe and Commonwealth territories aside from Canada. If, on the other hand, your MS has been purchased by a US publisher in the first instance, you would count yourself as an American for the purposes of working out the division of foreign rights. If your MS was bought by a UK publisher, you count as a Brit.

If you are British

Your agent is likely to sell 'home' rights in a bundle that includes Britain, Ireland, continental Europe, Australia, New Zealand, South Africa and a slew of other territories besides. Note that the right to 'continental Europe' gives your home publisher only the right to sell English-language work in those territories. So, if you are published by GodSaveTheQueen Ltd in London, and by Schwarz-Rot-Gold GmbH in Germany, then the former gets to sell English-language books in Germany. The latter possesses the rather more valuable right to sell German-language books in Germany. Historically, EU rules meant those rules extended automatically across the entire market. At the time of writing, it is totally opaque how things work from here on.

If you are Irish

You'll be treated as though you're British, so the above paragraphs will probably hold true for you too. And yes, I know. That colonial thing again.

If you are Australian, South African, a New Zealander or a citizen of another Commonwealth country

If you have a home publisher, then your publisher may have bought world rights (in which case, they'll be looking to sell them on at the big international book fairs) or UK and Commonwealth rights (in which case, they'll seek to have your book published by partners in London and elsewhere), or rights to the local market alone – in which case, you or your agent will be seeking to sell the book more widely.

If your publisher has bought world rights

Often a publisher wants to buy the world rights to your book, or 'World English' which means the right to sell your book any-where in the world, but in the English language only. If your literary agent is part of a well-resourced agency, I would resist this option. On the whole, agencies are better and more motivated when it comes to making those sales.

If all this seems pointlessly confusing – well, perhaps it is. On the other hand, you shouldn't be left to navigate these perils on your own. If you have an agent, they will simply steer you calmly through these things and let you know what's been done when it's been done. If you don't have an agent, you should certainly discuss international rights sales with your publisher. If your publisher is of any size at all, they'll certainly be involved in the international rights fest in Frankfurt and London, which means they should be able to guide you there. The NY Book Expo used to be a big deal, but currently seems to be in decline, which means London and Frankfurt are the fairs that matter.

And note that these overseas deals are not guaranteed. Yes, a hit American author will sell internationally just off the back of those American sales. But you could, for example, be quite a big author in the UK without having much of an international presence. And you could be a very big author in Norway without making much of a ding elsewhere.

FOREIGN-LANGUAGE SALES: WHO SELLS WHAT TO WHOM?

If the allocation of rights in the English language seems strangely complex, the sale of overseas rights is blessedly simple in comparison. If you have an agent, then they will look after foreign sales for you. Sometimes, they'll be working via agents in Germany, France and elsewhere. In smaller territories, they'll probably work directly with local publishers.

Many of these sales won't make much money. I once sold a book into China that earned me $500 before agents' commissions and tax. That was less than fifty cents per million of population. Back then, it's true that intellectual property rules in China were so feebly enforced that the $500 was in effect a polite way to say, 'We could have just pirated this book, but look how nice we are – we've paid for a couple of nice meals out for you instead.'

The same goes for most other international markets. Book sales in Germany can be a genuinely nice addition to an author's income. The same goes (to a slightly lesser extent) for Japan, France, Italy and Spain/Latin America. I do know authors whose books largely drowned in the UK but went on to become bestsellers in Germany. In such cases, you'll end up making more money from those overseas markets than from your home market, but these cases remain the exception.

KEEPING IT LOCAL

If you sell your work all over the world, it may have occurred to you that you'll end up with a huge number of editors, a huge number of publicists, a huge number of marketers, and so on. None of this should bother you too much. If you have an editor in both New York and London, you will get editorial feedback from both places and you'll need to juggle that as well as you can. If those editors are behaving professionally (which is not always the case), they'll find a way to merge their comments, or otherwise make it easy for you.

Mostly though, foreign publishers are buying your book. They're not buying you. You won't get editorial feedback from Seoul and Taipei. You won't be going on Radio Dusseldorf or giving interviews to *Il Giornale*. In short, you may have a dozen or more publishers who have invested in your work, but only one or two of those will make any material difference to your daily life. The rest of them are just there to chip in with a bit of extra cash. The only real exception will be if your books do extremely well overseas, in which case you'll be happy with the extra hassle involved.

HOLLYWOOD AND OTHER ILLUSIONS

Which brings us to the subject of film rights.

Almost certainly, as you've sat typing away at your novel, it has occurred to you – in the most objective possible way, of course – just what a tremendous film you have on your hands. You're not dumb enough to believe Tom Cruise would be *certain* to want the role that you have in mind for him. It's simply that, standing back and being coolly rational about it, you can see that it would be ideal for him. Likewise, it's just hard to see Jennifer Lawrence's agent not being wildly excited about that role which might as well have been written for her. As for directors, you're well aware that it would never be your decision to make, but you do have a shortlist in your bottom drawer, just in case anyone happens to ask.

Because I don't want to shatter any dreams, and because you are indeed being entirely objective and rational in your assessment of things, let's put your own particular case aside for the time being and consider instead the position that all other novelists are in.

The first point to make is that Hollywood doesn't make all that many movies – perhaps 700 or so in a typical year. Of those, around two-thirds will be based on original scripts, which means that there are around 150–200 adaptations. Of those adaptations, many will be of classic works (Shakespeare, Jane Austen, and so on). Others will be of short stories or comic books or newspaper articles or foreign films. That leaves a very small number of a dozen films which are based on the works of contemporary novelists. Of that small number, a majority will be the work of people who already have a significant name – Grisham, Pullman, Rowling, Clancy, etc. Since there are still a huge number of novels being published, simple mathematics suggests that all those other novelists are really going to struggle to get the film deal that they've oh-so-foolishly been dreaming of.

The second point to make is that there's a curious kind of assumption that the film world just sprays money over all that it touches. No doubt, by publishing-industry standards, there's some truth in that, but ordinary commercial logic does play its part, even in movies. As a rough rule of thumb, a movie budget will set aside 2–2.5% for the script or book, seldom more. If there is both a script and a book, the budget might run to as much as 5%, but it would be rare to see more than that in total. These percentages will need to pay for the rights purchase from the original novelist, payment to the screenwriter(s) who will be adapting that material, and all other script-development costs to boot. Though block-busting movies may well cost in excess of $100 million, a more normal amount for Hollywood would be somewhere closer to $30 million. A British, European or Australian movie would be more likely to cost in the region of £5–10 million, or the local equivalent.

As soon as you start to multiply these figures out, you end up with numbers that are attractive but not mind-blowing. Let's say your book is being turned into a movie by a decent independent producer, for a budget of $15 million. Let's also say that 3% is allocated for the total script budget (including rights acquisition). That means that there is $450,000 allocated to the script. Script writers and script doctors will eat well over half of that sum, which leaves, let's say, $100–150,000 left over for you. Now you'd need to be a pretty wealthy individual not to feel light-hearted if you suddenly scooped that kind of money, but you're also unlikely to find it life-changing. I know one author who has a very nice kitchen extension named after a screenplay he sold, and that's perhaps the way you should view things: selling movie rights may buy you a new kitchen; it's not likely to get you a villa in Palm Beach.

It's also worth noting that the film industry is a less probable buyer for your work than is the TV industry. While there just aren't that many feature films, the week-in, week-out demands of multi-channel TV are a monster that needs continual feeding. Because TV budgets are tighter than movie budgets, the payouts to authors are correspondingly lower – a new bathroom perhaps, or a very nice kitchen from IKEA.

My own work is currently under option in Hollywood for a possible TV series. The option fee was nice, but certainly not life-changing. If the option comes good, and a pilot is made, I get more money. If the pilot goes well, and a first season is made, I get more money. If that first season goes well, and multiple seasons are shot, I will accumulate quite a lot of money. But that's a lot of ifs, and Hollywood ifs mostly don't happen.

Since we're still talking here about other people, it may finally be worth noting that the film industry will flirt with numerous projects for every one it options, and it'll option a good many projects for every one that gets made. Even if you do get as far as selling an option (and most authors never make it as far as that),

that option will pay out (let's say) $10,000 on signature and $90,000 on the first day of shooting.

Needless to say, no one spends $10,000 without thinking that they have a realistic shot of going on to complete the project, but the film world is not like any other you've ever encountered. The phrase 'many a slip 'twixt cup and lip' is always a rather baffling one, taken literally. After all, most people are perfectly capable of lifting a glass to their mouths without spilling the fluid inside. In the film world, however, it seems that every market participant suffers from an uncontrollable, violent palsy. Time after time, glasses are filled and raised, in every expectation of taking a long refreshing drink – only for calamity to ensue. In Hollywood, getting from cup to lip is a long journey and one much stricken with accidents.

Since we're having a proverbial moment here, let's close it with a second one. In the film world, more than any other, it's as well not to count your chickens before they're hatched. In the publishing world, if a deal is agreed orally, then a contract will be produced – however slowly – and the money will finally arrive. The film world is not like that. Deals that were absolutely certain to happen have a funny way of disappearing into silence and emptiness. I would therefore recommend waiting until your chickens have arrived clucking in the safety of your bank before you start to celebrate on any scale. Go crazy with the fizzy water if you must. The champagne should wait until the cheque is cashed, cleared and counted.

A QUIET WORD TO YOU ON THE SIDE

Now, as mentioned earlier, all these cautions and caveats are important but, as we both know, they don't apply to you. I mean, sure, Spielberg is a busy man, but quality is quality and some projects simply sell themselves.

The question then is how you make it happen. In New York, the studios are fairly closely integrated with the books industry, through common ownership or via working relationships that function in much the same way. The result is that, if a New York-based publisher has an eminently filmable book, you can be pretty sure that the book will be looked at by someone in the industry. But elsewhere, those links function perfectly well too. Most of my work has not been especially filmable. Then I wrote something that was. My agent realised it was. He passed it to his colleagues at a film agency. They hawked the material around. We got multiple offers for it and picked the one we liked the best. The process felt businesslike, not magical – and businesslike is better.

The moral is twofold. The first is that the film industry *is* looking for strong new work. If your work is strong and original and happens to suit the marketing flavour of the moment, then you've got a more than decent chance that it'll be noticed. The second moral is that, if you are noticed, you need to trust your advisers. If your literary agent recommends a course of action, you will generally need to trust their judgement. Feel free to talk about what lies behind it, of course, but your default position should be to agree.

SELLING YOUR DAUGHTER

Last, you need to be realistic about both control and screenwriting. If you sell your rights, you are selling them. Tom Clancy has commented, 'I have been quoted as saying that selling a book to Hollywood is rather like turning your daughter over to a pimp. I will not confirm the accuracy of that quote.' The book you have in your head is not likely to be the one you see on screen. Doesn't matter. Don't watch the movie, just stay at home and count the money instead.

The same goes for actually writing the script. If you have worked professionally as a screenwriter for major production companies in the past, then fight – and fight hard – for the right to be named a co-writer on the project. If you haven't, then feel free to offer your services. Feel free to produce a sample script. But don't hold your breath and don't make a scene if people say no. There's an old Hollywood joke about the starlet who was so dumb that she slept with the screenwriter. But that screenwriter is way above your reach. You're source material, nothing more. Sell your work, cash the cheque and wave goodbye.

Part Five
TOWARDS PRODUCTION

Working with Publishers

You've sold your book. You've signed your contract. You're an author! Assuming that your book is going to be published in the relatively near future (let's say in the next six to nine months), your publisher will start to work simultaneously on three or four parallel tracks. Those tracks are:

Editorial

The editorial track deals with the final completion of your manuscript. There's likely to be a little editorial fine-tuning, and then the whole process of copyediting, page proofs and proofreading.

Design

The centrepiece of the design process is, of course, the development of a cover, but the layout and typography of the text will also play a part, as will any illustrative material included in the book.

Sales and marketing

For most books these days, the sales and marketing process is largely about the publisher's effort to secure store position with retailers. The 'sell-in' to retailers is where the most crucial battles are lost or won – and also the area where you will be least involved and least able to contribute. Amazon, though dominant as a retailer, isn't part of this game, partly because publishers tend to prioritise physical retail and physical book formats, but also because Amazon operates like a platform more than a store. You don't get into deep conversations with its buying team; you send a truck to the warehouse.

Publicity

Although it is part of the whole marketing campaign, the PR effort involves the author so closely that, from an author's point of view, it'll feel like a whole separate element of the publishing process and one that we'll deal with separately in this book.

The precise order in which you encounter the various different ingredients of the entire publishing process will vary somewhat with each different project, but – unless your editor is asleep on the job – the complete publishing pudding is being baked, nevertheless.

IT'S COMPLICATED

Before we get to the specifics of any of those processes, it's worth pausing a moment to reflect on a problem almost as old as publishing itself: the difficulty of the author-publisher relationship – a difficulty that arises from the very different perspectives that the two of you bring to bear. You, the author, are rather excited by your imminent publication. You probably believe several of the following propositions or possibly all of them:

- I have worked for months and years on this book, so I deserve to be closely involved in its publication.
- I have thought long and hard about matters such as title and cover design, so my editor would do well to consult closely with me.
- I have some unique and excellent ideas on marketing, which any sensible publisher will want to adopt in whole or part.
- I don't imagine that I'll be part of the core decision-making team as such, but I imagine that I'll be cc-ed in on any really significant emails and be invited to contribute.

- I will be kept informed of any promotional support from retailers, of intended print runs and of news on sales as it comes in.
- I will be collaborating closely with my publicist.
- I will get to see and comment on any press release relating to me or my book before it is sent.

I'm an author myself. I've certainly held many of the above beliefs at one time or another, and I think some of these expectations are reasonable. To take one simple example: if a large organisation is issuing a press release about me, I would expect them to clear it with me first. Partly that's a simple question of common sense. Press releases may contain errors which only the author will spot.

More to the point, though, it's basic courtesy. How can it possibly be polite for a corporation to release a statement about you to the national media without running it by you first? Obviously, if there was some major emergency – or you were lost for several months in a jungle, or you were busy running for the presidency of a medium-sized country – politeness might be obliged to give way to other considerations. But in the typical case, you are not lost in a jungle or running for president. Nor is there typically an emergency of the sort where a press release has to be issued by midday or else some PR-hostage is shot dead. Quite likely, in fact, you're sitting meekly not far from your home computer, only too eager to help if asked.

What's more, you know your book far better than any publicist. Perhaps they've nailed the salient point about the book in their press release. Perhaps they haven't. But since they're expert in public relations and not expert in your book, they'd be crazy not to want you to look at the release. It's just dumb not to include you.

Yet in the pressure to get things done, good business practice sometimes takes a dent or two. In my publishing career to date, I believe I've only ever seen one press release written about me in advance of its being issued, and then only because I made a point of asking to see it first. In fact, by way of contrast with the list of authorial expectations above, an editor is likely to think:

- We know how to sell books; an author doesn't; it doesn't make sense to involve the author too much.

- Authors can be notoriously prickly about such things as titles and cover designs. It's better to decide these things in-house, then sell the resultant idea to the author.

- Authors' views on marketing wheezes invariably involve ways of getting publishers to spend money. The answer is no.

- It wouldn't even occur to me to copy my author in on key decision-making emails. An author will misunderstand, get upset, require soothing – and waste time. The simplest thing is just to get on with the job.

- I certainly intend to keep my author reasonably up to speed with such things as print runs, retail uptake and so on, but I'm a busy person and these chores don't come at the top of my To Do list, or even close. Honestly? I'll probably forget.

- Publicists do involve authors as much as they need to; but authors have hopelessly unrealistic expectations of how much interaction is appropriate, and we'd be nuts to waste our time in trying to meet those expectations.

- As for that press release – heck, as far as I'm concerned, every morning is an issue-the-release-by-midday-or-the-PR-girl-gets-it sort of a morning.

The gap between the editor's outlook and yours may not always be yawning, but it will usually be there nonetheless. (And again, Amazon Publishing is, in my view, the most reliably inclusive of all the big publishers.) If you approach that gap in the wrong way, you risk riling those you work with and achieving nothing. If you instead adopt an entirely passive 'My Publisher Knows Best' approach, you may also end up disappointed. You need, instead, to aim at a posture which is assertive when it needs to be, sweet-tempered when it can be. You also need to start from a realistic understanding of what your editor can and cannot plausibly deliver. You need, in short, to be able to view the world through the eyes of a publisher.

THE EYES OF A PUBLISHER: MONEY

Publishing is not an industry that floats about on a sea of money. Although there's a media-created image of publishing as being all about long lunches, expense accounts, celebrity book launches, and the rest of it, the truth is more prosaic. Many small publishers barely break into profit. Even the largest publishers pay their staff relatively meagre wages and are hardly lavish with bonuses. One editor told me that he had recently been interrogated about puddings – the folk responsible for checking expense claims had wanted to know whether, at a recent author lunch, it had really been necessary to order a pudding as well as a starter.

What's more, your book is not a big deal. Let's assume you've been offered a $30,000 advance for your literary novel – which is a perfectly respectable offer in the current climate. If your book achieves 7,500 sales in hardback, 15,000 sales in paperback and a further 8,000 in e-book, it's done well. (Literary novels tend to be biased towards the hardback and away from the e-book. A thriller would have a very different pattern of sales.)

But just consider that result in a little more detail. Let's say that the hardback had a notional retail price of $28, the paperback sold at $17, and the e-book at $13. Let's presume that the publisher is selling the print versions to retailers at an average of 45% of cover price. Amazon will pay 70% of the e-book price to the publisher. The total income received by the publisher for this book, over the space of more than a year of selling, and more than two years of total involvement is:

- Hardback: 7,500 times $12.60 equals $94,500
- Paperback: 15,000 times equals $114,750

- E-book: 8,000 times 70% of $13 equals $72,800

The total income from the book equals $280,000 plus change. Knock off your advance and you have $250,000. That cash needs to cover your editor's time, as well as all the overheads (rent, heating, lighting, etc.) that go with it. It also needs to cover the time and overheads associated with everyone else on the project. It also needs to cover the production, warehousing and transport costs of getting your book printed and into bookstores. It needs to contribute towards the million and one things that a large and complicated corporation needs to look after. Board meetings, human resource functions, accounting, tech people, legal and compliance. If the book has been entered into any retail promotions, the publisher will have paid something for that privilege and the money needs to cover that too. What's more, most adult fiction loses money, so a profitable publisher needs to make sure that its profitable books do enough to compensate for the ones that fail.

Looked at like this, it seems miraculous that the book can turn a profit for anyone. It certainly won't turn a profit for anyone if the publisher starts sloshing money around on advertising and other consumer promotions.

What's more, paid promotion is hard to pull off. Big budget campaigns – posters on the subway and that kind of thing – are just too broad-spectrum to hit home. Those things are fine if you're selling Coke. They just don't work for the ultra-specific markets of individual books.

And sure: digital advertising is, in theory, a well to get to those ultra-granular markets, but that's much harder than it looks too. It's easy enough to drive traffic to a given book page, but only a small minority of that traffic will convert. At the high prices charged by Big Five publishers (a necessity, remember, if they are not to undercut their physical retail channels), the conversion rates are likely to be worse than one in ten, and probably much worse. Making ads pay when the conversion rates are that poor is essentially impossible. It's true that the most professional self-published authors do make good use of paid advertising. But those guys are highly motivated, they sell their books cheaply and they write in series. Almost always it's the series sellthrough which delivers the profit.

Most of the other marketing routes that authors think about have their drawbacks too. You want to make a book trailer for YouTube? Fine. Do that. But who will see it? You want a Twitter campaign in the voice of your lead character? Fine. But how will you get traffic? You want to go on a thirty-stop blog tour? Sure. But those things are expensive to set up and the conversion into sales can be terrible. You want to get on panel talks at major literary festivals? Fine. But all authors want the same, and you'd do well to hand-sell a dozen copies after one of those events.

In short, when publishers tell you that the budget does not permit a certain investment, they are almost certainly telling the truth.

THE EYES OF A PUBLISHER: TIME AND TIMING

An important consequence of the low-budget world of publishing is that time is also strictly rationed. Your book might be better published if everyone could spend more time on it. It's also true that, if you're a good enough writer to have secured a book deal, you yourself probably bring an obsessive degree of perfectionism to the project. That's as it should be, but you write from passion first and foremost. Your editor likes your book, but she's got twenty-three others to publish this year, and she likes those books too. She also has new submissions to consider, committees to sit on, book fairs to attend, and so on. She does not have a huge amount of time for you or your book.

You will encounter the same ruthless discipline when it comes to timing. On the PR front, you will (if all goes well) experience a burst of publicity activity around the launch of your book and then ... nothing. Dead silence. You'll find yourself thinking of other articles you could write, other interviews you could do, other news stories you could seek to engage with, but, if you try to contact your publicist to talk about these terrific ideas, you'll find that it takes longer and longer to get your phone calls returned, until you give up making them altogether.

From your perspective, valuable opportunities to promote the book are being wasted. From a publisher's perspective, there is only one 'sweet spot' for publicity, namely around the launch of a book. (Its first launch, that is: a launch in mass-market paperback following the hardback/e-book isn't news at all. It's a minor alteration to an existing product.) Because a publisher knows this, they'll focus all their PR efforts on the week or two when it's most needed and most fruitful. Unless the circumstances are unusual, any effort beforehand or afterwards will be a waste of time.

THE EYES OF A PUBLISHER: FASHION

Authors are, almost universally, oblivious to publishing fashions and disdainful of them. On the whole, they're right. No genuine-ly creative act emerges from focus groups and marketing analyses. The best books spring into being because, in the author's mind, they have to exist.

But that's authors. Publishers don't and can't and shouldn't think like that. Publishers sell to retailers who sell to readers. The books industry is as prone to fashion, excess, flippancy and illogic as any other industry where the consumer is boss. If celebrity cookbooks are all the rage, publishers will seek out celebrity cookbooks. If vampire books are selling like holy water and garlic, publishers will be seeking to sink their teeth into something vampiric.

At the same time, publishers can see further ahead than regular book-buyers. As an author, you can only look at what's on the bookshelves. You'll be a year or two behind the market, as viewed by the publishers who are buying manuscripts today. If the shops seem crowded with Dan Brown lookalikes (let's say), then it's a fair bet that publishers are already refusing to buy any more

Dan Brown-ish manuscripts that come their way. At Jericho Writers, I remember handling a really excellent kids' book whose theme was bullying. All the editors who saw that book loved it, but they turned it down anyway. Bullying had been done to death. They wanted something else.

BUT ON THE OTHER HAND ...

So far in this section I've tended to side with the publisher. Authors are often unrealistic about the extent of advertising support that is possible. They are often unrealistic about the amount of time that will be lavished on their book, unrealistic about sales expectations, unrealistic about the likely shelf life of their book, and so forth.

That unreality is not their fault. When I got my first proper job, I was given an induction course which told me what I needed to know to orient myself effectively in an unfamiliar world. Pretty much any competent employer will offer something similar to new employees. Yet no publisher that I know of invests any real time training authors to play an effective and useful role in the publishing process. If authors are naive, that's because nobody has ever made the effort to help them be otherwise.

Since authors are never divested of their naivety, their suggestions and desires are often inappropriate, counterproductive or unrealistic. For those reasons, publishers prefer to keep authors outside the publishing process. Decisions are made in-house, and those decisions are sold to authors. Indeed, one of the remarkable things about the publishing industry from an author's point of view is how nice everyone is. I've hardly ever met an unpleasant publisher and all my editors have been delightful. If I'm bothered by something, they're reassuring. If I'm upset, they're soothing. If I'm cross, they're diplomatic. If I'm optimistic, they're politely encouraging.

All this is remarkably pleasant ... until one starts to notice that one is being treated like a mental patient with an impulse-control problem. I remember once having lunch with my editor. We were talking about the books industry. Thanks to my work with Jericho Writers, I've engaged with thousands of writers, I know countless agents, and my contacts in publishing are eclectic and extensive. I'm not just an author; I'm an insider. My editor was much more open about the inner workings of the trade than I'd ever heard her be before or than any of my previous editors had been. After a while, she brought herself up short and apologised. 'I'm so sorry. I'd never usually talk so openly with an author, but then it's almost like you're an insider.'

I remember being astonished. Not only was my editor saying explicitly that being an author did not in itself render one a part of the industry, she was also saying that she would have censored her commentary if I had been 'only' an author. Those attitudes – those reprehensible attitudes – are, I would say, almost universal.

This book has two primary purposes: one rather routine, the other (in a mild way) revolutionary. The routine objective is to help first-time writers make a businesslike approach to agents and to navigate the first steps of an authorial career in a professional and commonsensical way. The revolutionary objective is broader and more interesting. It's to supply the training that publishers don't. It's to equip authors with the know-how to play their part in the publishing process constructively and creatively.

That objective is a revolutionary one, because it means encouraging you to clamber over the red ropes penning you into your area of long lunches and padded sofas and into the offices where decisions are made and campaigns are constructed. No publisher wants you on their side of those ropes. They will – in a thoroughly nice, diplomatic, encouraging way – seek to return you to the sofa. Much of the rest of this section and this book aims to supply a set of escape notes. If you follow them wisely, it's possible that you will gain a reputation for being an assertive author, but not an imbecile or difficult one. Your book may succeed or it may fail, because life is like that, but either way you'll have done all you can to shape its destiny in a way that makes sense for the book and that reflects your own knowledge, passion and enthusiasms.

ENGAGING WITH PUBLISHERS

The first thing to say about successful engagement with publishers is related to the lessons from earlier in this section. The key points to bear in mind are:

- Publishers have to sell a series of highly disparate products, few of which will achieve any great revenues.
- The fact that publishers succeed in making money at all is because they are disciplined and rigorous when it comes to budgeting for time and money.

Because you care more about your book than anything else, excluding (probably) your children and (possibly) your spouse, these facts are likely to exit your head almost as soon as they enter. They need to stay there.

If you are to engage constructively with publishers, you need to deal with the world as it is, not as you'd like it to be. Almost certainly, that means working within a smaller, tighter, narrower budget than you would like.

It also means accepting that your publisher is usually right. They know more about retailers, more about the print and broadcast media, more about printing costs and logistics, and more about a hundred other subjects than you can or ever will. If you start to argue on those fronts, you will instantly prove yourself a dunce, and your subsequent efforts to escape those enclosing ropes will become ever harder, ever less likely to succeed.

It's also important to be nice. Publishing is a *nice* industry. If you come over as arrogant (and many authors do), or overbearing (ditto), or aggressive, or demanding, or contemptuous or anything along similar lines, your editor will deal with you politely and firmly – while unhesitatingly and rightly, keeping you away from anything important. Assertiveness does not mean aggression. It means polite, businesslike focus on the point at hand. It means respecting your publisher's comments, seeking to see the world from their perspective. It means being grateful for points conceded. It means being generous with praise and niggardly with criticism.

These things do matter. I once worked with a publisher one of whose authors was a Very Famous Writer, with loads of bestselling titles to his name. The VFW was on the point of shifting his business to another firm and, far from being upset about this, everyone at the publisher concerned was delighted. They didn't like this man. Handling his work had been a chore, not a pleasure. When the time came to renew his contract, they made an offer – it would have been commercially crazy not to have done so – but the offer was pitched low. The VFW turned it down and went off somewhere else instead. Because he was widely known to be arrogant and difficult, it's likely that the winning publisher was also paying less than they might otherwise have done. If you value your arrogance so much that you don't mind getting underpaid, then by all means be arrogant. Just make sure that you have several top-ten bestsellers to your name first, however. Arrogant debut authors don't get underpaid. They don't get published.

Having said all this, you do need to be assertive, not simply nice. Many editors have perfected the art of soothing words and empty meanings. I knew one author who, for various reasons, was keenly interested in how one of her paperbacks was selling. She knew that the first print run had been 17,000 copies, but she also knew that she needed to sell some 50,000 if her existing level of advance was to be supportable into the future. As she saw it – and probably correctly – the sales of that book bore directly on her ability to continue in her chosen career.

Her editor knew her position. The two individuals had always got on well and had a strong and professional relationship. There was no reason why the editor in question should not have told the author whatever she knew about book sales. And the news that the author received was positive. The publisher had just ordered another print run. Things were looking good. The author went away from that encounter chuffed and happy. Her book was selling! It would need to go on selling strongly if it was to break through that 50,000-book barrier but, after a disastrous previous launch, things were looking up.

They weren't. The second print run which the publisher had ordered consisted of just 4,000 copies. The editor knew that when she told the author. She knew that if the author were to be offered a further contract at all, any advance would be precipitously down from what it had been in the past. She knew all that, but preferred not to tell the author, who would only find out much later after receiving a computer-generated royalty statement which put the news in cold black and white.

This kind of editorial 'niceness' is utterly phoney. It wasn't a kind act to withhold the truth. She was going to find out sooner or later, and she'd have much preferred to learn as soon as possible, so that she could plan accordingly. The trouble is that, because editors have been trained to soothe the author away from possible confrontation, they've never learned the art of relaying bad news in a straightforward, timely manner.

Since many authors come into the books trade from rougher, franker, more direct professions, the polite evasions of publishing are disconcerting. In particular, you may come away from a meeting believing that X is going to be done, or Y is agreed. You believe this, because you made an excellent case for X or Y, and your editor said something like, 'Yes, it's absolutely that kind of energy and imagination that we need to put to work here.' She might have said a number of other things along similar lines, all of them encouraging and supportive, but none of which precisely amounted to: 'Yes, we are going to do X and then, once we've done that, we're going to go right on and do Y.' You, of course, heard lots of supportive murmurs and nobody telling you that X or Y was a bad idea, so you concluded that X or Y are, at the very least, firmly on the menu. And they aren't. You just weren't told.

All this makes navigation unexpectedly difficult. By the time you find out that X hasn't been done, it's going to be too late. You can't get too brusque or too challenging, because that will get their backs up – and, remember, you'll be wrong more often than you're right. All the same, you are correct to think that your perspective, if correctly deployed, will add value and, if others don't want to include you, you will need to find a way to overcome their resistance.

THE MAGIC FORMULA FOR SUCCESS

There is no magic formula for success. The red ropes are there for a reason, and they're not about to be unhooked just because your editor likes you. All the same, the key elements of your strategy are already plain. You need to learn as much as you can about the industry. This book is a start (a very fine start, indeed), but you'll need more. In particular, you need to learn about your own particular corner of the publishing ecosystem. The way things are done at a small publisher of military history books is very different from the way a conglomerate publisher launches a new, big thriller writer.

You need to be businesslike in every aspect of your interaction with a publisher. Don't be late with deadlines – and, if you are running late, talk to your editor sooner rather than later to discuss things.

You should get into the habit of following up phone calls with a brief email to document what was agreed. Be courteous, friendly and responsive. The more positive and helpful you are in these routine interactions, the more scope you have to put your foot down on issues that bother you.

You also need to get to know and talk to your fellow authors. Face-to-face chats are great, but the very best solution is to find yourself a private online community of like-minded authors. Those things spill offline all the time – at festivals, at events, at raucous parties – but their online core gives you the chance to access the group's collective wisdom whenever and wherever you need it.

You should use every opportunity to make connections. Look to meet your publisher's other authors. Exchange phone numbers and email addresses. Approach authors at festivals. Introduce yourself. If that sounds scary – it shouldn't. Authors are lovely and welcoming to their own. They'll embrace you. And if you have the highest good fortune to be a crime author, that embrace will come with a brilliant sense of humour, a lot of commercial good sense and a quite remarkable capacity for drink.

You need to see the world from the publisher's point of view, and accept that any proposal you make has to look as good from that perspective as it does from yours – which means, above all, realism and cost-effectiveness.

Lastly, you need to pick your battles. From time to time, there'll be issues that are being poorly managed or that you care deeply about for some other reason. Focus your efforts on those issues. Engage keenly on those things. Be polite but assertive. Be reasonable. But push. You may or may not get the result you want – and the result you want may or may not make an overall difference to sales – but you will feel better with a campaign shaped, at least in part, around your ideas and convictions.

The rest of this book will focus on a whole series of topics, some of which are highly unlikely to concern you directly (though you do need to know about them to have a balanced picture of the publishing process), and some of which may well concern you deeply. What follows, therefore, is an escapologist's guide, a handbook for ducking under those red ropes and making a break for the office suites beyond. Good luck! You're going to need it.

EDITORIAL

At this happy stage of your career, you probably won't need to worry much about editorial feedback. Your work has already convinced an agent to take you on. A publisher has made an offer. If anyone had serious reservations about any central aspect of your work, you'd have heard all about it before now.

If you secured your original deal on the back of a book proposal, of course, the position is somewhat different. A proposal is only a sketch of a future work. If you deliver a work that seems to the publisher to fall short of the original intention, then you may well get tougher, more substantive comments.

HOW EDITING WORKS

Even for reasonably major projects, an editor won't have all that much time allocated to editorial work. For each book, they might have about a day and a half at their disposal, perhaps two. Since it probably takes a careful day to read something thoroughly, that leaves about a morning to compile a set of notes sufficient to steer a book from where it is to where it needs to be. If the book that emerges from this round of editing is not yet right, there will not be a further day and a half available to do the same again.

Obviously, no book will be sent to press with any really gross imperfections, but the emphasis at the second-round stage will be on a swift, practical tidy-up – the way teenagers clean up after a party, shoving the most visible rubbish into bin-liners and not worrying too much about the dark stains on the Persian carpet or those weird marks on the sitting-room ceiling. If for any reason the editorial problems are profound, a more intensive editorial approach might kick into action, but that's an exception.

Different editors deliver feedback in different ways. Most often, you'll get a long email. That'll start with praise – probably sincere, but also there to comfort your soul for the hardships to follow. You'll then get some paragraphs of general advice. Such-and-such a character seems a little too limp. The plot twist at Irkutsk seems a little contrived. The subplot involving the ghost of Cleopatra seems a little underwhelming at times. The criticisms you'll receive are likely to be on about that scale. Your editor will suggest remedies. You could talk more about such-and-such's childhood, to help the reader understand why he is as he is. You could deal with the Irkutsk problem by having the protagonist receive a key letter before, not after, she arrives there. And so on.

After you've waded through a page or so of such comments, you'll get to a long series of close notes or annotations (which may be marginal comments in the document itself). 'Page 23, you have Jan included in the conversation, yet it wasn't clear from page 21 that she had entered the room.' 'Page 34, some of the comedy seems a little thin. Maybe cut some of it out?' 'Page 38, you are repeating some of the info contained earlier in the chapter.' And so on.

While notes of this sort are typical, I've also had editorial discussions which were entirely oral, culminating in two or three bigger bits of advice. Once these bits of advice were dealt with, I then got a series of page-by-page close notes. On another occasion, an editor I worked with just sat with me in a room. We went through the manuscript page by page. She'd scribbled comments on various pages, and we just spent time talking through those comments in cases where they weren't already obvious. The whole thing took about forty minutes.

HOW TO WORK WITH YOUR EDITOR'S COMMENTS

When you get comments from your editor, be prepared for a certain amount of emotional reaction. Different authors react differently – and over time your skin will thicken – but it can be hard to hear anything negative about your work, even if criticisms come wrapped in plenty of praise (and, indeed, a book deal). If you're a sensitive soul, just allow yourself to have that first stung reaction and then, as it starts to pass, dig back into your editor's report to scrutinise it again. You may need to review it several times to let it settle and to get the fullest possible value out of it.

As you do this, you need to remember that your editor is there to advise, not to order. Though you'd be well-advised to take seriously your editor's niggles, you certainly don't need to adopt her proposed remedies. Editors are not writers. Some of them may approach your text with something like an author's intuition for how a certain approach would play out in practice. Many won't. In the past, I've received editorial reports where I understood precisely what my editor's concerns were and why she had them. At the same time, I was confident that, if I'd adopted the remedies she suggested, I'd have had a train-wreck on my hands, not a novel.

In that instance, the approach I adopted was more or less the direct opposite of the one my editor had suggested. (She had wanted me to add more about X, more about Y, more about Z. Instead, I cut 25,000 words out of the novel, tightening the focus and ratcheting up the intensity.) When I delivered the revised manuscript, she loved it. She wasn't bothered that I hadn't taken her advice, because the point was that I *had* taken it. She'd indicated the things she wasn't happy with. I fixed them. She did her editorial work as she was meant to; I had done my authorial work as I was meant to. Truth is, I doubt if she even noticed that I'd done the opposite of what she'd suggested. Why would she care? All that mattered was that the book was a good 'un.

If you're worried about heading off in a direction different to that recommended by your editor, then talk to her. As long as you have a plan and your plan makes sense, your editor is likely to embrace it. In twenty years of publishing, I've never once had a serious problem with my editor over editorial issues.

When it comes to dealing with the close notes, things are much simpler. The problems mentioned are more minor, the fixes more straightforward. Even with these things, however, there's room for differences of opinion. In case of doubt, just pick up the phone. Your editor will welcome you doing this. It's certainly better to spend fifteen minutes talking things through by phone than spending a day or two fiddling uselessly with your manuscript because you're hesitating over what your editor might think of this or that new idea.

EDITING TO THE MAX

Most editors in publishing houses are decent, capable editors. Most of the time, your editorial relationship will function very much as you want it to. But not always. Various different problems can arise.

Number one, your editor might not be very editorially minded. That sounds almost like a contradiction in terms, rather like accusing a plumber of not being much interested in plumbing. Despite the job title, however, an editor is about vastly more than editing. If I were obliged to choose between an editor who was editorially brilliant but useless at her other jobs, or one who was an editorial dunce but supremely gifted at co-ordinating design, production, sales, publicity and all the rest of it, I'd unquestionably opt for the latter. Some excellent editors are mediocre editors. Strange but true.

Number two, the level of editorial ambition in a modern publishing house is not very high. Again, that's not a veiled attack; it's the economics of publishing. Modern publishers just don't have time to engage in extensive, iterative, collaborative editing work. They have too many books to bring out. Time is costed remorselessly. And sadly, publishers have figured out that editorial excellence doesn't necessarily buy success. No one wants to diminish the importance of those old editorial skills, but getting the cover right, the launch right, the marketing approach right will all pay larger, faster dividends than tinkering with sentence rhythms or honing narrative structure. The commercial logic therefore tends towards the swift, decisive correction of obvious, correctable things, and that's it.

I once had a lengthy editorial conversation by phone with my editor. We'd discussed her general comments and the several pages of close notes that had followed. We chatted a little further and by this point had been on the phone perhaps forty-five minutes. She was getting ready to close the conversation, but I had one last question to ask before we ended. I said, 'But don't you think that the middle third of the novel is a bit saggy?' She said, 'Oh yes. Yes, it is a bit.'

I was gobsmacked. Her other comments had been accurate but minor, yet all the while she'd had a much larger reservation about the work and hadn't even thought it worth mentioning. Her attitude in that conversation wasn't, however, unusual. It's commercially responsible editing. Your artistic ambitions may be set higher, however.

The third problem that can mean the editorial process does not work as well as it ought is simply that the chemistry might not be right. Perhaps you and your editor just don't see your book in quite the same way. Or he can't get his points across in a way that makes sense to you. Or you find him domineering, or you think he finds you woolly. Sometimes, two people just can't work together.

If you encounter any of these problems, you'll need to decide what to do. One is simply to make the best of it. Use your own editorial wisdom. Use whatever you can get from your editor. Do the best job you can. That'll be the approach of most authors. It's not perfect, but it's generally good enough.

An alternative approach is to make full use of whatever other professional resources are available to you. I know one author who doesn't think much of her editor in the UK and relies heavily on her editor in the US. I know another who rates her agent exceptionally highly as an editor and works extensively with her. If you have access to such resources, then you're lucky. Most authors won't. (Anyone can access our editorial resources at Jericho Writers, but you do have to pay for them. An author with a book deal in their pocket shouldn't have to pay, so we should be a very last resort.)

One, somewhat nuclear, option is to ask your publisher if you can have a different editor. That's a perfectly reasonable strategy, or would be in most professional situations, but you may well find yourself feeling like the boy who asked for more. I know one author whose first novel had been shortlisted for a major prize and earned out her advance. The editor she'd worked with on the book left the firm. She was allocated another editor. She didn't get on with that editor and wrote a perfectly respectful letter to the publisher suggesting that she would work more successfully with an editor with whom she had better chemistry. (I know the letter was respectful: I saw it.) The publisher was not amused. For a while, it looked as though the author had jeopardised her relationship with that firm altogether. In the end, things were smoothed over, but it was an episode that left its mark on both sides. The author concerned would have been better off to have approached the situation via her agent, but I'm not sure she'd have secured the desired outcome. She'd just have avoided disaster. And, in any case, why should an author have to play these games? For my money, publishers should just get more professional.

GETTING ON WITH IT

Editing your book is not an endless process. By the time you've got an agent, got that book deal and got your first set of notes, that process is effectively at an end. Address any last changes. Reread your work. Then leave it. Your editor will certainly read your manuscript again. But really, your task now is to take your hand away from the keyboard.

Some authors, of course, will be only too delighted to drop their pen, stretch their fingers and never look at their manuscript again. Others are dyed-in-the-wool tinkerers, who'll have to exercise a mighty act of will to do likewise. So good: exercise that will. It's good for you. Apart from anything else, bringing an end to the editorial process means you're all ready to leap straight into copyediting, and how could that not be fun?

COPYEDITING, PROOFREADING, AND THE CLAN PEDANTIC

'Copyediting' and 'proofreading' are sometimes used interchangeably, but the former term implies more breadth than the latter. A copyeditor is there to correct spellings and typos, of course, but also to excise repetitious language, smooth out clunky sentences, ensure accuracy and consistency, make sure that dialogue formatting is done correctly, and so on. Proofreading is more restricted in scope. A proofreader assumes that the source text is fine in all its essentials, and his only task at that point is to correct any obvious mistakes introduced by the typesetting process or missed by the copyeditor.

You will be involved with both phases, and the degree of your involvement is up to you.

THE LAID-BACK SOUL

If you're not too fussed about the fine detail of your text, then relax. Someone else will do all the hard work for you. A typical copyeditor will find countless little slips of the pen through your manuscript, even if it's well-presented, and they'll fix them. They'll deal with it all. They will also compile a short list of questions – perhaps a dozen – which they need you to answer. (For example: 'Carly's eyes are described as "smoky grey" (p. 87) and "like the blue of far-off mountains" (p. 254). Is this OK?')

If you are the laid-back sort, who honestly wouldn't be bothered if you were described instead as 'laidback' or 'laid back', and really wouldn't notice or care if the word 'laid-back' was used five times in the same sentence, then you can just answer your copyeditor's questions and go back to burning joss sticks or listening to whale songs, or whatever it is that the truly laid-back do. You have an easy life.

THE PEDANTIC SOUL

If you're not that way inclined, you'll want to examine your copyeditor's corrections more closely. Your first reaction is likely to be one of shock at the sheer number of changes to your manuscript. You may well feel like the idiot child at school, given a D for English. Most of those marks, however, are of trivial importance. Contemporary manuscripts in the UK use single inverted commas ('like this scrawny pair'), but many authors continue to use doubles ("like these well-fed beauties"). The authors aren't incorrect, however. It's just a change of fashions. Likewise, many marks will simply be bringing the manuscript into the house style on a variety of presentational points.

Probe a little closer, however, and you may find some more substantial edits that you really don't agree with. For example, copyeditors are eagle-eyed when it comes to repetitious language. Their eagle eyes unquestionably help things most of the time, but often isn't always. Frequently, for example, a repeated word will be excised and replaced with a rough equivalent, thesaurus-style. The trouble is that some copyeditors have a tin ear when it comes to sentence rhythms; and the sentences that result from their often rather mechanical edits can be sentences that sound badly.

And of course, some repetitions are deliberate. The repetition of 'laid-back' in the sentence three paragraphs back was an obvious case, but it's easy to think of rather more literary uses too. T. S. Eliot's famous opening to *Burnt Norton* – 'Time present and time past / Are both perhaps present in time future, / And time future contained in time past' – would hardly have been improved by a heavy-handed copyedit.

Likewise, if your prose style is deliberately rough, casual, free and easy, it's not likely to fare well in the hands of a copyeditor who likes things tidied up in the manner of a 1950s librarian. Maybe you like your sentence fragments as fragments. Maybe you prefer the American 'like' to the British 'as if'. If a character of yours splits an infinitive in dialogue, then maybe you intended to split it, so it'll stay split.

These things don't matter to everyone. Indeed, they matter intensely only to a tiny minority – it's just that authors are hugely over-represented in that minority. If (like me) you belong to the Clan Pedantic, please feel free to express your pedantry to the max. This is your moment! If you have strong views on the Oxford comma, or whether the word 'hoover' needs a capital, or the correct deployment of the semi-colon, express those views to the full. You'll be in good company, because editors and copyeditors care about these things too. Indeed, they may care about them even more than you do. I once had a long email exchange with an editor about a single pair of inverted commas, whose use was certainly optional, and whose function in the manuscript was marginal in the extreme. But she cared! And I did! We were soulmates! (Or as we'd both, I'm sure, have preferred, soulmates.)

These joys can't, alas, last for ever. Your editor will want your own corrections of the copyeditor's corrections back sooner rather than later. Do what you're told to do. Do it by the deadline. Relish the hour.

DEDICATION, ACKNOWLEDGEMENTS, HISTORICAL NOTE

If you want a dedication, or a page of acknowledgements, or a historical note, or anything else, then (within reason) you'll be welcome to incorporate them. Your editor may already have asked for them. If not, then you'll be asked for them now.

Acknowledgements these days are terrifyingly cool. ('Thanks too to Max the Biker for his immense right hook, to Nadia for showing me her Ingushetia, to M. who didn't want me to mention his name for fear of retribution – and if I've forgotten to mention anyone, then thanks to you especially. The best nights go unremembered.') Personally, I've never mastered the art of the cool acknowledgement, but I understand that a willingness to lie and a hair-raising imagination are useful assets.

Do also be sensible about what your book needs. A novel does not need footnotes. A historical note should probably not run to more than two or three pages. A dedication should not be pornographic. If you really, really feel the need to explain the background to your work in twenty or thirty close-set pages, then do so and post it on the internet. A book is not the place.

INDEX

If your book needs an index, then you should already have discussed that with your editor, who'll make the appropriate arrangements. In some publishing contracts, you will be asked either to prepare an index yourself or to pay for the work. You should resist either option. Indexing is as much a part of the book's production as is copyediting or typesetting. It's not your skill. Don't get involved unless you want to – and have the skills to make a genuine contribution. (If you're authoring an academic text, of course, then footnotes are your responsibility. But you already knew that, I know.)

PERMISSIONS

If you are quoting copyright work or seeking to use illustrations that belong to someone else, you need to secure permission.

The whole permissions process is rather silly in my experience. If you are quoting a few lines of prose, you will need to locate the copyright owner (normally the publisher) and write to them asking for permission. Go to the relevant publisher's website and search it, using 'Permissions' as your search term. You'll find a page that sets out what you need to do. Often you need to write an email saying how many lines you want to quote, what the intended publication is, what the expected print run is in hardback and paperback, and a few other things besides.

Much of this is nonsense. These days, the print run of a work is decided very close to publication date and is of little significance anyway, as publishers opt for more frequent, shorter print runs than in the past. So why is a publisher asking a question to which they know you don't the answer and which doesn't matter anyway? I do not know and cannot say, I'm afraid.

In any case, you need to locate the hurdles you have to hop over, then hop dutifully over them. Make stuff up if you have to. In the vast majority of cases, no one will ask you to pay for permission, which means that you've wasted your time and they've wasted their time and no money has changed hands. If you want to quote a significant chunk written by a major modern poet, you will be asked to pay something – perhaps $100 or more – and quite right too. That money will theoretically come out of your pocket, but you may find that your publisher picks up the tab. Make sure you discuss things with your editor beforehand and work out some parameters that you are both happy to live by.

It's the same deal with any other copyright work – illustrations, quotes from film scripts, and so forth. If you can't trace the copyright holder, then say so in a note somewhere. Say that, if the copyright holder makes themselves known, you will seek to have them appropriately acknowledged in a future edition of the work … which in many cases is nonsense as well, since many books never make it into a revised, updated edition.

Leave plenty of time for all this. You don't need to start the process before you have a book deal – apart from anything else, you won't be in a position to supply most of the information that is asked of you. But, once you've got your deal, you've dealt with editorial matters and you're wondering what else you should be doing, then do this. It can take eight to twelve weeks to secure copyright permissions from some publishers, or even more. If you're on a tight deadline, you may need to start as soon as your deal is agreed.

Do also note that, if you do fail to get permission to quote something, any liability arising from that is yours, but in most cases any such liability is likely to be effectively nil. Most likely, no one will ever notice or care. You need to be much more scrupulous where your quotations are extensive, or where they are taken from books with obvious current market value.

And if in doubt, talk to your editor. Your publisher has encountered all these issues a zillion times and can advise. And, for all that it can be a headache, there are times when the permissions process works with surprising speed and ease. I once wanted to quote a chunk from *Monty Python's Life of Brian*. I was gloomily wondering just how painful and expensive it was going to be to extract permission from a bunch of millionaire anarchic comedians. Answer: it took a single email, which was responded to within twenty-four hours, granting me the permission for free. One more reason to love the Pythons.

PAGE PROOFS

From the corrections of the copyeditor and your own amendments of those corrections, your editor will compile a master document that goes out to be typeset. That process is now electronic, but electronic is not the same as automatic. There are still a host of decisions to be made about page layout, fonts, pagination, and so forth – but these are not your decisions.

The next you will see of your beloved is a set of page proofs. I used to get these as actual pages – and what lovely things they were! Alas, nowadays, you'll just get a PDF file through by email, which is a sad and sorry thing by comparison. Print it off and hug it, though. That'll help.

This will be the first time that you've seen your manuscript looking anything like a book, equipped with title pages, and proper layouts, and that page with all the tiny, boring detail at the front of every book. It's an exciting moment, a significant step.

It's not a step that need trouble you too much. The laid-back can simply admire the look of their new book, and flip through the pages if they fancy pretending to do some work. The Clan Pedantic will instantly get to work seeking to see if they can find a double space where there should be a single, and to see who won the War of the Oxford Comma. I gently recommend that you do reread your manuscript attentively, as this is your last opportunity to make any (minor) corrections, but it doesn't matter vastly if you don't.

Finally, don't expect to make significant corrections or write in any major new material at this point. You'll be messing a lot of people around if you do.

THE STRANGE CASE OF THE MISSING PROOFS

Oh, reader, if it has not yet become evident, let me state it bluntly:

> *Publishers are strange and wonderful creatures*
> *Their ways are mysterious.*

You have your page proofs, right? No publisher of mine has ever once failed to give me a set of page proofs. But only print books have pages. E-books do not.

Here are some other differences between print books and e-books:

- Internet links in print books don't work very well; they are very hard to click. Internet links in e-books just work like any link anywhere. They are easy to click.

- People who buy hardbacks presumably like buying hardbacks. People who buy e-books presumably like buying e-books.

- Tedious and longwinded copyright notices and corporate yadda are perfectly fine in the front of a print book, because your thumb can find any point in the text as easily as any other. Tedious and longwinded yadda at the front of an e-book reduces the amount of text that fits within Amazon's 'Look Inside' envelope.

- There's not much point having extensive blurbs for your other work in the back of your print book, because people can't easily access that work – or at least not without walking to a bookstore or picking up a laptop and going online. Blurbs in an e-book can be teamed up with a link that makes purchasing that book unbelievably simple.

Now, you would have thought these differences would have caused publishers to think of e-books and print books as interestingly different products. But far too commonly (still! after ten years of e-books!) publishers essentially take the print-formatted text and bung that into e-book form. The results can be simply ludicrous if considered from a half-sensible commercial perspective. So for example, it is still common to see:

- 'Also by this author' lists at the front end of a book. That can look nice in print but it's bananas in an e-book. The point at which a reader might buy another book by an author is after they've read and enjoyed the book in their hands. So the moment to present an 'also by' list is at the end of the book. Obviously.

- It's common to see those lists without links. So even though an e-book is effectively a website that can link to any other website in the world – such as (duh!) Amazon – publishers present those lists without any buy-link in place. You want your e-book to have a buy-link right where a user wants it.

- Print books don't tend to have extensive blurbs, but e-books should damn well have a short, enticing blurb for any of your other books. Plus a cover image. Those things are what pique people's interest in every other buying context. So why not here, in your e-book?

- A publisher of mine used to place full page, black-and-white advertisements for a hardback book of mine in the e-book that people were reading. But if people are reading an e-book, they probably like reading e-books. So images should show your book on a Kindle (or similar). Those images will remind your reader that they could download that book on their device right now, this minute.

And so on. All this says that publishers should routinely give authors copies of the draft e-book file for authors to look through, in the same way as they dish out page proofs. With luck, that might be changing, but it remains the case that I have never had an e-book draft file from a publisher without asking for it. Repeatedly.

Please do likewise. Months before your book is due for release, you need to ask for and get that e-book file and make sure you are happy with it. Don't assume that because a publisher does things in a certain way, that way has been adopted after extensive experiment. Too often, it's because no one is actually thinking about an e-book as an e-book.

Oh yes, and you also want your e-book to offer a reader magnet – a free story, written by you, especially for your reader. That's a whole big subject in its own right and provides the fodder for a very important later chapter. For now – hold the thought.

WAVING GOODBYE

And that's it. The journey that began with your opening sentence, that reached its mid-point when you reached the final full stop, has now ended. There is plenty yet to do, but what follows is a marketing challenge, not a literary one. You may holster your pen, wipe down your keyboard and remove the orange plastic troll from the roof of your computer monitor. It has done its duty. The luck and perseverance that you needed have come your way and brought you the rewards you yearned for. It's time for other things, the things that matter – the things that will sell the book.

COVER DESIGN AND TITLE

At some point, and overlapping with the processes of the last couple of sections, you will be presented with a draft cover design. You might receive it nicely printed on card. More likely, you'll get it as a PDF or JPG file sent online. You might see it first on A4 sheets printed off from an ordinary office colour printer. If it works logistically, you'll be presented with the concept when you're next at a meeting or lunch with your publisher.

Mostly, you'll just see a single design. You're being asked to choose from a menu with only one option. ('Would you like the oysters, sir?' 'Um. What else is there?' 'Nothing, sir. You could just have the lemon slice on its own, I suppose.' 'Uh, OK. I'll take the oysters.' 'An excellent choice, sir. Thank you. And you, madam? Will you be having the oysters?')

Occasionally – very occasionally – you might be invited to air your thoughts about a set of possible options, but those 'options' will almost certainly be variants on a single theme: in effect, the same design concept, but tweaked this way and that for the sake of variety.

The one universal, however, of these moments is a slight air of tension in the room as they happen. You're the author. This is a genuinely nice industry, where people want you to like what they've done. They want you to be happy with the approach to publication. But they also want you to say 'yes'. The image that you're shown has evolved from meetings, discussions, experiments, comments and revisions. It's the version that has the house seal of approval. Your 'yes' will be very welcome. Your 'no' will not be popular.

There's tension in the air for another reason besides. You have no say on cover design. In a typical contract, your publishers are obliged to 'consult' you on the subject, but they would certainly have met their legal obligations in full if they said, 'Here is our cover design,' you said, 'I loathe, despise and detest it,' and they said, 'We note your opinion but are going to go ahead anyway.' In formal terms, you are powerless.

Nevertheless, life is about more than contracts and so is publishing. Editors will want you to be happy. What's more, while the consensus house view hasn't been arrived at lightly, if your argument against a given design is cogent and persuasive, your editor may well change her mind anyway. Because cover design is a critical element in the approach to market, all these things matter intensely. This section is here to help you manage them as best as you possibly can.

TA-DAA!

The best place to start is with the moment of revelation itself.

It's common for editors to turn the unveiling of a cover design into a 'ta-daaa!' moment during a lunch or meeting. The impulse to do it that way is perhaps understandable, but it's also a bad one, a terrible one. The cover design is the most important single decision of the entire publishing process. It should no more be made the centre of a 'ta-daaa!' moment than should a corporate budget or a crucial marketing plan.

In particular, it's fantastically hard for you, the author, to respond sensibly in the handful of seconds after the curtain (metaphorically) falls. That's no way at all to produce a smart business decision. What ought to happen, in fact, is that a draft cover design is sent to you, probably by email, at an early stage. That way, you can be involved when decisions are still malleable, when the timetable still has plenty of room. Because your editor may not play it that way of her own accord, you need to nudge her as far in that direction as you possibly can. You won't move her as far as you'd like, but, if you don't nudge, you won't get anywhere. So start nudging, politely but early. Just say that you're bad at thinking these things through quickly, and you'd like to see a draft cover at the earliest possible stage.

If you're lucky, you'll get what you asked for. If you're not, at least you'll have prepared the ground for a guarded reaction when the moment arrives.

In any event, just be prepared in advance *not* to be too nice, too helpful, too quick to say yes to that cover. Everyone around you will want you to do just that. There'll be a gentle but unrelenting pressure on you to do it. Yet now is almost certainly not the moment to make a final decision. So just make yourself say, 'Yes, interesting, do talk me through your thought processes here ...' Whatever else you go on to say, just be certain that you leave yourself room for manoeuvre, so that, if, on reflection, you think the cover is not as strong as it ought to be, you are able to say so without having to backtrack. Even if you find yourself absolutely loving the cover when you first see it, make sure that you leave yourself wiggle-room. First impressions matter a lot (especially with book covers) but thoughtful reflection will often add significantly to that first reaction.

Above all, remember that in a large majority of instances your publisher is looking to secure your agreement, not solicit your commentary. Your publisher doesn't *want* any reaction other than, 'Gosh, fantastic!' Sometimes, of course, that reaction will be absolutely appropriate. Other times, it will not be. When it isn't, you need to do what you can to improve things – while all the time bearing in mind your meagre bargaining position and the importance of not rupturing your relationship at this early stage.

THE IMPORTANCE OF COMMON SENSE

In any debate over book covers, it's easy to be over-impressed by the authority of those who publish books for a living. Publishers know so much more about the attitudes of retail buyers, image libraries, production possibilities and so forth that it's easy for a mere author to defer to the weight of all that superior knowledge.

Yet authors are experts too. Presumably you tend to read the kind of book that you've just written. You've spent hours browsing in bookstores. You know which book covers work for you and which don't. If you're a crime writer, then you'll be decently familiar with the state of the art. That is, you know the 'look' of contemporary cover. That doesn't give you more authority than anyone else, but it does qualify you to have a view.

And my own experience has been that ideas that seem to be bad are bad. I don't think I've ever encountered an exception to that rule, either when it comes to my own work or anybody else's. Indeed, it's often been the case that, when a book hasn't sold, at the post-mortem afterwards people will point to a jacket design that missed the mark. In the large majority of such cases, the problem was obvious beforehand and was the very thing the author had been uncomfortable about.

I've also noticed an understandable drive in publishing to seek ideas that are new, different, edgy and clever. Apart from anything else, a jacket designer doubtless loves to express his own creativity to the max and would love to see a design award coming his way at some point. You, however, care less than nothing about design awards.

You, I humbly suggest, are interested in book sales. If the new, different, edgy and clever cover is going to help sell your book, fantastic. If not, get the cover changed. For one of my books, my designer wanted to wrap the book's title right round the hardback jacket so that, in order to understand what the book was called, a browser would actually need to unpeel the jacket (including its inside flaps) and spread it out flat. It was dazzlingly clever in some sense but threatened to deliver no book sales at all. (And how it would have worked in e-book form was altogether mysterious.) In that instance, I'm pretty sure my editor was pleased by my horrified reaction, because it gave her a chance to combat a design that she didn't like herself.

You also need to use your common sense when it comes to deciding whether a particular design is going to work. Book designers are quite likely to be young, metropolitan, design-oriented, left-of-centre, cool types. Your book might have its natural market among older, conservative-minded, deeply uncool, right-leaning types. You need to make sure that the designers are producing a cover that suits the book's target audience, not one that suits their own tastes. Naturally, an editor will make the target audience clear to the designer as part of the design brief, but that brief may not always be followed.

And beware any cries of procrastination. If you think a particular design is misfiring, then you're very likely to be told that you just need to wait until you see the cover in its completed state, that it'll look so much better with the foil, that they've got new effects technology which looks amazing, yadda, yadda, blah.

All this is nonsense. It's true that jacket designers do now make imaginative use of the various new technologies open to them. Jacket covers can now have special metallic-style effects, gold foil can be embossed or dimpled, covers can be snipped through allowing you to peep beneath the surface. And so on. But the final copy that emerges from all this cleverness will look almost exactly the same as the one now in your hands, just a bit shinier. It is just not true to suggest that you can't judge the one by the other. You can. The main reason why you are being told to wait is so that, in three or four weeks' time, when you have the cover in its impressively metallicised version, there will be no time left to change it. You need to combat that kind of procrastination by putting your foot down early and firmly.

One last point – the most crucial of the lot perhaps – is that you need to be careful to distinguish between a cover that you like and one that you think will sell the book. It just doesn't matter whether *you* like the cover. What matters is that you feel the book will have its commercial appeal enhanced by its jacket. Making that judgement sensibly requires you to put your own feelings aside and view the cover as neutrally as you can.

The key checks here are simple and critical.

First: does the book convey its genre simply and accurately? That probably matters more than anything else. Penguin Random House once published a crime thriller of mine. It was British-set.

It was a police procedural. In many ways, the book was a down-the-line crime thriller. And the cover? Looked like a high-end psychological exploration of something. Or a reprint of some classic French existential noir. Or … well, something that wasn't a simple crime thriller. That book got amazing reviews – and sold atrociously.

These things matter a lot in supermarkets and bookstores. Online, the importance of genre-signalling is almost greater. If a reader is looking for a book of a certain type, the easiest way for a lazy eye to browse is simply to look for the right sort of cover amongst a given set of search results. It's not merely that your book cover must attract that eye. Your *thumbnail* must attract the eye. And that means obeying the rules of your genre. Completely. Every time. No exceptions.

Second: does the mood suggested by the cover echo the mood of your book? If your cover has a gentle nostalgic feel and your book is a contemporary slasher-horror piece, the cover just doesn't work. You might find some buyers, for sure, but you'll get horrible reviews and any sales will be quickly over. Your cover has to make (and your text needs to deliver) both a genre promise and an atmospheric promise. There can be no compromise on either count.

Third, and this is more optional, is there some interesting reverberation between title and cover? The very best covers raise questions with their title ('Where the Crawdads Sing', let's say). A terrible cover is one that answers that question directly: perhaps by showing a crawdad (a crayfish, or freshwater lobster) in its natural environment. That closes the question opened by the title and does nothing to entice the reader's further exploration. Instead the cover designer showed us a moody waterscape with a lone figure in a canoe. Who is the figure? What is a crawdad? Can crawdads even sing? What is the figure doing in that landscape? Why is he/she paddling alone? The questions multiply and gain a kind of urgency, precisely because the cover takes only a most oblique approach to its subject.

Finally, and this again is *not* optional, is the text of your title clearly visible if the image size is reduced to thumbnail? Designers love sending you huge files in massive resolution. They'll send you files via Dropbox or WeTransfer because ordinary emails sag under the weight of data that those designers want to send.

And sure. Big images (especially on a black background) look wonderful. But the competitive arena that matters most to you is of tiny images competing on a white background. If in doubt, paste a thumbnail sized version of your draft cover design onto a screengrab of Amazon search results in your genre. Can you read your title? Does your book look like its genre sisters? Do you feel motivated to click to find out more?

These tests are all more crucial than the one that is burning in your head right now. *Yes, yes, yes, but does the cover encapsulate my book?* That's what you want to ask, and the answer is – I don't care. No one does. No one should.

I'll give you two examples. My first Fiona Griffiths novel did so-so in hardback release (in the UK). Not horrible, not good. Then a major retailer said they loved the book, wanted to promote the paperback big time ... but they hated the hardback cover. If we wanted the promo, we had to change the cover. That was fine with me and the publisher, and they came up with some acid green text, a dark and foreboding background and – a scary tree. Trees had no particular relevance in my book, scary or otherwise. But the book looked like a crime novel. It looked moody and dramatic. So I approved the cover and that book sold like hot cakes on the first day of winter. No reader has ever asked me about the tree, and no reader ever will. The key promises (regarding genre and atmosphere) were made and kept. That's all that matters.

Another example. A friend of mine, a crime bestseller, was presented with a cover that showed a shattered wine glass against an attractive yet moody background. The image was dazzling and contrasted brilliantly with the book's title. But there was no broken wine glass in the story. The author saw the excellence of the cover, but she didn't like the lack of connection between image and text. So she changed the text. She altered a key scene to include a broken wine glass. Boom! Her soul was happy. The book had a great cover. And it went on to be a bestseller.

IF SOMETHING ISN'T RIGHT

If, on reflection, you feel that your draft cover design is not working, then say so. The calmer you can be about this, the better. A good strategy is to make clear how you see the target market for your book and how you think the cover is missing that market. For example, let's say you've written a crime novel that includes the compulsory murder or two, but which is fairly light in nature – more Miss Marple, let's say, than Scarpetta. Let's also say that you've been given a cover which is sombre, black and splashed with blood, guns, syringes and the like. You may well feel that the cover and the book are missing each other. Say so.

Go to Amazon and put together a group of the kind of covers that you think would work. That research may teach you that the book designer was right and you were wrong. But if you still feel the same way, put together a short email explaining your view. Set out who you think your target readers are (in terms of favourite authors, demographics and so on). And say who you think your comparable authors are.

Remain reasonable and unemotional. Ideally, your email needs to be something that could be forwarded to the cover designer without creating a stir. Making it easy for the editor and designer to take action is a big part of winning this war. If the tone of your first email is angry and difficult, your editor has to write a whole new email and act as a creative go-between – a much harder and less attractive task. So say what you think. But say it gently.

TITLE

As an author, you probably think of your title choice as part of the manuscript itself: an aesthetic choice that shines its light over the book as a whole. As you approach publication, however, you need to lock such thoughts firmly away. Your book title is no more than an aspect of cover design. The title needs to be part of a package which intrigues and attracts your target audience. From that point of view, it doesn't really matter if the title neatly encapsulates the book or not. All that matters is that the cover design and the title form an instantly attractive package for the potential reader. If your publisher tells you that your chosen title isn't working, then they're more often than not right.

That last sentence may strike you as inconsistent with the tone of this section. When it comes to cover designs, I've argued that your publisher may well be wrong and that you have enough expertise to be confident in identifying those errors. When it comes to title, however, I'm telling you that you need to trust your publisher. The underlying logic is the same. When it comes to cover design, it becomes very hard for a publisher to avoid group-think – that process by which dissenting voices are unwittingly choked off. It can also be hard for a design team to rip up the best first idea they had and start again from scratch. The issue here is that it is hard both to create something and not be over-attached to that creation.

The same goes with you and your title. You love your title. You've lived with it. You got excited when you thought of it. You love the tune of it in your head. It just strikes you as implausible when your editor tells you that it's not working with the design concept that they have. Nevertheless, you'd mostly do well to listen. My fourth novel, a book about flying in the 1920s, ended up being entitled *Glory Boys*. I think I had wanted to call it *Heaven and Earth*, or something of that sort. I liked my title. I hated *Glory Boys*, which I thought sounded camp and under-whelming. Nevertheless, I was wrong. The designers were right. The design they chose just worked with that title. The title *Glory Boys*, in fact, became part of the look of the cover, which was attractive and buyable.

Occasionally, publishers will actually suggest a title. Mostly, however, they'll ask you if you have any other suggestions. If they don't like those other suggestions, they'll ask you for more. And so on. The best way to generate a good list of possibles is to use the method discussed already: essentially just force yourself to compile a list of some hundred or more options, the good and the bad all together. From that long list, strike out the obvious bad ones, then give the remaining ones ample time to call to you. Sometimes, the best titles are ones that you thought of immediately and dismissed.

SUBTITLES IN NON-FICTION

Another important ingredient of some book covers is a 'shout line' or subtitle. A subtitle is more for use in non-fiction, and it expands or explains the meaning of the title. Thus, Steven Pinker's bestselling *The Language Instinct* was explained and amplified by the words that followed the title in smaller type: *The New Science of Language and Mind*. With non-fiction, you're more than likely to have developed such a subtitle already. If not, you can do so in collaboration with your editor.

Pinker's subtitle is a good example of the genre. Non-fiction mostly sells itself on the basis of its subject matter, so simply advertising the topic of the book is a good start. At the same time, that word 'new' functions in much the same way as it does when stuck on to a new formulation of washing powder or a rebranded mortgage product. The word teases and attracts. It teases, because its coded message is, 'You may think that you know this subject, but you really can't do because everything you thought you knew is out of date.' It attracts because it promises to let you in on something that others don't yet have. If you can find a subtitle that simultaneously describes and attracts, you're on to a good thing.

SUBTITLES IN FICTION

The earlier version of this book did not have a section talking about fiction subtitles. After all, fiction doesn't have subtitles, does it? Well no, it didn't. But Amazon, in effect, rewrote the rules, because its search layouts give weight to both title (*The Girl in the*

Ice) and to the subtitle (*A Gripping Serial Killer Thriller*). That's not a real subtitle. It's an advertising slogan. But if Amazon is happy enough to glue an ad slogan to the title, you should contentedly glue away.

You can put pretty much anything you like in the subtitle. The only real restriction is that Amazon requires you to display the subtitle on the cover itself. So you can't put that stuff about a gripping serial killer thriller into Amazon's database and not put it on the cover. You have to do both. (Historically, Amazon has been very sloppy about enforcing its own rules. It's not as bad now.)

In any case, it is well worth thinking about Amazon here. What would look good on Amazon? What do your peers do? Can you find something attractive and distinctive here? You need to think not as a novelist, but as an advertising exec. The sharper and stronger your shout line, the better. The best way to prompt thoughts is to run appropriate searches on Amazon and gather ideas from the various approaches there.

A FINAL WORD

As you mull over these thoughts in the context of your book and your draft cover design, you need to bear two things in mind.

First, nothing matters more than the cover design. It quite possibly matters more than the content of the book itself – not in building a word-of-mouth bestseller, but in giving you an initial sales platform that could support such a bestseller. That early sales platform cannot come from your book's content, simply because people haven't yet read it. It will not come from book reviews because you are unlikely to have many, and in any case, they don't generate many sales. And, if the initial sales platform is lacklustre or worse, your book will vanish from the promo slots so quickly that any word-of-mouth sales momentum will never have the chance to take off. So design matters. It matters hugely. Your success depends on it.

Secondly, you have no right of veto. Publishers aren't general-ly looking for you to play a constructive and collaborative role in determining the look of the cover. On the contrary, in most cases, they'll be pressuring you, nicely but persistently, to approve the design that is put in front of you. Mostly the draft design will be either excellent or good enough. Sometimes it won't be. In those instances where the design is poor, you need to do something – and that means leaping over the hurdles that are put in your way, whilst managing to avoid destroying your relationships before they've even begun.

That isn't an easy brief, but then, if you are after an easy task, you should never have become an author.

THE BLURB

The novelist and playwright Michael Frayn once created a character who, in theory, was hard at work writing a novel but who, in practice, spent his whole time writing and polishing the blurb. Frayn was making a joke, not recommending a strategy, yet there are things one could learn from his character all the same.

The previous section talked extensively about cover design. The look of the cover should be enough to entice a reader to pick the book up or click through to the relevant sales page. Once they've made that first move, their next step is to learn more. That's where your blurb comes in. On Amazon, the little bit of text about your book is technically called the book description and can run to as many as 4,000 characters. But to avoid being annoying, I'll mostly use the word 'blurb' for both forms of sales text.

DESIGN ASPECTS (PRINT)

The main themes of the cover design will pull through to the back of the book: the same fonts, the same colours, the same background. There'll need to be room for an ISBN, barcode and a website address.

This still leaves plenty of room. As a debut author, you are unlikely to have any book reviews or usable book puffs, but it's quite likely that your jacket designer will want to make the book look a little as though you have such reviews, by setting opening and closing phrases in a different colour, font, size or style from the rest of the text. For example, the original blurb of John Grisham's first novel, *The Firm*, had as its opening sentence: '*The job of his dreams is about to become his worst nightmare.*' It closes with:

'*Now; Mitch is in the place where dreams end and nightmares begin …*'
Both those phrases were picked out in a font and colour to
separate them from the remaining text. If the phrases had been set
in exactly the same way – and at the very outset of his career
before the positive reviews started to pour in – then the back of
the book would have looked rather bland, no matter how
interesting the text.

These thoughts are worth bearing in mind, because whoever
comes up with the blurb needs to ensure that the cover designer
has material to work with – notably a very 'sales-ey' first and last
sentence. Accuracy here is not the point. Nor is subtlety. Sales,
brevity and punch are your watchwords.

WHO WRITES THE TEXT?

On the whole, publishers write the blurb, not you. I've seen some
excellent publishers' blurbs in my time; I've also seen some limp
ones. At the same time, writing blurbs is a chore for your editor,
and, if you volunteer, they're likely to be responsive. Better still, if
you simply offer them some text, then – if it's strong enough –
your editor will most likely be only too happy to accept it.

If you care to write the blurb yourself, then do so early and
email it to your editor sooner rather than later. If your editor has
already composed some text and got approval for it from the sales
and marketing types, and from the folk over in design, then that
text may have an unassailable lead over yours, irrespective of
which one is actually better.

GETTING THE TEXT RIGHT

Writing blurbs is an utterly different art form from writing a novel
or non-fiction manuscript. Everything you so painfully learned
about writing over the last few months and years needs to be
forgotten, or at least ruthlessly suppressed.

For one thing, a book blurb is extraordinarily brief. It's worth
checking the length of blurbs in comparable works. You're likely
to encounter an average of around a hundred words, including

header and footer text. You just can't say anything detailed or layered or complex in such a space. You need to set up the premise. Throw in a dash of intrigue. Maybe a dab of self-praise ('this moving and beautifully told tale …'). Then quit.

If your blurb leaves lots of questions unanswered, then fine. Unanswered questions are a reason for someone to buy a book. If your blurb isn't quite accurate in setting out the premise or developing its implications, it doesn't matter. Readers know perfectly well that the back of the book is not some legally sanctioned summary of the content. Think of the blurb like a tiny story with mounting jeopardy/complexity and ending in a cliffhanger. You need to establish what kind of story yours is (e.g.: crime fiction, police procedural, set in Wales). You need to establish something about your premise and set-up: 'A young female corpse has been found in a country churchyard, with no marks of violence.' You need, ideally, to introduce one little twist or complication, much as you would in the story itself: 'But she is not the only young woman to have gone missing recently …' And leave yourself room for that final cliffhanger: 'Fiona Griffiths must solve the mystery … or risk becoming the next victim …'

Though a good blurb is short, you shouldn't try to write it in a single sitting. You need to work more the way that a poet might: cutting out unnecessary words, honing phrases, trying out different strategies. Spend several hours on the project over several days. If you end up with more than one version, offer both to your publisher. With a little luck, you'll be on your way.

PUFFS

Because you are a debut author, the first edition of your book (probably a hardback, or e-book, or both) will emerge into the world with no book reviews to garnish it. There'll be nothing reading, 'Praise for Joe Schmoe'. Nothing promising that you're scarier than P. G. Wodehouse, funnier than Faulkner, wiser than the Kardashians, more up-to-the-minute than Homer.

Without these things, however, your book risks looking a little naked. A little clever blurb-writing combined with some sleight-of-hand typography will help a little, but ideally you want more. The theoretical solution is the 'puff'. A puff is an authorised comment from some celebrity or influencer in your genre, endorsing your book. *'I laughed till I cried'*, *Oprah Winfrey* – that sort of thing. The quotation doesn't need to have appeared in any publication or any media outlet at all. All that matters is that the celebrity is happy to endorse the statement.

The huge, almost insuperable, challenge is how to get the darn puff. The starting place is likely to be a bound proof. A bound proof is simply a proof (i.e. unfinalised) copy of your work, quite possibly just encased in plain covers. The plainness doesn't matter. The book is never going to go on sale, it's simply going to be used as something that can be introduced to the trade more feasibly than a bundle of loose-leaf paper. Not all books will ever see a bound proof. A major launch for commercial fiction certainly will. A minor launch for a niche book certainly won't. The decision on whether to commission a bound proof won't be yours, and it'll be driven by whether the good folk of marketing feel they need it as a selling tool.

But let's say that your book is going to experience life as a bound proof. You've therefore got the kind of thing that could be sent out for a celebrity endorsement. Often enough, I've witnessed my editor diligently compiling a list of people who could be asked for plugs. For my book on British history, for example, I believe we approached upwards of thirty people. I don't know if any of them ever responded (because it was my editor who sent out the letters, not me). I do know that we drew a total blank.

What is to be done?

Well, the first thing to say is there's no point in radically lowering your aim in terms of what kind of names to approach. The only names worth having are big ones: ones that you can expect your reader to recognise and respect. Too often, I see authors struggling to get blurbs and end up soliciting blurbs from the wrong people. So if, for example, you've written a medical thriller, you might end up soliciting a puff from (I don't know) the consultant obstetrician at your local hospital. You might get that puff too. *'A very interesting and well-researched novel about what could go wrong in a complex, modern hospital.' – Jiminy Jolly, Consultant Obstetrician, St Jude's Hospital.* And absolutely nothing about that puff is worth having. The good Dr Jolly might be the world's best obstetrician, but most readers don't know that, so his name is irrelevant. His puff feels heavy and worthy and dull, which means it's actually dragging down your text. A bad puff is much worse than no puff at all.

So if you are going to chase these beasts, aim high. Did your brother-in-law go to school with Jerry Seinfeld? Wasn't your sister once a classmate of Lena Dunham? Be brash. Be assertive. And know that you'll fail at least ten times more often than you win.

But critically, do this. Talk to your editor. If she's about to fire off a batch of books to a list of authors, then you should add a handwritten note to each book, kindly soliciting a comment on the book. The authors will know exactly what you're after – and that handwritten touch will make a real difference. I know a million-plus-selling author who used to get at least ten proof copies of novels every week. If the books came with a simple compliments slip and nothing else, she just threw them away. If they came with a personalised note from a publicist, she put the book to one side for consideration. If it had a note from the author, she read that book whenever her time permitted – and she was generous with her blurbs.

And look. If you draw a blank, you draw a blank. There's nothing to be done about that. At least you tried.

Part Six
PUBLICATION

The Holy Land of Sales

You've now got a text that everyone is happy with. You've got a jacket design that you have pasted above your computer and that you look at about three dozen times every day. You've lit candles to St Francis de Sales who, let's face it, isn't a heavy hitter among the company of the blessed, but he is the officially appointed patron saint for authors and (less flatteringly) journalists, so he's the chap you need to light candles to. If you are slightly more New Age about things, you have consulted fortune-tellers, enjoyed a Reiki healing, placed crystals under your pillow, rubbed the right kind of essential oils into the soles of your feet, gone macrobiotic and redecorated your house with state-of-the-art feng shui. That's all excellent. All the more so because the single most important element of the publishing process is about to take place – and it's about to take place out of your sight, and beyond your control.

THE HOLY QUINTET

The Bookseller, the British equivalent of *Publishers Weekly*, once described a seminar held by Waterstones, the UK's leading bookstore chain. The purpose of the seminar was to tell the assembled agents and publishers all about the great things the group was up to. The magazine reported widespread consternation when the speaker said that the four key considerations when ordering a book were its track record, support from the publisher, market context and pricing/cover. According to *The Bookseller*, one attendee said, 'Half the people in the room put their hands up and asked, "What about the writing?".'

I don't want to make too much of this. Truth is, the quality of content has always mattered and always will. Nevertheless, the anecdote is telling about the importance of all those other things that you, the author, do not have control over. We'll take them in turn, splitting the last of the Waterstones criteria into two – a holy quintet.

Oh, and although e-book pricing is fantastically important, the issues there are distinct from those affecting print, so I'm going to split that discussion off for the next chapter.

Track record

If this is the first time you've been in print, you don't have a track record. If, on the other hand, you're launching a paperback when your hardback has already been launched, or if you've published broadly similar work before, then you certainly have a sales track record and you will be judged on it. That's not necessarily good news. If your publisher puts a misjudged cover on your hardback, that could potentially injure your career almost beyond redemption, as paperback buyers look at the hardback failure and decide against backing a loser. Your sales of book #2 won't exactly be great either, not unless your publisher can come up with a great reason why retailers should ignore the fate of its predecessor.

Support from the publisher

This criterion translates roughly into an assessment of how much money the publisher is putting behind a book. The more money is spent, the more the retailer is likely to promote the book. There is something weird about this metric. It's really not clear, for example, how much even quite substantial social media campaigns directly affect user behaviour. I've seen evidence, for example, that suggests Big Five Twitter campaigns aimed at supporting non-brandname authors have almost zero effect. But those big campaigns can work in another way too. If a supermarket chain sees a publisher putting a heck of a lot of activity behind an author, they may place a huge order and offer generous shelf space. That shelf space will then, for sure, deliver sales, simply because of the footfall and visibility. So in a way, that social media campaign did generate sales for the author ... even if it failed directly to influence the purchasing decisions of even a single consumer.

Market context

Retailers are selling to a market, and they need to be responsive. Misery memoirs might be all the rage one year; they may fall away drastically the next. Dan Brown knock-offs may be huge sellers in one season, impossible to shift the next. There have been other huge rises and falls in the sales of vampire fiction, of erotic fiction and (to a lesser extent) of Young Adult dystopian fiction. Retailers have to take these things into account when placing their orders. For you, who may get the idea for a book years before the date of actual publication, those things aren't easy to manage ... except that if you're starting to write a copycat version of whatever book is currently causing a sales sensation, you are likely to find it unsaleable when it's done. Copycat as a strategy works badly, thank goodness.

Print pricing

Pricing means two things. First of all, the cover price the publisher has placed on the book; and second, the price at which the publisher is prepared to sell your books to the retailer. If a supermarket is being offered two books of similar quality and appeal, and they can get one at a 65% discount to the recommended retail price, and the other one at a 55% discount, they will go for the former every time, irrespective of the quality of writing. They are there to make money, not advance the cause of literature.

Cover

Retailers are right to care about the quality of your cover. These things are vastly fashion-dependent too. Fonts, colours and themes have waves of popularity. There's been a recent trend for crime covers to favour blue backgrounds (especially creepy houses) with yellow fonts that nod towards Helvetica or Open Sans. The covers look nice enough to the author ... until they notice that five out of ten books in their genre look identical. And yes, a supermarket wants to respect the trend, but it doesn't just want to stock blue-and-yellow books, so some of those dedicated followers of fashion will fail because they were too samey.

These thoughts are sobering, because you start to realise how much of your destiny lies in hands other than yours. You remember the time you read through your entire manuscript, concerned that some of your sentence rhythms were a little abrupt? Well, good for you. You sound like the right sort of author, meticulous and perfectionist. But none of that matters at this stage. There are more important things in play.

TRACK RECORD

Of the holy quintet above, perhaps the only element that calls for somewhat fuller explanation is the concept of track record.

Many readers of this book will have no track record. (Academic, business or other specialist publications don't count in this context.) That doesn't matter – indeed, it may even be a good thing. Debut authors are recognised as such, and the trade will be perfectly open to promoting strong contributions by first-timers. Retailers will, of course, be able to look at the track records of books on similar subjects or in similar genres, so they aren't entirely in the dark when it comes to guesstimating sales.

On the other hand, as soon as you get into print, you do start to accumulate a sales record. Assuming your novel comes out in hardback first, those sales will be assessed. If this is your second book, the sales of your first will be closely scrutinised. Because most authors do not clamber straight on to the bestseller lists and stay there for weeks on end, there will be many pro authors who'd prefer it if they could relaunch themselves with the virgin whiteness of an unspotted sales record. (And do: they change genres and, if necessary, change their names.)

In short, sales records matter and they matter more now than they ever used to. The brief moral: you'd do well to push as hard as you can to maximise the sales of every book, in every edition. It's not simply that you may earn out your advance and achieve some royalties by doing that. It's that you are working to build the foundations of a career that will sustain you long into the future.

A DECENTLY SIZED SUV

Important as these issues may be, the crucial discussions will take place where you can't hear or influence them. You will not even be told – except perhaps in extreme summary form – the upshot of those discussions. Still more scarily, perhaps, the physical retail market for books has both consolidated and disintegrated.

The consolidation is more obvious. Barnes and Noble in the US and Waterstones in the UK have either acquired, or witnessed the collapse of, almost every specialist competitor. Those two firms are now united by a common CEO and a common owner. The supermarkets remain huge. Amazon is even vaster.

That doesn't sound like an especially healthy retail market, but you'd think that publishers would secretly be rather pleased. After all, in a highly consolidated market, your route to creating a bestseller looks pretty easy. Step one: bully or buy your way onto the front tables of the big chains. Step two: listen to those sales registers ring.

Except that things have changed. When James Daunt became the CEO of Waterstones, he stopped the practice of centralised buying completely. Instead, local store managers got to choose the books that they loved and thought their local customers would love too. When James Daunt subsequently also became the CEO of Barnes & Noble, he instituted the same practice there too.

Readers loved those changes. Publishers were horrified. Their entire corporate structures had been set up to drive sales through a handful of retail buyers – as many, say, as you could fit into a decently sized SUV. How did that sales effort now work when the two largest bookstore chains in the English-speaking world had, in effect, split itself into a huge number of independent stores? The consequence was that publishers, driven by that search for scale, became increasingly dependent on the supermarkets – and on Amazon.

That's scary. For sure, those supermarket buyers are smart, book-loving individuals. I've met a few of them, and I've always been struck by their range, knowledge and passion. But still. They buy terribly few titles because they don't have a lot of shelf space. Additionally, supermarkets have no sense of committing to an author – building profile, building sales, book after book after book. They could place an order of 30,000 copies for one of your books and then, for no especial reason, place no orders at all for your next one. That pothole could easily burst your career.

The result of all this upheaval is that when publishers are seeking to sell their wares to retailers, the conversations will not simply be about how many books are being ordered. Sales conversations today are multi-dimensional and interlocking. What discount is the publisher offering? How much consumer advertising? What kind of PR effort is being made? Is the publisher willing to pay for promotional slots, and, if so, how much and for how long? And what other competing books are out there at the same time? And what are *their* publishers saying about discounts, and promotions and all the rest of it? For your book to achieve a strong sales platform, retailers will need to be impressed by the entire package and be relatively more impressed by your package than by any comparable offerings from rival publishers. It is in these discussions that many a crucial battle is lost or won. And you're not there to fight them.

THY REFUGE AND THY STRENGTH

So what can you do?

The first, best, most certain answer is a simple one. You need to sell your book for the highest possible advance in the first place. The more money a publisher has riding on a book, the less they can afford to see it bomb. There are no guarantees, but this remains your best protection by a country mile.

If, like so many authors, you don't really care about the money but just want a decent career and a committed readership, then you would do well to chase the money anyway. That doesn't mean that you need to write commercial fiction instead of literary fiction, or mass-market non-fiction instead of your own cultured highbrow work, but it does mean that you need to be attentive to the market for these things. There's highly saleable literary fiction, and there's highly unsaleable literary fiction. If you are determined to write the latter, don't be surprised if your publisher finds it hard to shift it.

While securing a strong advance is, for sure, your best bet, it remains a bet, a gamble. The fact is, power has shifted from publishers to retailers. A couple of decades back, publishers essentially instructed retailers what to stock. Those days are long gone. Now, if a retailer doesn't like a title, it won't give the book significant support – or perhaps any at all. If that sentence isn't clear, let me make it more explicit: the biggest retailer in your home market may choose to buy exactly zero copies of your work. That does happen. It is not uncommon.

If a buyer likes a title, it may (for a price) offer quite extensive support. Because publishers will be having at least eight or ten important conversations with key buyers at the same time, predicting the end result of these is like determining the answer to a set of simultaneous equations with eight ever-shifting variables. In the best case, all retailers will think positively about the same title. That means that the publisher can be confident of offering strong support for the book, knowing that it will be sold with sufficient prominence through enough outlets to justify the investment.

But in the event that one important buyer suddenly withdraws support, the publisher will have to reconsider their investment. That reconsideration may nudge other retailers into reducing their degree of support. In the worst case, two or three major abstentions from key buyers will be enough to force your publisher to scale back severely their intended support for the book. The result can easily be that a book which seemed hot six weeks ago is effectively dead right now. That outcome may well be heartbreaking for you – if you get prompt and honest information from your publisher, that is – but the process leading to that outcome had its own commercial rationale at every step.

It may or may not help you to know that the buyers who abstained from supporting your book most likely never read it.

GETTING DRUNK WITH THE MONEY

At my very first meeting with a publisher, I was introduced to various people: the editor, the publisher, the publicist – and the sales guy. It wasn't hard to understand all those other jobs but, maybe because I was being a little dim, I didn't quite understand the task of the salesperson. Publishers print books. Retailers buy them. I could see that you needed a catalogue and some discussion over what that catalogue contained, but a bookseller was no more likely to stop ordering books than a supermarket is likely to stop ordering baked beans. I didn't quite get it. My bafflement must have been obvious, because the sales guy was patient with me.

'I talk to buyers about the book. I get them excited by it. We get our reps to spread the excitement. We want to have your book as strongly positioned as we possibly can.'

Ah! I was beginning to get it now. There'd be earnest conversations about the market for adventure fiction (in my case), discussions of trends, a committed pitch for my style and approach – like a college discussion about literature, only played out for real. I started to nod my understanding, but the sales guy was still talking.

'Basically,' he said, 'my job involves getting drunk with buyers.'

Ten years on from that conversation, I've grown increasingly sure that the sales job involves more than just strategic alcohol abuse, but there's no question that (erm) informal sales techniques play their part in the books trade, just as they do anywhere. Many authors will see out plenty of book deals without ever encountering trade buyers, but many is not the same as all. If you do get the chance to meet the trade, then make the most of it.

The evenings I've attended have involved buyers from the supermarkets, from the big chains, and from some of the wholesalers and other operators. If your work is more literary, you'd be meeting a group with a more upmarket bias. Other than that, the exact shape of the evening will depend on the way your publisher happens to arrange it. Quite likely, however, your publisher will have arranged a get-together at some nice hotel somewhere. Quite likely, there will be an opportunity to show that you know how to find the bottom end of a glass. You will probably be called on to make a brief speech – a few minutes long, no more – but the real business of the evening will simply be socialising with the people who have the power to buy your book by the thousand, or reject it altogether. You won't be the only author there, but there will only be a few others present. You're lucky to be asked.

So be nice. Be as interested in them and what they do for a living as they are in you and what you do. As a matter of fact, what they do is not simply important to your future career, it also gives you a precious opportunity to understand how they think, how decisions are made, how the retail end of the trade thinks about consumers and buying habits. That's scarce information and you should squirrel it away (before, of course, you become so drunk that you've forgotten where you keep your head).

After the evening, and after you've crawled miserably down from Mount Hangover, send a 'nice meeting you'-type email to the people you met. It's so easy, at these things, for authors to come across as snobby and pretentious. That's almost certainly a misleading impression, yet it's worth combating anyway. A short, friendly email that touches on some aspect of the previous night's conversation is easy to send. It's personal, and it'll help you to stand out from the crowd. Don't allow these things to stay on the bottom end of your 'to do' list. Retail buyers are, by far, the most important people in your life right now, so take them seriously.

E-BOOK PRICING

The price of print books is, rather obviously, constrained by the cost of printing, storing, and shifting the things. All that, plus the risk of collecting and pulping them if they don't sell.

E-books are different. Amazon is happy to sell e-books as cheaply as $0.99. In practice, because Apple is happy to 'sell' them for free, Amazon will generally price-match, so the price range is anywhere from nothing at all to $12 and more.

Where your book lives on this spectrum is essentially a matter of commercial strategy. Yes, your book has to contribute to the various fixed costs of publication (your advance, the editing process, and all that). But does it make the biggest contribution by shifting a load of units at $2.99? Or not very many units at $11.99? Or does it contribute best by attracting a zillion readers into your series, with rock-bottom pricing of $0.99 and $0.00, on the basis that those readers will love your work so much they'll buy your subsequent books at full price?

That's one set of questions, but here's another. Let's say, for example, that your sales team has got you great placement with the supermarkets, who have ordered some great volume of hardbacks. The sales team has probably got a great order like that by discounting heavily, thereby squeezing the publisher's own take, and yours. At the same time, you really, really want those hardbacks to sell, because that'll earn you money, it'll set up the paperback very nicely, and it'll start to build your readership right where you want it. Great.

But if the supermarkets are currently trying to shift hardbacks at (say) $19.99, discounted down from $27, they're not going to be thrilled to find that your publisher is simultaneously offering the e-book at $0.99. For that reason, publishers have typically stuck a 'do not buy me now' price on the e-book. For example, as I write, I'm looking at *Blowout,* a new release by Rachel Maddow. The sticker price for the hardback is $30, but it's being discounted down to as little as $17.99, online and in store. Because the publisher wants to shift plenty of hardbacks, the Kindle price for the book is $15.99 – just two bucks less than the hardback. That's a horrible way to sell e-books, obviously, but the publisher isn't trying to sell e-books. They are trying to defend the print market.

If you have the temerity to complain, publishers will remind you that the e-book price can always be pulled right down when it comes to the transition to paperback. Which is correct as far as it goes, but also misses the point. The launch of a book is a sacred thing. That's the moment at which it's easiest to attract traffic to the Amazon page. That's when it's easiest to clamber onto bestseller lists, to get 'hot new release' promotions and the rest. So if you murder the e-book's chances at launch, your chances of reviving it down the road are seriously impaired.

In addition, the step down from those $15.99 type prices is often very modest. Perhaps just a step down to $11.99 or $9.99. You won't generate much of a sales revival with those prices either.

So what to do? Well, the controversy has a simple resolution – in principle. If you have a ton of bricks-and-mortar retail uptake, you support their sales by pricing your e-books high. If, on the other hand, you don't have a ton of retail uptake, there's no point in continuing to price the e-book as though you did. Under those circumstances, then, publishers should switch seamlessly from a physical-first strategy to an online-first one. Under both strategies, you'd continue to sell books through every outlet you could. It's just that the lead motor would be different.

IN PUBLISHER LAND

Alas, however, things are not always so easily resolved. In Publisher Land, low-cost e-books feel like a threat to the ecosystem. The apocalyptic scenario runs like this: publishers price e-books cheaply for authors who don't have great uptake in physical retail. Consumers drift from hardbacks to e-books. Everyone makes less money from hardbacks than they did. Supermarkets shift their shelf space to other products. A few independent stores go bust. Print runs get smaller. Unit costs go up, forcing prices upwards and increasing the gap between hardbacks and e-books.

A death spiral looms.

It can therefore happen that your publishers – the same ones who were so friendly and excited when they took you on – will choose to restrict your digital sales in order to shelter the hardback sales accruing to some other lucky author. That's not conspiracy theory. The CEO of Hachette, for one, has given interviews explicitly setting out this strategy.

But this approach may be terrible for you. If physical retailers don't do well with your book, you want your publisher to prioritise your sales on Amazon. (I mention Amazon relentlessly in this context because it is 85% or so of online sales. Apple and the rest are also-rans.) The first huge step in that re-ordering of priorities would involve dropping your e-book price to $5.99 at the most. If they don't do that – if they keep the e-book price in excess of $10 – your publisher is deliberately injuring your sales on Amazon, in full knowledge of the fact that physical retail cannot save you.

The implications for your career? Probably fatal. In short, if you are not one of those authors whose books are piled high in the supermarkets, you may have a fight on your hands.

And you need to fight it.

That short sentence gets a whole paragraph to itself, with some hand-twirled italics to boot, because it's so damn important. You *must* fight for low e-book pricing for your debut novel, unless your book commands a ton of retail space (in which case, just let your publishers do what they do). You may not get what you want with sweet words and gentle reason. You may need to make a pest of yourself – and a pest who pushes hard at the same issue, week after week, month after month.

Don't be afraid to do it. Your career may depend on it.

You mustn't just secure that low pricing; you need to position yourself to benefit. And how do you do that? Simple: you build a great author platform. I'll just zip through a couple of chapters on publicity and other marketing, then we'll talk about platform.

Sit tight. The next few chapters are important.

PUBLICITY

Publicity, publicity, there's nothing like publicity
It's the goal of every writer, it is market-electricity.
You may find it in the papers, you may find it on TV,
But you must not fail to find it, for publicity's the key.

And should you find an author with a suicidal air
Unshaven and unwashed, with an alcoholic glare,
His sickness is a fatal one; its cause, alas, too clear –
When publication day arrived, the publicity wasn't there!

With apologies to T. S. Eliot,
full-time publisher and part-time poet

Publicity matters. For a book to succeed, it needs excellent content. It needs a strong, clear, attractive cover design that is appropriate to the target audience. It needs an excellent retail platform. And it needs the oxygen of publicity, because publicity is likely to be the only means by which potential readers have their attention drawn to your book.

All larger publishers have in-house PR specialists. In my experience, these people are usually good and often excellent, but your book will constitute a small part of their overall workload. You won't have their concentrated attention for more than a limited period, and effective collaboration is crucial to a successful outcome. Whereas no author can have more than a limited influence on the sales and marketing process, an active author can make a huge and potentially vital difference to how the publicity pans out. It's the purpose of this section to ensure that you make as much of this process as you possibly can.

HOW PUBLICITY WORKS

Ideally, you'll meet your PR person a fair few weeks before publication – perhaps three to five months beforehand. You need this advance preparation because different media outlets require very different amounts of lead-time. A major news programme on radio or TV will make its crucial editorial decisions the day before the show, and likely adjust those in the hour or two before the show goes out. At the other end of the spectrum, a glossy magazine needs weeks or months of lead-time. Because you want your publicity to fire in one concentrated burst around publication date, you need your own PR team to juggle all those different lead-times and launch dates as best they can.

In the best of all possible worlds, that meeting with your publicist will be one-to-one; it will not be time-limited; it will be discursive and collaborative and allow plenty of room for brainstorming and lateral thinking. Those kinds of sessions work best because the best ideas don't always emerge first. Curious little facts about you that you've never seen to be of much consequence can come to make all the difference to the PR opportunities available. Larger ideas can grow out of casual comments. A campaign can take shape in a way that it never could have done had the meeting been brisker and more agenda-led.

Many authors will never have such a meeting. Most meetings are time-limited and not one-to-one. In most cases, your publicist will approach things with something like a plan of action already sketched out. That plan will certainly be based on your book. It will also be based on some discussions with your editor over strategy. It may also be based on a questionnaire about yourself that you've been asked to fill in and return. The result, most likely, will be a pretty decent set of ideas about how to proceed. The purpose of the meeting with you will be in order to check that you are available to do what needs to be done, and that there is no obvious impediment to the ideas under consideration. You are there to respond, not to initiate; to approve, not to instigate.

Either way, you'll end the meeting with a list of ideas to explore. If you are a novelist, those ideas are likely to centre on you rather than on the novel. You may well find that somewhat disconcerting – after all, it's the book that's meant to be the star of the show, not you – but the truth is that the publication of yet another novel by yet another debut novelist is not, in itself, a particularly newsworthy story. On the other hand, if there is a good human-interest tale in the making of the novel, there's scope for publicity there.

I turned to writing when my wife became seriously ill. I gave up my job as an investment banker to look after her and, in the process, wrote my first novel. That story, limited as it was, lay at the heart of a highly effective PR campaign. As far as I can recall, we achieved absolutely no publicity for the book itself. Every single element of the campaign centred in one way or another on my own personal story, which achieved a considerable degree of publicity.

If you are writing non-fiction, those strong personal stories are still potential ammo, of course, but you can also look to your subject matter. Thus, if you happen to have written a book about (let's say) the experience of Spanish flu in 1918, there is, to the world of 2020 and after, some obvious interest in what you have to say about pandemics.

Once you have your list of ideas, it will be your publicist's job to see how many of those can be made to happen. You should be on standby to do whatever is asked, but it's your publicist who has the contacts and the authority, so your role is merely supportive. On some occasions, a newspaper or magazine will want to send someone to interview and photograph you. On other occasions, the newspaper or magazine will want a 'first-person' piece, authored by you, and written to a particular brief. If you write something for a newspaper, you should be offered payment – and you should certainly take it, if so. If you are asked to write something and no one mentions payment, feel free to ask.

When it comes to the broadcast media, you're not likely to achieve significant national exposure unless your story is particularly remarkable, or your book particularly topical. Nevertheless, if you have something special to offer, there are opportunities, and you should gladly take them. In most cases, TV appearances will require you to travel. Radio appearances can usually be handled either by phone or (better still) by hooking up from your local radio studio.

Writers are often somewhat nervous of the whole PR enterprise, but it's generally a fairly pleasant experience. For one thing, the kind of journalists who come to interview writers are a different breed from the sort of journalists who hound politicians, expose celebrities and invent things. I've done a lot of stories with journalists specialising in human-interest stories and they've been a warm, lovely, sympathetic bunch. If you have specific concerns – things you do or don't want to talk about, for example – just say so. I've never once had a journalist betray a confidence or ignore any reasonable request for discretion.

Photographers are likewise easy. Any photographer who comes your way will specialise in features, not news – the basic difference being that a news photographer specialises in subjects who are running away from the camera; a features photographer is dealing with someone happy to stand and look at it. Photographers won't be expecting you to be the world's most beautiful or glamorous person. Nor do they need you to know what you're doing. Your job is to make the coffee and smile on command.

When it comes to interacting with the news media, no one will be out to stitch you up, make you look bad or interview you aggressively. Your book simply doesn't constitute that kind of story. At the same time, any relationship with the news media is apt to be a little jumpy, rather like dating somebody who suffers from attention deficit disorder combined with an acute inability to maintain personal relationships. You may talk enthusiastically with a radio editor on Tuesday about your projected contribution to their Thursday show, only to find out in the course of Wednesday evening that their attention has moved elsewhere. Or you may have been commissioned to write an article on your specialist subject for inclusion in a Sunday newspaper only to find that your article has been ditched at the last possible second and without anyone having had the courtesy to let you know. Don't take these things personally. It's not you; it's them. The pace of the modern rolling news cycle is so frenetic that these abrupt switches of attention are commonplace. All you can do is hope to ride the rollercoaster for long enough to get something from it.

TIMING

The ideal timing for all these things is simple. With non-fiction, you'd hope to be serialised in a newspaper a week or two before publication. (Serialisation, by the way, doesn't usually mean that a *series* of extracts will appear. If you're not already famous, then serialisation is almost certainly going to be a one-off.) Fiction is seldom serialised, so there's not quite such an obvious kick-off point, but most PR concentrates around publication date or just a little before. Either way, the aim of a strong campaign will be to have as much publicity as possible appearing within two or three weeks of launch. In practice, some compromises will be required. If, for example, a major women's magazine wants to run a feature on you in their November edition (which will go on sale in October), but your book comes out in early September, you'd be nuts not to agree to the proposal, simply because the dates aren't ideal. Occasionally, book release dates can even change.

You should also be aware that media folk are very touchy about priority and exclusivity. If *The Daily Yadda* has profiled you for their health page, *The Morning Blah* won't even think about using your story, no matter that *The Yadda's* readers don't overlap with *The Blah's*. Having said that, a major regional newspaper won't feel upset if a national has previously run a piece, and a minor regional newspaper won't care if the entire world has already run a piece. Equally, the women's magazines see themselves as distinct from the newspapers, and tabloids to some extent regard themselves as different from the broadsheets. To human beings of normal sanity, these prickly feelings of jealousy and precedence are all rather hard to understand – but who cares? You have a publicist whose job it is to enter the jungle and deal with its beasts. Your job is to do what you're told.

Finally, if you're concerned that two weeks after the publication date everything seems to have gone quiet, you needn't be. It certainly will have gone quiet, but it's gone quiet because by this point your book is no longer newsworthy, and neither *The Yadda*, nor *The Blah*, nor the *Women's Chitterchatter*, nor even your reliable friend the *Shawangunk Clarion* has got time for you. The good ship Publicity has now steamed on by. You may bid it farewell.

SUPPORTING THE PROCESS

For all that the media game is best played by specialists, you can do a lot to help. Sometimes – in the best cases – you'll find that your publicist spends real time with you, collaboratively working out a plan of action. This, however, is unlikely to happen. It's much more likely that the meeting with your publicist will be relatively cursory and non-collaborative. If you are well-prepared, you may end up coaxing a genuine (albeit temporary) partnership into being or, at the very least, tabling some ideas which wouldn't have been there otherwise.

One tip is that you should try to arrange your meeting with the PR person so that you have real time with him or (more likely) her. If you are trying to discuss a PR campaign when your editor is in the room, along with someone from marketing, someone from the rights department and someone else called Becky who seems really smiley but whose job function you didn't quite catch, then the meeting won't have much patience for a long discussion. Therefore, either ask beforehand if you can book an hour or so's slot with your publicist, or politely suggest that the person from marketing, the person from rights and Smiley Becky all make a move, because you want to focus for an hour or so on PR. Everyone will greet your suggestion with relief, except for Smiley Becky, who will simply smile.

Second, the more you can do to generate ideas, the better. The trouble with most authors, of course, is that they're deeply ignorant. Not ignorant of the important things in life – mass unemployment, Victorian parlour games, the life and loves of Jackie Kennedy, or whatever else it is they've written about – but ignorant of the media world. The key to success in PR is to find the right intersection between what the media wants and what you have to talk about. The more realism you can bring to what the media are interested in, the more usefully creative your ideas will be. It's difficult for a book like this to suggest the sort of ideas which will work for your particular situation, but the following list should at least get you thinking on the right lines.

Human interest

If there is a human-interest story that lies behind your writing, then it's a very strong angle for publicity. For example:

- You have two children with learning disabilities – a subject that lies at the heart of your novel.
- You suffer from a rare but colourful condition. Writing a novel has been the only thing that kept you sane.
- You ended an abusive relationship after being hospitalised by your husband. You found that only through writing could you deal with your experiences.
- You competed in the Olympics, but realised that you are a writer first and foremost and gave up sport to focus on your art.
- You have breast cancer; you've been treated for it; you're in remission. While undergoing tests and surgery, you started to plan and write your novel.

You'll notice that there's a certain mawkishness in most of these examples, and it's perfectly true that 'human interest' normally involves an illness, a disability, a lousy relationship or a Triumph Over The Odds. It's also true that you may well feel that, when your story is condensed to a soundbite, the truth has somehow evaporated away in the process. For example, perhaps your breast cancer had damn all to do with the novel. Perhaps you always wanted to write a novel and it so happened that you had just begun on chapter 1 when you were first diagnosed and treated. You never connected the two; you don't see why anyone else should either.

Don't worry about such details. No one else will. Really, the template for your story has already been written. It is the job of the PR industry and the feature-writing media to find subjects to fill that template. If they can shove you into it, smile gracefully and let yourself be shoved.

A corollary of these comments is that you shouldn't be too shy about volunteering information that might be relevant. You once played for the XYZ Football Club? Then that's of interest. You nursed your father as he died of Hodgkin's? Say so. Your mother was a noted politician? Mention it. Depending on the exact circumstances of your situation and your book, these things may or may not be relevant, but it's not for you to decide. Your job is to give your publicist the fullest possible view of the available materials and let them pick the ones that work for them.

Features

Widening the net, you should muse about what kind of features you could write. Ideally, those features will be clearly related to your book. If you have written about a tropical paradise, pitch a feature which looks at the environmental degradation that's currently threatening the area. If you've written a book about the death of community in a coal-mining area, offer to write about the human costs of environmentalism.

You needn't, however, be too hung up on relevance. I was once seeking to promote a novel that dealt with aviation in the United States in the 1920s. Quite separately, the *Financial Times* asked me to write a travel-style piece for them covering a ceremony in St George's Chapel in Windsor Castle. The *FT* article had nothing at all to do with my novel, but the opportunity was too good to turn down. I wrote the piece. I stuck in a section at the end that linked the (rather elderly) Knights of the Garter who had just processed down the aisle with the (rather youthful) fighter aces of the First World War. The connection was forced, but the article read well, the *FT* paid well, and the piece got something about my novel across to numerous readers. Any publicity is good publicity.

In coming up with ideas for possible features, don't try to make a list in a single twenty-minute session at your computer. Ideas will bubble up over hours and days. Make a list of possible ideas. Discard ones that sound awful, but leave the rest. Also, try to broaden your media consumption, at least for a while or until insanity beckons. *The Daily Yadda* will have specific slots on a Tuesday that they don't have on any other day. *The Morning Blah* will have openings that *The Yadda* wouldn't consider. *The Sunday Tree-Destroyer* will have a host of regular features that need to be filled every week ('Me and My Pet', 'Like Father, Like Son', 'My First Car', What's in My Wallet', etc). Identify the slots that exist, then check to see if you've got anything that might plausibly fill them.

When you've assembled your list of ideas (which will, ideally, be as specific about possible media slots as possible), you should show them to your publicist. She may well leap on ideas that you thought weak and discard ones that you thought strong, but that's her job. Your task is to be bountiful. Hers is to be selective. If none of your ideas are rejected, you should have thought of more.

The news

Not often, but occasionally, it is possible to shoehorn your book into an existing national debate. Let's say, for example, that the media is abuzz with some story about declining standards in schools. You just so happen to have written a memoir describing your schooldays in the late 1950s. If you can find a way to tie your memoir into the national debate, then so much the better.

You need to watch the news story as it develops day by day. Propose ideas to your publicist. Don't say, 'I could write something about my memoir.' Say, 'I could do a 1,200-word piece for the 'Well Schooled' column of the *Boston Bugler*, looking at the best and worst of old-fashioned education.' That gives the publicist an outlet and an angle. All she needs to do is make the call.

Still better, it sometimes happens that you can – in a very modest way – seek to *create* a news story. You won't be able to create one from scratch, but let's say that a senior politician has called for a return to the values of the 1950s in education. You could perhaps write a direct attack on that politician and seek to place the piece in a newspaper where it will attract the maximum degree of attention – the politician's local newspaper, for example. Your attack then becomes fodder for rejoinder, debate and discussion – and presto! your campaign has taken on a life beyond the humble author-writes-book story. Articles may start to appear that you and your publicist did not yourself initiate. This is the sweet spot of all PR. It's rare that a particular book and a particular news story coincide well enough to achieve this happy outcome, but it's worth reaching for if you possibly can.

Special interests in mainstream publications

The appetite of newspapers for content is never-ending. The property sections need to create new features on property every week. The motoring sections need something on cars. The money pages need their column inches filled, as do the travel pages, the health pages, the science and technology pages, and so forth.

One of my books was promoted by, among other things, a front-page article in the property section of a Sunday newspaper about our impending house sale. Most of the article was about the house, but there was a column inch or two in which the journalist gushed about what a wonderful place it had been for me to write my novels. At the end of the article, there was some blurb in italics giving the title and cost of my latest book. The article hardly constituted the world's most accurately directed publicity, but who cared? It was on the front page of its own section and landed on the brunch tables of 1.2 million readers.

Again, the way you need to operate is by generating ideas for your publicist to amend, use or discard as she sees fit – but, if you don't mention that you are selling your beautiful home, or restoring your beloved 1920s Harley-Davidson, or have learned Balinese cookery from an acknowledged Balinese master, she won't even be able to get started.

Specialist journals

One of the reviews I've had which gave me the most pleasure was a small piece in *Accountancy Age*. The review gave me pleasure not because it was flattering, but because it was there at all. No one ever thinks to give interesting books to *Accountancy Age* to review. They review books all right, but the majority have titles like *New Approaches to the Pricing of Untraded Securities*, or *FIFO vs LIFO: The Everlasting Debate*. My book wasn't about accounting, but it was a financial thriller and either my publicist or I had the bright idea that maybe, once in a while, accountants would like to read a financial thriller. So we sent them my novel and asked them to review it. And they did. No ask, no get.

Bloggers

Publicists these days will take as much care with the major bloggers in your niche as they used to take with the major newspaper book editors. And 'take care' here means quite literally. A prominent crime blogger at a crime festival would be able to get wined and dined by publishers at every single mealtime if they chose. A big blogger can shift books.

Most of those bloggers will simply be authoritative online reviewers, in which case your task is mostly to write a great book and hope the blogger reviews it with kindness. It would be nice if bloggers respected your publication schedule in terms of timing, but those guys have TBR piles higher than their heads, and it's not uncommon for a review – your cherished review – to come out six months after your book is published. That still helps – it's fodder for your Amazon page and your paperback cover – but it won't directly create any meaningful sales. Other times, bloggers want author interviews or other items designed to fit specific content slots in the blog. ('My influences' or 'How I come up with ideas' or whatever else.) If the blog has reasonable traffic and authority, it's well worth doing what you can to grab those slots.

Equally, if you go to festivals and other places where writers, readers and bloggers congregate, you should regard bloggers as being amongst the most important people in any room. It's important to network with other authors and essential to network with anyone there who is from the retail side. But bloggers matter too, perhaps even more than authors. Offer to buy them drinks. Make nice. Be interested in them. Don't push yourself forward. Email a nice-to-meet-you after the event. You don't even have to make a request. The bloggers know who you are and what you want. If they liked you and liked your book, they'll probably do what they can for you.

Oh yes, and if you are not a crime author, you have made a very serious error, because crime bloggers are the best.

Local outlets

Lastly, don't forget your local newspaper and local radio stations. These outfits love local authors. The papers will come and interview you for every book you release. The radio station will happily give you a fifteen- or thirty- minute slot chatting with Radio Nowhere's favourite DJ, and all you'll have to do to earn it is sit through the various easy-listening tracks that will intersperse your musings. These outlets aren't going to make a vast difference to your book sales, but they may make some. The engagements are also both fun and local – a good combination. Your publicist will probably be happy to set these things up herself, but, if she's reluctant, just make the calls yourself. Don't be shy. Local outlets are hungry for local celebrities and, if you're not much of a celebrity, you can comfort yourself with the thought that they're not much of a newspaper or radio station either. You guys were made for each other.

These suggestions should certainly be enough to set you on your way. Above all, bear in mind (1) that you are the story as much as your book; (2) that you need to be proactive in developing ideas; and (3) that you need to shape your suggestions around the needs of different media outlets and the existing slots that require daily or weekly content.

GOING GRANULAR

Your main route to sales will be your publisher's sales team. If those guys attract a lot of retail support, your book will be on a lot of shelves. Sheer footfall will be enough to make your book drop winningly into a lot of shopping baskets.

If you have had success on the publicity front, that will also help. It's not even that buyers are driven to buy a book because (let's say) they saw a mother-and-daughter piece in a woman's magazine. It's more that, when buyers are surveying a table of books, your name is the one that pops out, because it's already faintly familiar from that article.

All that still leaves plenty of scope for additional marketing activity.

A lot of that marketing takes place online. Unless your publisher actually hates you, there'll be some activity on Twitter. Ditto something on Facebook. Ditto something in terms of newsletters and house blogs.

But you need to distinguish between marketing aimed at keeping you happy and marketing aimed at selling books. 'Hey, author, look at our wonderful cover reveal Tweet. Isn't that *great*? And we've had five retweets already. *Amazing*.' The trouble with this kind of guff is that marketing of this sort costs nothing – and doesn't work. I talked with one head of digital marketing at a Big Five house who told me that she thought Twitter didn't sell books. Which would hardly be surprising: no one buys a book because of a sales pitch that takes place in 280 characters or less. (The exception? If an author already has a large following, Twitter functions as a notification tool. 'Author X has a new book out. You know you're going to buy it, because you bought all her others. So you may as well buy it now.')

That's not to say, though, that digital can't work. It's just that you have to have a strategy which starts with the book and its particular promise. That means figuring out which readers to target and which channels are going to work best for those readers, then putting together a multi-channel campaign which will touch your ideal readers in the right way and at multiple points in their online/offline life.

SHEILA, WHO LOVES ANIMALS

You can and should help to get that campaign organised and effective. You need to think hard about your ideal reader. A lot of professional marketers (and self-publishers) like to visualise an actual person. 'Sheila is an aspirational thirty-something, with a college degree in pharmacy. She is now a stay-at-home mother-of-two. She loves animals and the outdoors ...' That kind of thing doesn't work for me personally, but I recommend you at least consider the strategy. Lots of people who are better marketers than I am swear by it.

Then you need to figure out the available touchpoints. Where can you connect to Sheila? Yes, Sheila probably watches *American Idol*. She also probably loves the latest big show from Netflix. But your publisher isn't about to take TV ads out and, in any case, no mass-market show offers a granular definition of your reader – and you want granular. You're always looking to find locations that your ideal reader *does* love and that other people *don't*. The key of marketing success in an online world is total specificity.

Let's say, for example, you're writing a crime series involving a mother-of-two detective based in Little Rock, Arkansas. You're going to be on the search for such things as:

- Bloggers who write about crime set in the American South.

- Bloggers who are stay-at-home mums, and like reviewing crime.
- Bloggers with an interest in true crime set in Arkansas. (They might not have an interest in your book because it's not true crime, but the Arkansas connection might be enough to sway it. It's worth the email.)
- Facebook groups with an American south/crime focus.
- Facebook groups that focus on female protagonists in crime.
- Facebook groups that somehow combine stay-at-home mothers and crime fiction.
- Any well-populated Twitter hashtags that somehow bind together your themes.
- Any local radio shows that work well for your themes.
- Any local print media that might work.

The closer you can get to your ideal targets, the better. You'll get more enthusiasm from the blogger and much higher conversion rates from your audience too. But it's not enough just to take your publisher a list of blogs and Facebook groups. You need to find routes into those things ... and in most cases, the route in question is you.

So, let's say you find a blogger with a well-populated blog in your target area. Yes, your publisher could write a corporate email offering a review copy or two. And that might work. A bit, sometimes. Much better though, you could seek to e-know the blogger. You offer review copies. You offer a Facebook Live, 'ask the author' session. You run a quiz. You send the blogger a review copy wrapped in a map of Little Rock and fastened with a chain. And so on. The Holy Trinity of this kind of marketing is simple. First, you need to find the right partner – the blog or chat group where your ideal readers, your Sheilas, assemble. Next, you need to find the right approach route – the gimmick or hook that excites your audience. And third, you need you. You're the face of the brand. You are its Coco Chanel.

The best campaigns work with seamless unity between marketing team and author. You find the blogger. The marketing team comes up with a nicely packaged gimmick. You work your contacts according to who has the best entrance route.

And stay granular. It always works best. It's easy to think that your potential readership won't be defined by boxes on some stupid checklist. (Stay-at-home mother? Check. American South? Check. And so on.) You're right – but also wrong. Although your readership group will extend far beyond that core, you can't easily reach them, and you'll almost certainly be unable to find the five to seven touchpoints that are said to be necessary before a purchase takes place. So build your core. That's been the secret behind the huge success of indie authors. It's the secret behind almost any successful online marketing. Build your core. Build your brand ambassadors. Sales will work outward from there, the same as a fire builds from the red-hot core at its heart.

TWO POSTERS AT GATWICK AIRPORT

Once upon a time, many moons ago, I wrote a book. It was a rather good one: called *The Sons of Adam*. It was to be published by HarperCollins and, when my agent and I negotiated a contract with them, the firm listed out in a schedule all the great marketing stuff they were going to do. Not *intending* to do, please note, but going to do. Committing to do.

The items on the list weren't stupid little free things, like doing cover reveals on Twitter. They were socking great expensive things, like full-size posters at mainline rail stations. The firm had big hopes for the book, and they were intending to push it hard. The plan was to establish me as a properly bestselling brandname author.

But …

(All good stories about publishing have a 'but' and, luckily, that wicked little conjunction is never in short supply.)

But the key retailer for the book – WHSmith, a massive British bookseller – decided not to buy it. It placed an order of exactly zero copies. Quite why this was, I don't know. The firm had been highly supportive of my earlier books, and we'd sold a lot of them. But there had been management changes at the firm, and I guess the new managers needed to show they were doing something different from the last lot.

In any case, our core retailer just bailed out. That shouldn't, in fact, have altered anything much. HarperCollins had contracted to fulfil a certain number of marketing pledges and had undertaken that if it couldn't, for example, fulfil item (d) on the list, it would replace that item by something of equal value. And a contract, remember, is a sacred thing. A promise, enforceable in court. A company's most sacred promise.

The firm's most sacred promise, however, turned out to be worthless. They did virtually no marketing. Told me, not very apologetically, that it wouldn't be cost-effective. When I threw a full-scale Authorial Tantrum, they agreed to put up two paltry little posters at Gatwick Airport. Those posters didn't even remotely amount to the campaign I'd been promised. HarperCollins didn't pretend otherwise. They just didn't care.

I didn't seek enforcement action via the courts. I couldn't have afforded it. It would have destroyed my relationship with the firm that was still my publisher. The book, which was a good 'un, didn't bomb exactly, but sold far below its real potential. That sales failure basically ended the first spell of my fiction career. It was a crash from which I was unable to struggle out.

I tell this depressing little story to make a point. If your publisher decides – probably because it's disappointed by bricks–and–mortar retail uptake – to withhold any serious attempt at marketing, your book will never sell well. You probably won't be told that your book has been quietly murdered. You'll only start to suspect something when you notice your publisher's early enthusiasm has altered into a kind of fixed, muted politeness. But you can't do anything. You've sold the rights. Marketing decisions lie with your publisher. The best you can do is seize the initiative yourself. To seize the marketing reins and gallop that horse as fast as you can.

It's to that subject we now turn.

Your Digital Platform

Ah! Finally.

We delay no further. We've reached the whole complicated and disconcerting matter of your digital platform. It's become a truism that authors have to take on more of their own marketing than ever before. It's also become a truism that social media and other digital channels are more important than ever. At the same time, publishers never quite come out and say it. They say, if pressed, that they'll design their marketing campaigns around the book and the author. So if, for example, you hate Twitter, publishers would simply deploy other channels instead.

Not all those propositions can be true at once, but there's a second nest of issues in any case. If author-led marketing does matter, what exactly are you expected to do? If you don't currently have a Twitter account, it'll only take you a minute to get one. But then what? An authorial platform isn't about what accounts you have. It's about the followers you have: your audience. It can take years to build a real audience on any platform you care to think about – blogs, Twitter, Facebook, whatever else. Not just that, but mere statistics are pretty much worthless. It's not numbers which count, but engagement. You don't just need an audience, you need an *engaged* audience, a loyal audience. And that takes months and years of hard work.

These issues are murky mostly because the answers aren't quite clear and satisfying, but I'll do what I can to clear them up. Oh, and there is one bright, shining lamp of truth here – a digital strategy which any sane author should adopt as fully as possible and as early as possible. It's not a lot of work and it doesn't involve endless, stupid self-promotion on Twitter. We'll get to that bright and shiny object very soon.

WHAT'S THE POINT OF DIGITAL?

Let's start, however, by stepping back. The purpose of any kind of digital strategy is to sell books. That's it. If a certain element of your digital strategy furthers that goal, then good. Go ahead. If any element does not further that goal, don't waste your time.

That message might risk making your gums bleed from sheer obviousness, but bear with me. Far too many authors haven't detached their real-self from their author-self. So let's say your real-self enjoys shouting about politics, trolling celebrities, and exchanging vegan recipes online. That's fine. Please do all those things with my blessing. But those things won't help sell your books unless they directly engage your audience. So if you're a talk-radio host with a political book about to hit the shelves, your author-self should absolutely be using Twitter to yell about politics. But if you have a sweet romance about to hit the shelves, then an abrasive online political identity is utterly unhelpful.

So your first task is a simple one. Split your real-self from your author-self. You should have a Facebook page for each. You should have a Twitter account for each. (Or, better, you should let your author-self take over your Twitter account.) The specifics of how you handle this matter less than the overall purpose, which is to make sure that anyone going online to encounter author-you will find a nicely curated version of just that. The sweet-romance novelist will present to her audience as a sweet-romance novelist. What you get up to with your real-self accounts will be hidden or muzzled.

So much for basics. But Facebook and Twitter aren't going to lie at the heart of your digital strategy. We'll turn to them in more detail before we clamber to the end of this chapter. First though, we get to the heart of your digital strategy: the huge, beating motor that lies at the heart of all good author-led marketing.

We're talking websites. We're talking mailing lists. And we're talking Amazon.

YOUR WEBSITE: WHY IT MATTERS

Your website matters. It matters a lot. It is the most precious digital asset you will ever have. And most authors, more than 90% of authors, get it wrong. That sounds scary, perhaps, but most authors mess up because they don't understand the purpose of a website.

So, recite after me: *the purpose of your website is to collect email addresses.* That's it. That's why you have one. That's the central pillar of your entire digital strategy: the purpose of your website is to collect the email addresses of readers so you can contact them again in the future.

It's OK if your site has other purposes too. A bio, so people can find out more about you. A contact page, so people can reach you. And so on. But the primary purpose of your site is just what I said it is. It's to collect email addresses, nothing else.

Now some of you may be a bit perplexed. Shouldn't 'selling books' be a primary purpose of the website? Isn't that the whole point of our digital strategy anyway? Well, yes. Duh! But also no, because no one in the whole world ever has gone to an author's website in order to purchase a book. You go to Amazon to do that. (Or Apple Books or an actual bookshop.) So readers come to your website not to buy a book, but to engage with you in some other way. Some of those ways will be the secondary ones (making contact, find a bio) but the one that matters to you the most is collecting the email addresses of readers.

To understand why that is quite so wickedly important, you need to understand the way Amazon works. In particular, you need to understand that Amazon is a bookstore quite unlike any physical store you've ever entered. When you walk into a Barnes & Noble, the books laid out on the front tables are the books that the store manager thinks will most appeal to most book-buyers. It's a deliberately average, middle-of-the-road selection.

Amazon isn't like that. When you're logged in to Amazon (as you are by default), Amazon magically re-arranges its entire store to present the books and other items that it thinks you personally are most likely to buy. There is a different Amazon store for every visitor. The 'recommended for you' titles are algorithmically picked from your history of past purchases and past searches. And that's just a part of Amazon's zillion-and-one marketing channels. It also deploys marketing emails, 'hot new releases', granular bestseller lists and much more.

You kind of know all this. But here's the thing: Amazon's little marketing robots need fodder. And your mailing list is going to supply that fodder.

Here's what you do. You're going to build a mailing list using the tools I'm about to give you. Then, when your next book comes out, you are going to email your readers to say, 'Hey, I've got a new book out, and I know you love my work because you signed up to my mailing list, so go and buy that book now.' If you are a delicate, professional and eloquent author, you may wish to adapt the text of that email, but the gist will be the same. You are asking your readers to go and buy your book. You can do the same thing on Twitter, but you would be actually lucky to get a 0.1% conversion rate. The same thing delivered by email can easily achieve a 30% conversion rate. What's more, those conversions will be delivered over a very narrow window, with most people either buying or choosing not to buy your book within twenty-four hours of your mail-out.

So let's say you have a mailing list of 1,000 names. And let's say you have a conversion rate of 30%. You have taken 1000 pre-existing readers and achieved sales of 300 copies. That sounds good in a way, but not spectacular. Those 300 sales were always going to be the easiest to achieve, so it looks like a long haul still lies ahead of you.

Except that logic forgets about Amazon. What you've just done is trigger a surge of sales in your book. That sales surge blasts you up the bestseller lists. In thinking about this, it helps to know that the Amazon bestseller lists are updated hourly and that they are very sensitive indeed to recency of sales. The sales you made in the last twenty-four hours account for a full 50% of your entire sales rank. The sales you made over the last five days accounts for 97% of it. Therefore, a quick blast of sales delivered via your mailing list will achieve real visibility on Amazon, even if you have no past sales history to draw on.

Amazon loves and adores that visibility. I said that its marketing robots are always anxious to adapt the store to the specific tastes of those entering. If, let's say, you write sweet romance, and you've just shifted 300 copies in twenty-four hours, Amazon's marketing robots are going to think, 'Wow, this book is really selling well. It won't interest those looking for computer textbooks or steampunk fantasy, but all those sweet romance readers will love it. We have to get this book under their noses right now.' All of a sudden, your book will be shown to the readers most likely to love it.

Oh, reader, that sentence is so beautiful I am compelled to repeat it:

Your book will be shown to the readers most likely to love it.

If you like, you can add another little clause to the end of that sentence: *'by the marketing algorithms of the world's largest and most sophisticated bookstore.'*

So you get the largest audience of readers in the world. Plus you get some incredibly sophisticated marketing tools analysing that audience to find the very best readers for you.

And visibility delivers sales. The reason why supermarkets are good at selling books has nothing to do with the supermarket environment which is, in fact, a terrible one for books. Supermarkets achieve the sales they do because of footfall. Send ten million shoppers past a bookstand featuring your book and even a tiny conversion rate will end up delivering a big heap of sales. It's the same with Amazon, only better – much better – because the readers who come to see your book are the group that you would most choose to target.

That is why any competent author-led marketing project starts with a mailing list. That mailing list delivers visibility. And visibility, delivered Amazon-style, will deliver sales. Indeed, the sales you can achieve via your mailing list are vastly greater than the size of the mailing list itself. More bluntly still: the simplest way to achieve sales success on Amazon is to have a strong and well-functioning email list. It's the most precious marketing commodity you can have.

That email list will last you from book to book, and from publisher to publisher. If ever you choose to quit traditional publishing, that email list will mean you step straight into a self-publishing career that is, more likely, more lucrative than the traditional one you left behind. I recognise that you can't fully absorb the truth of these comments until you've witnessed them in the context of your own work and your own sales, but you can take me at my word. Your mailing list is critical. It should be the central plank not just in your digital strategy, but in your sales strategy, period. Twitter and Facebook and all those other platforms? They're secondary. Forget the hype and focus on what works.

YOUR MAILING LIST: HOW TO CREATE IT

The way you're going to collect those email addresses is simple. It works like this:

1. *You write a story.* That story will be set in the world of your book – it's often a prequel, but anything that deploys the same style, characters and world is fine. The story wants to feel rich and satisfying, but it shouldn't be unduly burdensome for you to write. I'd suggest that anything in the 10–15,000-word drop zone feels about right, but you can write a bit shorter or a bit longer, as you prefer. If you write non-fiction, then you can really offer anything. A spreadsheet. A cheat sheet. A set of swipe copy. Whatever you like.

2. *You turn that story into a properly formatted e-book.* You need a professional-looking cover. Try Googling 'pre-made book cover' for a low-cost solution. You then need to

create the e-book file (which is different from a Word document or a PDF). The easiest way to do this is probably via Draft2Digital, which offers an easy and free con-conversion tool. You now have a properly formatted e-book that can be viewed on any e-reader. To avoid confusion, I'm now going to call that file your 'reader magnet' – it's the free gift that you're going to use to attract readers and their email addresses.

3. *You get your publisher to set up your for-sale e-book correctly.* We're talking now about your actual book: the 70,000–word labour of love that you've worked so hard to write, edit and now publish. You are going to make sure that the e-version of that book says, loud and clear, 'Hey, readers, if you loved this book, you can get a free short story that is available only to members of my Readers' Club.' You want to make the offer at multiple points in the front and back matter of your e-book. (You may as well make the offer in the print book too, but the conversion rate will be vanishingly small.) Do not under any circumstances allow your publisher to make those decisions for you, as they are quite likely to bury your offer. Love and revere publishers though I surely do, I will say that their understanding of author mailing lists is on a par with that of your Aunt Mildred who lives in a nursing home in Albuquerque and believes that a computer is what you get when you add a human being and some slide rules. Getting proper calls to action in your e-book is going to be a task for you. Insist on seeing a preview of your draft e-book as early as possible in the production process. If it's not right, ask for it to be changed. Go on asking until it's right.

4. *Your publisher publishes your actual, for-sale book.* When the publisher launches your debut novel, your mailing list has exactly zero names on it. Your mailing-list-powered contribution to sales is also nil.

5. *Readers read your book and love it.* They also encounter a message which says, 'Hey, reader, do you want a free story?' Naturally, they realise that is precisely what they want.

6. *Readers click the link in your e-book which passes them through to your website.* You've promised readers that free reader magnet, so you need to deliver it. Your website is the place that makes this exchange. It's where readers submit an email address and start the automated process that puts your reader magnet right onto their Kindles or other device. This exchange – email for story – is the crux of the whole mailing list strategy, and it takes place on your website. That's why getting your website correct is so utterly important. And when you collect all those lovely emails, they're not going to sit in a spreadsheet on your computer. You're going to sign up with an email service provider (ESP) to manage all that for you. Mailchimp used to be the ESP of choice among authors. It's just recently fallen a little out of favour to be replaced by Mailerlite (currently the best simple, low-cost service around) or Convertkit (a fancier service for the more ambitious author). Truth is, though, they all work fine. Pick whichever one you like.

7. *You deliver your reader magnet.* You could, in theory, do this just by pointing readers to a PDF document somewhere on your site, but that's a horrible way to engage with text online and, these days, looks really unprofessional. What you want to do is put a properly formatted e-book right onto their device itself (and in the right folder and all, so it opens up just as expected). You also want to do that in a way that means you don't get annoying tech questions from readers for the rest of your life. The solution to that is simple: it's called bookfunnel.com. The service is excellent and wonderfully cheap. Go for it.

8. *You continue to talk to readers.* Collecting emails is only part of it. If you only ever communicate with readers when you have a book out, your conversation will seem jumpy

and self-serving. Fiction authors should aim to write once a month. Non-fiction authors should write about weekly. (You can read my weekly emails via Jerichowriters.com as an example of how to manage the non-fiction mailings: sign up here.)[2] Your job with those emails isn't to sell anything. It's to build a relationship. If the relationship you create is strong, the selling email, when it comes, is the easiest one you ever have to write.

And that's it. That's how you collect reader emails, honestly, ethically and very successfully.

The super-fantastic and utterly brilliant thing about this technique is that it gets stronger every time you use it. Every time you launch a book, you use your mailing list to drive visibility on Amazon. That means a whole heap of new readers coming to your books. A good proportion of those new readers will join your mailing list, thereby beefing up its power and might. So when you next launch a book, you get even more visibility, even more new readers, even more sales.

Oh yes, and while we're listing the super-fantastic and utterly brilliant aspects of the author mailing list, I should mention that the technique works very well for traditionally published authors and even better for self-published authors. So creating that list early and maintaining it properly is a task that will sustain you, no matter what the ups and downs of your traditional career.

For that reason, if your publisher asks you if you would like them to build a website for you, you should be very wary indeed. I know one author, a bestseller across the English-speaking world, whose publisher asked her if she wanted a free website. I urged her to look at the small print of that offer very carefully ... and sure enough, although the website would have collected reader emails, that email list would have belonged to the publisher, not the author. If the author ever wanted to move on from her publisher, she'd have had to leave behind her entire mailing list.

---

[2] https://jerichowriters.com/sign-up-news-updates/

The publisher couldn't even have offered it to her for free; to do so would have breached basic data privacy laws.

Luckily, that author refused the offer. I know another author who did leave her publisher for another, more committed, one. But because she hadn't checked the ownership of her email list nearly early enough in her career, she found that moving publishers meant losing her entire list. You must not let that happen to you.

Please do understand that this chapter outlines the basic strategy you need to follow in creating the mailing list. It falls far short of giving you a detailed roadmap. That said, a few specific pointers will help.

First, I do recommend that you set up your website in Word-Press, and that you use Parallax for Writers (from gocreate.me) as your theme. If you don't know what I've just said, then pay someone to create the site for you, but using WordPress/Parallax for Writers. There are a million reasons why that's the right approach, but I'm not going to tell you what they are, so you'll just have to trust me.

Second, I do also recommend that you learn enough website basics that you can handle the ordinary, modest operation of your website yourself. It isn't hard, and if you always have to go through a third party to make minor website changes, your site will soon be as stuck as a campervan in a bog. That's not a good look, I promise.

Third, when you bring people from your actual for-sale e-book to your website, they need to come to a landing page, not a normal web page. So if you care to go to my author site (harrybingham.com), you'll notice that it looks pretty much like any author site ever – except cooler, because I have a great web designer. You'll also notice that the free e-book offer on my home page is rather prominent, to put it mildly. (But what's the point of a website? That's right: it's there to collect emails.) You'll also notice that the main navigation is in place. If you want to poke around the website, you're perfectly free to do just that.

Freedom and liberty are all very well in a way, but not when it comes to capturing emails. When readers of your paid-for e-book click that 'Get my free story' link, you don't want them to poke around your site. You want them to give you their email address. So readers of my e-books are directed not to my home page, but to a specially designed landing page.[3] If you click through to that page – and you blooming well should – you'll notice that the main navigation has vanished. It's not there. There is literally nothing you can do on that page except submit an email address or close the browser tab. That lack of distraction is absolutely critical to optimising conversions – and unless you are relentless and perfectionist about maximising conversions at every single stage of your process, you will end up with a mailing list that operates at about 25–50% of its maximum capacity. If the mailing list ends up being the primary motor of your sales, as it well may, then your laziness at the set-up stage has killed as much as three-quarters of your sales. Moral: don't be lazy.

Fourth and finally, this is a book on getting published. It is not a full and detailed primer on mailing lists or other elements of your digital strategy. But you do need that primer. A modern author cannot sensibly remain ignorant of these things. I strongly recommend Tammi Labrecque's book, *Newsletter Ninja*, which tells you how to operate your list to maximum effect. You also need a considerably more detailed guide on how to set up your e-book, your reader magnet, your website, and so on. The best source I know for all that is (sorry!) via a Jericho Writers membership, which gives you complete access to our self-publishing course. And yes, I do know you're publishing traditionally, but it's the self-pub course which goes into complete detail on mailing lists and all that. A Jericho membership doesn't have to cost much. Just buy a one-month subscription, grab the material you need, then cancel. We'd love you to stay longer, of course, but if you just grab-and-go, that's fine too. Oh yes, and we offer a complete course on getting published too, so if you have any

---

[3] https://harrybingham.com/lev-in-glasgow/

questions left after reading this book, a Jericho Writers member-ship will almost certainly sort you out.

And with that 'there's much more you need to know' caution ringing in your ears, we'll dive off to survey all those other digital platforms you probably want to know about.

OTHER DIGITAL PLATFORMS: BASICS

Your mailing list is by far the most important element of your platform. If you do only the most elementary set-up on Facebook and Twitter, and set up a mailing list correctly, you've done fine.

But, even if you want to stick to basics, there's no reason not to be professional. These days, any author should really have a website, a Twitter account and an author-page on Facebook. You don't need to be especially active on social media if you don't want to be, but you do want to make yourself open to the world. If readers care enough about your books that they want to contact you, you risk losing a loyal ambassador if you make yourself hard to reach. Some people will choose to reach you via email. Others will instinctively reach for Twitter or Facebook. If your book is something that's naturally visual, a cookbook or something on interior design perhaps, you'll probably want to be on Instagram and perhaps Pinterest too.

Nor is it only readers who may want to reach you. The chief executive of a major TV firm once contacted me via Twitter. He was interested in optioning one of my books for screen – a book where I'd already sold the rights, dammit – and chose to reach me via Twitter. That kind of outreach is something you deeply want to encourage, and that means keeping every door as wide open as you can manage. You also want to hear from journalists, bloggers, other authors in your sphere, festival organisers, broadcasters, after-dinner speaker agencies, experts in areas that your book touches on, creative writing organisations and many others. As you move from aspiring writer to emerging novelist, you are also moving from a deeply private sphere to one that is at least semi-public. You need to welcome that new world. And that means having the accounts that people expect you to have. As I say, for most authors, that will be website and Facebook and Twitter, at a minimum. I don't go beyond that minimum myself. Most authors don't need to.

Good. The next step is to manage your digital footprint as an exercise in branding, not one in self-expression. If you are a sweet-romance author, your profile photo doesn't want to show you dressed as a Goth and riding a Harley-Davidson. Likewise, the banner image you have on Facebook and Twitter wants to echo the look you have on your books. It's very common for first-time authors to make use of the cover image they have for their first book. That's fine, but you're leaving a hostage to fortune. If your paperback comes out with a different image, your Facebook/Twitter images will be out of date or off-message. And when you have multiple books to talk about, picking any one of them for that opening banner image seems like a wrong choice. A simple way to get round these issues is to echo the mood of your cover, but be rigorous about adopting the fonts and colours of your covers. As a sweet-romance author, you might use a banner image of woman-in-white-dress-in-spring-garden, let's say, and adorn that with a message written in the fonts of your book cover itself. That will look utterly consistent with the world of your fiction and will stay timelessly up to date even as you bring out more books.

While we're on these basics, you should also get used to look-ing at images in multiple formats. It's very common for authors to spend a lot of time getting their Facebook page looking just so on a desktop view ... but forget to look at the same thing on a phone. Very often words are sliced off or tops of heads go missing, and the effect, to put it mildly, is amateurish and clumsy. So just check, mobile and desktop, on everything always.

That said, if you're not very digitally minded and you're al-ready feeling daunted, remember this. Your product – the book – matters intensely. You need to be perfectionist about every detail. The same is true about everything in your list-building sequence. But it's not really true of anything else: the rest of your website, your author-page on Facebook, your Twitter profile and so on. With all those things, if you are roughly on-brand and moderately competent, you're doing fine. Truth is, you could do the whole lot, including your site, in an afternoon if you wanted to. A high level of digital polish just doesn't matter. You're not Coca-Cola. On-brand and not-incompetent is a low enough bar that you can wriggle over it with ease.

FACEBOOK: CREATING CONTENT

We've covered the elements of set-up, but we haven't yet talked about what content you should put out there.

The answer is simple. The content you are going to distribute will be material that your ideal reader really wants and *material that no one else really does*. A perfect Facebook page will be like a plateful of hot buttered toast for your ideal readers … and actively off-putting to everyone else. That might sound odd but think about it.

Let's say, for example, that you write fiction set in the American West during the Reconstruction era. Your ideal content could include any great pictures from that time. Little stories. Little things you've found from your research. Maybe any audio or video recordings that relate to that place and that period. So for a while, that's how you build your Facebook page, and your likes counter ticks slowly up.

Good. But then – tragedy! You notice that your paranormal-romance writing buddy has five times the number of likes you have … and you have a great idea. What about including a really funny cat video, because everyone likes a really funny cat video? You have some cute puppies at home as well, so how about including some home-video clips of those little cuties? You experiment along those lines, and soon enough you have more likes than your paranormal-romance buddy. So you've won, right?

Yes. You've just won a stupid and pointless contest that no one except you cared about. In the process of doing that, you've just corrupted your Facebook audience, probably beyond repair. Organic reach on Facebook is now heavily driven by engagement, and you have now just about killed it. When you come to your next book launch, you'll write a post that says 'Buy my book – it's great' and Facebook will experiment to see if anyone wants to hear that message. Yes, it'll show that message to some of your American West/Reconstruction fans, and those guys will go out and buy your book. But it'll also show the message to that horde of cat-lovers who never gave a damn for your books or your period. Those guys will murder your engagement rates, and Facebook will decide, quite rightly, that your post has no great organic reach potential, so it won't show your message to those you most want to see it.

That's bad, but it gets worse. Because while it's easy to purge your mailing list of non-clickers, there's no way to clean your Facebook likes of the dead wood. You'll have to scrap your page and start again. You have the exact same issue if you ever want to run ads to your Facebook audience. If you run those ads to your audience of combined lovers-of-Westerns and lovers-of-cat-videos, your ads will perform incredibly badly, because of all those damn cat-lovers.

So keep your content extremely narrow and extremely focused on your target readers. Those guys, and no one else.

How much content do you want to put out there? It's up to you. My own digital strategy is so heavily focused on my mailing list that I don't really bother with Twitter and Facebook. I'd get more sales if I did, but I have a young family. I'm heavily involved with Jericho Writers. And I can't do everything. If you have more time and more ambition, regular Facebook posting would be great. Two or three times a week would be ideal. Once a week would be absolutely fine. What you publish is much more important than how often.

TWITTER: HOW TO USE IT

With Twitter, your strategy will be different. You need to figure out where your community lies and what it talks about. Then you need to participate.

I know an author of Young Adult fiction who's really engaged in the Twitter chat that relates to YA fiction in general. There are agents and publishers involved in that chat. Also booksellers and bloggers and other opinion-formers. With YA fiction, there'll be plenty of teens engaging too. The topics will sometimes be excited ones relating to an upcoming launch. ('Hey, I've just seen a proof copy of X by Famous Author Y and I can't wait to read it.') Other times, it'll be talking about topics that matter to teens – for example, issues relating to mental health or cyber-bullying. And at other times, the topics will have to do with YA publishing in general. Whether, for example, the advent of sensitivity readers is a boon or a curse.

A good digital strategy here is simply – participate. Discuss the issues. Pass on the excitement. Make friends. Retweet things you care about. Share the love. And when you come to have a book out, you can hope that your community tweets and retweets and shares the love in its turn. It's not even that those tweets drive book sales directly. It's more that they drive them indirectly. Booksellers know you (or e-know you) and they want to support you. Your book gets picked for slots it wouldn't otherwise get. Librarians talk about you to schools. Bloggers ask to do interviews. And so on. You don't quite know how that map of digital connections drives sales, but the more you have, the better your chances of winning.

As it happens, I'm pretty much Trappist on Twitter myself – take a look if you don't believe me – but again, my time is limited, so I do less than I should. And simply having an open Twitter account means that people can contact you.

THE LONGEST CHAPTER

This has been, by far, the longest chapter in this book. It is also the one that most skims its subject matter. It is also, no question, one of the most important.

So please, let this chapter be your launch point for further exploration. A Jericho Writers membership[4] gives you a great way to do just that. If you prefer to explore elsewhere, you should do just that. The one thing you really shouldn't do is ignore the topic. I know far too many authors who start to recognise the importance of these topics two, or three or five books into their career. At that point, they start to address their omission, but what a tragic waste of opportunity! Even if you do the most limited basics with Facebook, Twitter and your mailing list, those five books could have given you a selling platform so strong, you could be confident of launching any book you wanted to write (so long as you're not genre-hopping) without any support from a publisher at all. You might still want that publisher support – why not? – but you could have built a sales motor that you own, control and operate.

So start now. That means: learn the ropes – don't just turn the page.

---

[4] https://members.jerichowriters.com/bazaar/full-membership/

THE DAY OF PUBLICATION AND AFTER

A Very Short Section

When your book is published – nothing happens.

You may just possibly get a bunch of flowers from your publisher, which is surprising and nice. Or champagne in a fancy box. There probably won't be a launch party, unless you have had the wit to arrange one for yourself. (Which I heartily recommend that you do. They're fun.)

More surprising, perhaps, is that you won't even find that your book necessarily appears in bookshops on publication day. Some retailers may have taken it a few days early. Some won't be taking it yet. Others won't be taking it at all. Or perhaps a major retailer has taken your book and entered it into one of their major promotions … but, when you actually try to find your book in its appointed position in store, you may well realise that it's nowhere to be found.

You can try speaking to the shop staff, or you can let your publisher know and they'll chase it up themselves. Alternatively, and better still, if you happen to be in possession of a mother, then my experience is that letting her loose on any rogue bookshops (in very loud voice: **'why haven't you got the EXCELLENT new book by that *FABULOUS* new author _____'**) will do vastly more to procure change than any publishers rep ever will.

That's it. The excited to and fro you've had with your editor these past weeks is now mostly gone. He's moved on to other books, other authors. You can ask for sales information and you'll get it. But after a certain point, those emails will stop coming.

You of course want to know how your book is doing. The modern author-data portal, which most big publishers now offer, is a partial solution to that black hole of ignorance, but they all have their weaknesses. The only author-portal which is truly comprehensive and reliable is the one offered by Amazon, but since only self-published authors get access to that feast of statistical goodness, you'll have to make do with what your publisher supplies.

It's not just about the data either. Too often, publishers will largely stop communicating with you once your book is launched. That's not intended to send you a message, it's just that their interest has always been with the book rather than with you and, once the book is launched, it's launched. If the book does well, there will be more to be done on the publishing side – negotiating an extension of the book's time on the promo tables, providing further marketing assistance, sorting out reprints and the like. There may even be bits and pieces that involve you – a gig at a literary festival, for example. A book-signing, perhaps. Mostly, though, your involvement is over.

If you do get invitations to address festivals or go to book-signings, then accept by all means, but keep your expectations firmly anchored in reality. Some speakers can draw enormous crowds to these events. You most likely can't. If a literary festival asks you to talk but doesn't offer you any cash, feel free to ask about payment. If it's travel expenses and a sandwich only, go if you want to, but don't expect to sell so many books that you'll make your money back that way. The most important part of these things is connecting with other authors and bloggers in your niche. The more of that you can do, the better. And it's damn good fun as well. (Especially if you're a crime author, because crime writers are the best.)

Quite apart from anything else, book sales will only benefit you if and when you've earned out your advance, which may well be never. I once drove seventy miles to a literary festival to find that I was talking to the local library society. I must have spoken well, because after my talk a number of people came up to me and promised me faithfully that they'd be searching out my books in the local town library. Which was nice, but hardly a route to fortune. That said, these events are enjoyable, no matter how humble. You also get to feel in your own tiny way like a star. Which, indeed, you are.

Lastly, you should call to mind my earlier comments about the shelf life of your book. By around six weeks from publication, your book's destiny has most likely already been determined. If it's selling strongly, it'll stay on those promo tables. It'll rise up the charts. It'll gather attention. It'll stick around long enough for word of mouth to do its bit. If (which is much more probable) your book hasn't sold in any great quantity, then it'll creep from those promo tables to the shelves round the side of the shop. It won't appear on the charts. It won't get any further media exposure. Any nascent word-of-mouth muttering will be stillborn. Your book will sell a little from the side shelves, but the time will come when the bookshop is restocking and your book will need to be cleared away and returned to the warehouse whence it came.

On Amazon, of course, shelves are eternal, and so is your book. If a good digital-first publisher encounters disappointing sales first off, they're not likely to leave it there. They may rejacket the book. They may adjust the blurb, or price point, or metadata. These things are smart. For the right product, they can definitely work – indeed, they can tip a book from mediocre sales to bestsellerdom. It's not just fiction either. Let's say you have launched a non-fiction book about the fine sport of rugby. Perhaps it sells a bit. Perhaps not much. But then, a year or two later, the Rugby World Cup is in full blast. Rugby fans are re-energising their interest in the sport. An attentive digital-first publisher should be using that opportunity to boost sales of your book. You should be looking out for those opportunities, communicating with your publisher, and doing whatever can best be done from your side.

And if that sounds good, do just bear in mind that print-oriented publishers who sell mainly through bricks-and-mortar stores don't usually have that kind of mindset, or that kind of nimbleness, though they are certainly improving. The most digital-oriented imprints inside a Big Five house might be able to play those rapid adjustment games with their backlist titles.

But mostly ...

Enjoy those flowers. Have a great launch party. And work hard on your next book.

Part Seven
LIFE AFTER PUBLICATION

FROM HARDBACK TO PAPERBACK

Fifteen or twenty years back, there was an industry rule of thumb which suggested that a typical book would sell five times as much in paper covers as it had done in hard ones. Still further back, it was common for hardback publishers to be quite distinct from paperback ones. The hardback crowd would buy a book and then sell the paperback publishing rights to a wholly different company.

These days, of course, your paperback publisher will be the same as your hardback publisher, though the imprint will change. (If you are published in hardback by Viking, for example, your paperback will be published by Penguin. If you're published in hardback by Macmillan, your paperback will come out as a Pan book. And so on.) The rules of thumb have become less certain too. A book that sells 10,000 copies in hardback (a fairly standard number in the US) might sell just 15,000 in paperback, or it might go on to sell in the hundreds of thousands (with huge e-book sales as well). There are a million different factors here, but the main one is probably: is your book more of a hardbacky sort of product (literary fiction, or the kind of non-fiction that gets serious reviews in serious newspapers)? Or is it happily paper-back/e-book – commercial fiction and the like?

Your own involvement in the paperback launch will be like a small-scale reprise of the hardback launch. It'll all be on a smaller scale because, whereas the launch of a new book has some news value, the re-emergence of that same book with a somewhat bendier jacket isn't generally news at all.

If you can find a genuinely new angle for the publicity, you can try to get your publisher's attention for it – but you will be fighting uphill. The assumption among publishers is that hardbacks have news value, paperbacks don't. The jacket, likewise, is more than likely going to be a reprise of the hardback jacket. Perhaps a designer will play a little with the fonts and spacing. Perhaps there'll be an icon included, or something surplus removed. On the whole, though, no one will be inclined to invest much time and attention at this stage. The fate of the hardback looms over the paperback like a prophecy. If your hardback sold poorly, your paperback won't have secured significant promotional slots, and without a strong retail platform, your paperback won't sell in any quantity. Therefore, it makes no sense for the publisher to fuss too much over it.

Conversely, if your hardback sold strongly, that retail platform will exist, but your publisher is likely to conclude that their sales strategy for the hardback must have been a good one, so they'll simply redeploy it as appropriate for the paperback.

To my mind, publishers take this inattention a little too far. If a hardback was originally sold into a Christmas market, for example, the blurb on the paperback is unlikely to feel right if it's coming out in July. More generally, if the book sold below expectations in hardback, the paperback edition should provide an opportunity for second thoughts and a second assault on readers' wallets.

It's worth mentioning here that, in theory, your original editor is still your editor. In some houses, you'll find that the same person is in charge of both hardback and paperback editions. In others, you'll have a separate editor for the paperback, though your original hardback editor is still your main and most important point of contact. The publishers who most firmly separate hardback and paperback publishing like to say that it allows them to publish with a fresh eye and an undogmatic attitude. Maybe. My own preference would be to have the same editor all the way through, but, since the decision won't be up to you, it's not one you need to fret about.

Overall, my advice to authors would be to review blurb and jacket carefully. If there are things that could be tightened or improved, then press diligently for them to be altered. When it comes to jacket design, you're likely to achieve some success. When it comes to procuring publicity for the paperback, you'll do well to get anything at all.

THE NEXT PROJECT

Almost inevitably, then, most authors sense a kind of low-level disappointment around the time of second publication. When you're writing a book, it seems like the most important thing in the world to you. When it arrives on the shelves, and after a flurry of PR activity, it seems like no one really cares.

And they don't – or at least in nothing like the way you care. Your agent and editor both genuinely like your book, and probably like you too. But they handle numerous books every year and, in the end, the publication of yours is just business. The best solution for most authors is to live in the warm bath of future hope, not the chilly waters of present reality. Be diligent and persistent in doing what you can to guard the welfare of your babies but be aware that you can't do all that much for them.

In any case, you should, by now, be hard at work on your next project. Bid farewell to your firstborn, rejoice in its successes and don't take its failures to heart. After all, they're not really failures at all. I once spoke to my agent about a book of mine that had sold below expectations. The question I wanted answered was, *why?* Why hadn't it sold? Was it the cover? Was it the blurb? Was it the content? Was it the PR campaign?

Her answer was a wise one, namely that a failure to do well at the tills is the default outcome. When a book doesn't sell as many copies as it could do, no publisher sits around asking why. It hasn't sold in shedloads, because books mostly don't. The question *why* is usually only asked in the exactly opposite situation, when all of a sudden a book starts selling in huge volumes. Was there something about the cover that appealed to the public? Some trick of the author's media profile? Some clever bit of positioning? Publishers are keenly interested to understand the magic, in the hope that they can bottle and re-use it. When they reckon they've found that bit of magic – the pale, mawkish covers that once ruled the misery memoir market, for example – everyone uses it, everyone copies it, and the magic vanishes. I had a starkly depicted tree on the UK edition of my first Fiona Griffiths book. Orion's marketing manager told me proudly that their team had invented the 'scary tree' as a trope for crime fiction, but added, 'now everyone's doing it, so it doesn't have the same effect'.

So be professional when it comes to that paperback edition. Work hard on your next book. Don't stress too much – and remember why you became a writer in the first place.

Working with Small Publishers

Thus far, the discussion of the publication process has largely assumed that you are working with a major publisher. That assumption hasn't been explicit, but it's been there nonetheless – lurking in the discussion about promotional slots, the notion that you'll have a dedicated publicist, the idea that there are enough staff knocking around that you might attend a meeting with Smiley Becky without actually knowing who she is or what she does.

Smaller publishers are unlikely to get access to the promotional slots of major retailers. Those smaller publishers won't have their own PR department. They can't afford a floating array of Smiley Beckys. And even supposing that those retailers entered into discussions in the first place, smaller publishers just can't afford the outlays involved. (Retailer: 'Great news! We'd like to buy 20,000 copies at a massive discount to the retail price. We'll have them on our shelves for two weeks. If they don't sell, we'll send them all back to you for a full refund. Oh yes, and you'll have to pay for all printing, warehousing, logistics and other costs along the way. OK?' Small Publisher: 'Uh … Can I just take a moment, please?')

Which means that, if your publisher is smaller, the discussion of the previous pages is simultaneously true and false. It's true in the sense that smaller publishers have to deal with all the processes of normal publishing – design, production, publicity, sales, marketing, and so forth. It is, however, false in its implication that your publisher will have abundant resources to promote your book. It won't. These days, a smaller publisher is doing well to get decent uptake from retailers. Publicity is likely to be scanty.

341

There might be some social media activity, but the gap between 'sent a Tweet' and 'made some sales' is a long one. Those promo tables are likely to seem a long, long way from your book.

Yet there's good news in all this as well as bad. The bad news is something you already knew: namely, that huge sales are unlikely. The good news is everything else. Because your publisher is low on resources, they'll want real input from you. They may even have approached you to write the book in the first place because of who you are. What's more, if your book is a subject-led book of some description – a 'how-to' book on parenting; a memoir about mental illness; a book on flower identification – then you almost certainly have access to certain micro-communities that your publisher very much wants to reach. For example, if you're writing about flowers, then perhaps you're a member of a botanical society, or are involved with some local botanical gardens. More than likely, you know someone who edits a newsletter, runs a website or arranges lectures and garden visits. Those contacts are precious, and your publisher is likely to make the most of them. The marketing exercise can almost become collaborative, in a way that is usually less true for authors working with the larger houses.

Indeed, though those promo tables host the fastest sales, they seldom host the longest. A book on (let's say) working through your tax returns, negotiating divorce or caring for cats can sell year in, year out. If there's material that needs updating from time to time, then you'll be asked to do just that, but the book itself can endure.

This book, as it happens, is a prime example of just this phenomenon. I first wrote this book for a large traditional publisher about ten years ago. It has sold steadily in every year since. The book needed a wash-and-brush-up to keep it current, and I decided I wanted to publish this edition directly via Jericho Writers, but there's no reason why it shouldn't keep selling well for another ten years to come. Over time, it'll have been one of my most lucrative ever books, and that's without ever receiving the tarantara of publicity that has accompanied some of my others.

Maximising those long-term sales is a matter of doing the small things right and, where necessary, regularly. So, for example, pick a title that instantly communicates the purpose of the book. If your book is about how to wax your moustache, then might I suggest that *How to Wax Your Moustache* might be a good title. If you go for something flaky and imaginative – *The Handlebar and the Horseshoe: A Gentleman's Guide to Perfection* – you simply won't communicate the purpose or value of your book in the few seconds available before the browser's eye moves on.

Equally, you should keep an eye on such things as the book cover. If the cover you and your publisher first chose starts to look dated, then give the text a quick frisk to update it, pop on a new cover, and bring the book out as a revised and expanded second edition. That kind of makeover lends authority and gives you the ability to change those things that need changing.

Equally, if you are still a big wheel in the world of moustaches, or whatever your niche may be, then continue to use your book both as calling card and sales opportunity. The sales you get will never be huge in any month, but the month-to-month income can really build into something of value.

Of course, if you are writing fiction (or most forms of narrative non-fiction) with a small publisher, those long-term sales are unlikely to materialise. In which case, just enjoy the ride whatever it is and wherever it takes you.

You wanted publication for the validation and the pleasure of it all. You have both things. You've already won. These aren't the kind of outcomes which will make a hedge-fund manager sick with envy, but then, if poisoning hedge-fund managers is your goal, you took a wrong turn by becoming a writer.

Vanity Publishers

Now then.

The snake in the publishing woodpile. The hissing serpent. The cold-blooded poisoner with dead, reptilian eyes.

Here's the issue. You've sent your book off to agents. You didn't get anywhere. You looked for advice. Didn't find anything helpful.

And then – hey up. You have just, for the millionth time, Googled 'How do I get my book published,' when you notice all those little ads. They say things like: 'We want to publish new writers. We are open to new submissions.'

And you're not a dummy. A publisher who advertises? That sounds a bit weird. But you click through and you find what seems to be a genuine publisher. It has a ton of book and authors on its site. The whole thing seems nicely designed and profession-al.

You submit your manuscript. You get an email thanking you for a submission. You're told to wait.

You do everything recommended in this book. You find obscure saints and light candles to them. You avoid walking under ladders. You tie black cats into knots and practice sacred chanting.

And then The Email arrives. And it's a good news/bad news kinda thing. On the one hand the email says that the editorial board loved your book. *They loved it! The editorial board!* That's the good news.

On the other hand, there's a bit of boilerplate yadda about what a tough market it is out there, and how the publisher is forced to consider the risks very carefully. So on this occasion, the board has decided against making a full offer for your work and would instead prefer to publish it on a partnership basis. You firkle out what that means exactly, and in essence it means that the publisher pays a chunk of the launch costs and you pay a chunk as well. Royalty terms and all that seem favourable and the offer seems sincere.

That's not quite the process you had imagined. This 'partnership' arrangement might cost $3,000, or $5,000, or even more – but these guys seem serious. Advertising in *The New York Review of Books* seems like it might be possible (for a further sum.) And these guys might take your book to the London Book Fair, or BookExpo, or Frankfurt. They're already talking about marketing packs, press releases and options for Australasia. Gee!

Though you go through the motions of inner and outer debate, the truth is that your mind is already made up. You want to publish this book and these guys are for real. Yes, it's expensive, but there's every reason to hope that you'll make your money back from sales down the line. The game feels excitingly entrepreneurial in a way, and you've never stopped believing in your book, so you decide to go for it. Nothing ventured, nothing gained, right?

Given a menu of marketing choices, you end up ticking slightly more options than you'd intended, and your upfront cost starts to approach $10,000 or more, but if you're going to do this, you might as well do it right. Bill Gates and Steve Jobs and Jeff Bezos and Mark Zuckerberg – those guys didn't think small, did they?

I already know the end of this story, however.

Your book will be produced. It might even have decently edited text and an adequately competent cover. It'll be available through all the book wholesalers. It'll be sitting there on Amazon and the other e-stores. If you paid for nonsense like a place on the stand at BookExpo or those dumb ads in *The NYRB*, those things will be delivered as requested.

But sales? Actual sales? You'll be lucky to break into three figures. A median estimate of sales might be perhaps forty or fifty copies sold.

You've lost a ton of money, but more than that: you've lost some pride. This thing you cared about so much feels like it's ended in some kind of low-end fraud.

WHY VANITY PUBLISHERS ALWAYS FAIL

Vanity publishers fail for a simple, inevitable reason. They don't want to sell your book. They don't care about it. They don't try. I mean, sure, if they can pop a book up on Amazon and some sales come in, then great. They'll scoop their share of the royalties and be happy with that.

But putting a book on Amazon is easy and free. Any idiot can do that, and millions of idiots already have. But books don't sell just because they're available. They sell for two reasons: they're good, and they're being properly marketed.

Trouble is, vanity publishers just don't care about the quality of the books they handle. If they can find a sucker to give them 10,000 bucks to produce a book, they'll take the 10,000 bucks and not care about the quality of the book. I know this is true, because I once sent a manuscript off to a vanity publisher and asked if they'd publish it. They said yes.

Now, OK, I'm a pro author, so my books are typically quite good. Only on this occasion, what I sent out was five pages from a dishwasher manual. The company concerned wrote back to me congratulating me on my 'excellent commercial potential'. When, using a different name and email address, I sent them the full text of *Pride & Prejudice*, they sent an identical email.

In short, vanity publishers know that their books are mostly dross. I honestly doubt if an 'editor' reads the book before accepting it. My guess would be not. It would be a crazy waste of money to start marketing those books. Sure, there will be some genuinely good work in amongst the rubbish, but a vanity publisher would have to utterly upend its business model to dig those books out and start marketing them.

So they don't.

The books are 'available for sale' everywhere in the world – meaning that you could in theory go into your local bookshop and order a copy – but that's not how people buy books. Books need to be on the shelves of physical bookstores, or prominent in the Amazon search results, or both. If neither thing is true, your book will die.

The vanity publishers don't care, because you've already paid them.

EIGHT POEMS

I'll finish this chapter with a true story.

I once received an enquiry from a woman who was dying of cancer. She had written eight poems. They weren't, to be candid, very good poems, but they were from the heart and they were perhaps the most important creative act of this woman's life. They deserved to be cherished for that reason alone. She had sent her work off to a publisher and got back a letter precisely as described. The author of that letter commented that he had been particularly moved by this woman's poems, because he had been very sick himself once. He said that the market for poetry was tough, but that there could well be strong demand in the UK, America and Australasia. This woman, who was not rich and who was also dying, was being asked for £8,000 (about $12,000). She was flattered by the praise and tempted by the proposition.

The truth is that everything about that letter was deceitful. You can't sensibly publish a poetry collection of eight rather short poems. A poetry collection needs to be ten times longer than that. What's more, even the very best debut collection is unlikely to sell more than a few hundred copies. The market for poetry is almost vanishingly small, and this woman's poems weren't remotely right for whatever market does exist. *The simple, nasty truth is that somebody consciously sought to deceive a dying woman out of £8,000.* The deceit might technically have been lawful, but most street muggers have better ethics. That company was loathsome, and it's still in business. I'd guess that the company concerned sends out letters like that several times a week.

It's fraud – a legal fraud, admittedly, but still a nasty, stinking, venomous fraud.

The short advice that ends this chapter: Avoid, avoid, avoid, avoid.

SECOND-NOVEL SYNDROME AND OTHER AFFLICTIONS

Writing is an unusual profession for many reasons, but here's one more. If you choose to become a baker or a banker or a footballer or a call girl, you are probably expecting to bake, bank, kick balls and – uh – make calls every day of your professional life. That's presumably why you entered the profession. Writers, on the other hand, normally feel impassioned by the particular story which drove them to pick up their pens in the first place. They complete their manuscript, find an agent, make a sale and proceed happily towards publication. Then, blow me, the publisher wants another book.

The writer often receives this news with an inner amazement. The first book begged to be written. It was an obsession that captured your waking thoughts and often your dream worlds as well. For most writers, the second book just isn't like that. It's a contractual obligation. It's a matter of craft as much as passion. For sure, you would like to be a writer, so writing another book seems like just the right thing to be doing, but this second assignment simply doesn't *feel* anything like the first one did.

Unsurprisingly, this is the point at which many authors foul up.

A CAUTIONARY TALE

Because it's mostly novelists who have a two-book deal, and because second-novel syndrome is most acutely suffered by them, I'm going to talk about only novelists in what follows. But if you're a non-fiction author with an alarming two-book deal to satisfy, what follows is for you as well.

Once upon a time, there was an author – let's call him Harold Bingley – who wrote a novel, found an agent and got a nice fat deal from a well-known publisher. He hadn't found that first novel particularly hard to write. Everyone told him it was terrific. He was confident that he knew what he was doing.

Then he was asked to write a second novel. Fine. This author, a friend of mine, wanted to write a second novel, but he had no idea what he was going to write about. There simply wasn't a story clamouring to be written the same way the first one was. But still, he was good at this, right? The first novel had come out easily enough, so the second one would presumably come the same way.

Alas, it did not. The first draft of that second novel was horrible. It was a car crash wrapped in a plane wreck. It did not please Harold Bingley's publisher. They were very nice about it, but they were very clear that the book needed major surgery. Surgery that involved the Ctrl-A ('select all') function followed by an itsy-bitsy tap of the Delete key. That wasn't quite how the publisher put it, but Harold Bingley at this point was back on the straight and narrow. He went back to his computer, opened his novel, hit Ctrl-A, then Delete. He rewrote that novel from scratch. It still wasn't as good as the first one, but it was a solid, professional, dependable piece of work.

He never encountered that same problem again. From there on, his novels were born either of passion and craft working together, or of a disciplined, worldly-wise craft working alongside enough joy and pleasure to substitute for true passion.

Harold Bingley's travails were perhaps a little more extreme than normal, but without trying very hard I can think of half-a-dozen novelists of my acquaintance who experienced something similar. First novels aren't asked for. They arrive. Your fingertips burn with the desire to set them down on paper. Second novels are seldom as insistent. You have to jump from an art informed by desire to one informed by excellent technique. What's more, though it's easy to believe that your technique must be good enough, because that first novel came out all right, you are still very much learning the ropes – a phrase which has its origins in the Georgian navy, when the ropes in question might stand a hundred feet above a storm-tossed deck; falling off had ugly consequences.

NOT FALLING OFF

The most important lesson from these meditations is simple. You need humility. You need to remember that you are still a relative novice, that you haven't proved you can do anything until you can do it twice in a row, that you still have an abundant amount to learn of the novelist's art.

Following straight on from that, you should get as much help as you can. Your agent and your editor will be perfectly familiar with second-novel syndrome. Even if you have a high degree of confidence in your second novel, I'd urge you to put together a detailed proposal. A detailed outline, plus the opening 10,000 words or so. There's no particular format that the outline has to take. If you shun detailed plot outlines (as I do), then you can still say plenty about the overall shape of the plot, the nature of the action, where the narrative drive comes from, who your characters are, and so on. Put down everything you know about the book and everything you think someone would need to know to make sense of it.

Don't allow yourself to think of this as a working document, in the sense that you can be at all slipshod about presentation or salesmanship. Agents and editors are all fine people, bless them, but they are not authors. Whereas authors know all too well how slow progress can be from first draft to final draft, and how sloppy things can look in between, agents and editors are not similarly inured. If you send them something that feels first-draftish, you're likely to terrify them.

So take your time. Work on your proposal at least as carefully as you would if you were submitting work to an agent for the first time. In one sense, this is wasted effort, in that you yourself don't need anything more polished than a first draft at this stage. Yet the act of polishing will teach you something, and the feedback you get will be more reliable.

Once you've sent out this proposal – either to your agent or to your editor or to both at once, depending on your own pattern of working relationships – wait for feedback. When it comes, it'll be the usual combination of illuminating and frustrating. The illumination will come from insights that you needed and hadn't yet reached. The frustration will come from comments that you know to be true and don't know how best to take on board.

You don't need to treat this feedback process as a one-off. It doesn't need to be. Your second novel *matters*. Yes, for sure, you've got a contract. Unless you make a real pig's ear of it, the novel will be published, and you'll be paid. But, if the second novel stinks, it'll be much harder to sell, your sales history will be trending downwards rather than upwards and, if your career is not quite doomed, it's nevertheless looking a little doomy.

Your agent and your editor understand all this. If you need time to get that next novel right, then ask. For the most part, you'll get the support that you need. You may also find that all those books on writing technique, which seemed irrelevant to your first novel, are suddenly feeling rather valuable now. You don't have to agree with all that they recommend; the process of disagreement can be a mighty enlightening one. If your agent, editor and written resources aren't enough, then feel free to reach out to Jericho Writers. That's not a route I advise – as a pro author, you should be able to get the right help, free, from your publisher – but sometimes it's good to have the fallback. Jericho Writers helps a handful of professional authors every year, so you will not be alone.

Finally, once you have a concept that works, stay closely in touch with your agent or publisher as you proceed. They should prefer to offer input at this stage than have to tidy a car crash at a later one. With just a little luck, your second novel will be at least as good as your first and, perhaps, even a little better.

That friend of mine, Harold Bingley, wishes you well. It turned out all right for him in the end.

TAXES, MORTGAGES AND OTHER PLEASURES

One of the most excellent and wonderful things about being a writer is the ease with which you can minimise your tax bill. The steps involved are threefold. They are (1) become a writer, (2) have very little income, (3) pay very little tax. These simple rules should suffice for most writers. Indeed, the only possible room for error comes if you foul up on step 2. It's possible to think of writers who have managed to make a mess of things here – J. K. Rowling, James Paterson, Barack Obama, teenage YouTube vloggers of weird name and baffling appeal – but the vast majority of writers will be able to negotiate this stage without undue difficulty.

Because of the ease and simplicity of this strategy, the amounts of money involved in step (3) are not great. Nevertheless, there's no point in giving more money to the taxman than you really need to, so do bear in mind the following points:

- All your income is taxable. Not just income from writing books, but income from journalism, income from speaking engagements and the like. Don't forget these additional items, as the taxman is likely to feel narked if you do.
- You have plenty of expenses that are allowable for tax purposes. Agents' commissions, travel and subsistence, re-search materials, computers and printers, phone calls, and so forth. Because writing seldom feels quite like work, many of these expenses may feel to you like cheating. The cost of travel to New York or London for lunch with your publisher? Buying a few crime novels as you con-template your next book? Poking around the museum at

Gettysburg as you contemplate a historical novel? These things may be fun, but they're work. For you, they really, truly are. You're not conning anyone by claiming for these things. You're just lucky enough to have a job that you like.

- In addition, and most importantly, if you work from a home office, the costs of that office are offsettable against tax. An office is the place you work from. Doesn't matter if that room is also a place that your husband uses to watch late-night wrestling or a place that your teenage daughter wrecks every few weeks when she has one of her parties. If you use it to work in, you have costs that are allowable for tax purposes.

You do of course need check the rules of your own tax jurisdiction as to exactly what costs are offsettable, but the normal rule of thumb is that if you use 10% of your house for work and work only, then 10% of associated costs are tax-deductible. But again: do check the small print. Taxmen tend to lack a sense of humour.

In some jurisdictions, there are special rules available for creators of artistic works. The idea is that you may find yourself with significant income in one year, and much less in another. If you rise into a higher tax band in the first year, then the amount you pay in tax is likely to be higher overall than if your income had come in steadily over the two years taken together. For this reason, authors are often allowed to average their income when it benefits them to do so. If any of that applies to you, you probably want an accountant to run their slide rule over the numbers. You don't need to go to any fancy-pants accountant to do this. It's basic stuff from their point of view. You *will* need a fancy-pants accountant when you stumble blinking to the top of the bestseller lists in four continents. Till then, I'd recommend a lower-budget solution.

Likewise, if your accountant recommends that you incorporate as a limited company, register for VAT, re-categorise your grandmother as a special-purpose vehicle based in the Netherlands

Antilles, or that you indulge in any other exotic financial manoeuvre, then stay sceptical. If you completely understand what you are letting yourself in for, then make the best decision you can. If you don't – and you're a writer, so numbers terrify you, remember? – keep it simple.

MORTGAGES

If the matter of taxation can seem to have a blissful irrelevance about it at times, the same happy claim cannot generally be made about writers and their mortgages. If you are a self-employed writer, and you don't have a steady part-time job or (better still) a steady full-time spouse of the income-earning variety, conversations with mortgage companies are apt to be a little disheartening. They run a bit like this:

BORED MORTGAGE CLERK: So, are you currently in employment?

WRITER: No.

BMC: Self-employed?

WRITER: Yes.

BMC: Nature of the business?

WRITER: I'm a writer.

[First pause.]

BMC: I'll put writing. The name of the business?

WRITER: Well, it's not really a business, as such. I'm a writer. I write novels. You know. Novels. So I suppose the name of the business is me.

[Second pause.]

BMC: Do you have audited accounts for the last three years?

WRITER: Audited? As in auditor? Well, not as such, no.

BMC: I mean, are you able to verify a steady income from self-employment for a three-year period or more?

WRITER: *Steady* income? [*Small high-pitched giggle.*]

[*Third pause.*]

BMC: Look, I'm sorry, Mr—

WRITER: No. Wait, wait. I've got this amazing idea for a screenplay …

I don't exactly have a solution to offer to these conundrums, except to remind you that they exist. In the happy days before the financial crisis, you only needed to prove you had a pulse and there'd be someone out there who'd be happy to lend you money. In the colder realities of today's world, lenders are a little more demanding of their borrowers, and you'll need to factor that into your calculations. If your family is largely dependent on writing as a source of income, then I'd gently suggest that a fairly flexible mortgage is likely to suit you better than the kind designed for those tedious folks with their jobs and their monthly pay-packets.

In the same way, when it comes to pension planning and the like, you probably want to make your plans more rather than less prudent. I've no doubt at all that your screenplay concept is the most wonderful idea since someone had the brainwave of combining nuns, Nazis and singing, but it's still not the kind of pension plan you should be looking at to keep you warm in old age.

Staying Alive and Staying Published

You've written and published your first novel. You've written and published your second. If you first bought this book when you were thinking about your agent letter, then it's now a dog-eared copy knocking around your study alongside some Bulgarian royalty statements (which are, it has to be said, only slightly more bewildering than those that come from your home publisher).

Now what?

That's not an easy question. Of course, if your first books have sold hugely, your publisher will be hurling large bundles of money at your head and it's easy enough to know what to do. You say thank you very much and pick them up. But few authors will find themselves in this position. For most of us – whether we're talented, average or plodding – writing is not an easy way to make money. Several options offer themselves, and you need to think hard and be fiercely realistic about how to proceed.

MOTIVATIONS

This book started with a discourse on motivations, and it needs to end that way too. Why do you write? Did you have a story to tell – a story that is now told and done with? Did you have a passion for writing? Did you want to make money? Did you want fame? The questions may be the same now as they were at the start, but your answers will have changed. You know more about the industry. You know more about yourself. All good writers are driven by passion, but that passion can take several forms. Here, for example, are some of the forms it can take. (As always, the stories are true, though some of the details have been altered to protect privacy.) I should say as well that all these authors are talented and have, between them, won or been shortlisted for a number of serious literary awards.

ANNABEL wanted to tell a story. Her first novel was stunning, her second novel – written in fulfilment of a two-book deal – was no better than careful. She stopped writing, moved house, got married, had kids, thought about other things. Years after she laid down her pen, another story began to nibble at her, and she was happy to let it nibble. She started to flesh out her ideas, she talked to her agent, and things started to get moving once again. Annabel never wrote for money in the first place. She isn't writing for money now.

BERTRAND is a writer. If he isn't writing, he isn't complete. He has never made much money from his 'proper' writing – though it's always been critically acclaimed both in London and New York – but he's managed to secure himself regular work with various children's educational publishers, writing historical and other books for them. He also does bits of editorial work, various teaching gigs, and the like. None of this pays terrifically well, but it's all writing-related and satisfies him. His 'proper' work fits in around the rest. He loves his life.

CATHERINE wrote women's fiction. She's had bestsellers to her name in more than one country. She's had a decent TV deal for one of her books. She loved writing more than anything else she's ever done. And she's given it up. The money, at its best, was good, but it was utterly unreliable. What's more, though she loved the writing process, she wasn't a particularly speedy writer and found the work more exhausting than anything else she'd ever done. In the end, she decided that she'd rather do other things. She now mostly lives off the income from property investments she made from her brief sojourn in the big time. She keeps her literary muscle alive by doing freelance editorial work and the like, but mostly those muscles have been allowed to lose their fitness. She's happy to let them.

DANIEL is a literary author who simply has to write. He's migrated from large, prestigious publishers to small, passionate ones. He makes next to no money from his literary work but is fiercely committed to it. He's an immaculate stylist who can turn out maybe 250 words on a good day, so he's not merely working for very little money, he's working slowly for very little money. Daniel also finds other minor sources of income to keep body and soul together – a little journalism, some translation, the odd ghost-writing job – but mostly he's adapted his life to need very little money at all. He lives in a self-build home that is little more than a fancy shed. He gets his electricity – such of it as he uses – from a solar panel. He grows his own veggies. Every now and then, he finds himself dining off fresh air and sunshine.

EDIE has taken a classic authorial route. She writes novels and teaches creative writing. It doesn't matter too much if the novels sell or if they don't; they've always been more of a decently paid hobby than a real profession. She likes writing and expects to go on doing so, but it wouldn't kill her if her publisher stopped taking her books (and nor would it bother the authorities at the university where she teaches). She admits that there's something a little weird in teaching others how to write when her own relationship to that profession is a little ambiguous, but she enjoys her students, enjoys her teaching and enjoys her writing. For her, the combination works.

Those are their stories. Here is mine:

AN AUTHOR'S TALE

I wrote five novels for HarperCollins. Those novels were broadly in the same genre – old-fashioned adventure yarns, in which there were no vampires, no violence, no trays of dissected body parts, just flawed heroes and heroines struggling to meet their goals. The novels morphed gently from financial thrillers to historical dramas, but the tone and approach was broadly similar. It's true that with my last book (a historical romance), my German publisher wanted to change my name to a woman's name because they reckoned it had strayed too far from my original brand identity, but on the whole I played by the rules of the marketing game. (I offered to write as Emma Makepeace, but the deal never came to fruition, alas. I still mourn my female alter ego. She'd have been great.)

The sales of my first book were excellent. The sales of my second book (which was less good than the first and had a feeble cover design) were lacklustre but solid. The third book was all set for a major launch when a critical wholesaler went bankrupt, knocking out a swathe of potential sales. At the same time, a major chain retailer underwent a violent series of corporate upheavals, in the course of which I went from being one of their most heavily promoted authors to one they weren't even going to stock at all. This abrupt reversal had nothing to do with my book; it was simply that the new person had only just got his feet under the desk and hadn't yet had time to survey his new domain. Not his fault, not my fault, not my publisher's fault; just one of those things. My publisher, who had planned a major national launch campaign, withdrew the whole thing because of the sudden gap in the retail uptake.

The sales of that book – probably my best novel to date – were shocking. Two more novels followed. My sales were still decent, but I'm not an author who's happy to accept a mediocre income, and the advances I demanded were more than my publisher was ever going to pay.

So I switched tack. I put together a non-fiction proposal, for a work of popular history. The proposal had nothing whatever to do with anything I had written before. My existing agent liked it, was happy to continue representing me, but told me that this kind of non-fiction wasn't her main enthusiasm or strength and said that, if I wanted to move elsewhere, I should feel free. So I did.

That first-draft proposal was reshaped under the beady eye of my current agent and we ended up selling that proposal for a ton of money to a different bit of HarperCollins. The fact that I still happen to be published under that same lofty Hammersmith roof was pure coincidence. The editor at Fourth Estate who offered for my book hadn't even spoken to my former colleagues in mass-market fiction before she made her offer.

When I completed my non-fiction deal (and hurled together a couple of 'how-to' books for Bloomsbury), I had a yen to return to fiction. So I did, but in an utterly different way. I re-invented myself as a crime writer. I spent about two years letting a character form in my head. This was the first time a book had come to me led by character rather than plot, and I loved it. I loved *her*. Fiona Griffiths, my crazy but rational, vulnerable but dangerous, little Welsh detective. Once I started to find her voice (expressive but fractured, present tense but reflective), I knew I had discovered my own literary gold.

I wrote the first draft of that first Fiona novel in about two months. (Beautiful, un-English snowy months when we got snowed in and I walked the dogs in fields of ice a-glitter with golden January sunshine.) The novel needed a bit of tidying up, but not much. And plotting that book was easy-peasy, pudding and pie. My technique: I went to bed each night and dreamed the chapter I would write the next day.

That first book sold to publishers in the UK, America, France, Germany, Spain, Italy and a spray of other countries as well. It got lovely reviews. It bonded with readers. It got optioned for TV. The TV show was made and aired in near record time. It did well.

But?

(All stories need a 'but', and all stories about writing are stuffed full of that wicked little conjunction.)

In my case the *but* was simply this – publishers in both the US and the UK failed to find a cover design and route to market that really worked, so in both places the series ended up selling at way below its actual potential. That's not Disappointed Author spitting out the Sour Grapes of Rage. That's simply a statement of empirical fact. My US publisher was keen to continue with the series, but on terms I found unacceptable. So I said no.

I self-published the third book in the series. (The publisher, Penguin Random House, had published the first two.) It did moderately OK, not well.

I self-published the fourth book, using the teeny-tiny mailing list I'd acquired via the previous book. That book did more than well. It earned money and found readers on a scale I'd not had before.

So I asked PRH if they would, pretty please, allow me to revert the rights in the first two books in the series. They were under no obligation to do anything of the sort, but they were kind enough to say yes. They weren't all nice – their 'yes' came with a request for $10,000 attached to it – but I was happy enough to pay what they asked.

I got the rights back, rejacketed the books, improved the Amazon metadata, rebuilt my mailing list collection and much else. The fifth book did better than the fourth. The sixth book and its sisters earned me $100,000 in a calendar year, without much marketing input on my part. If I hadn't taken a break to deal with Jericho Writers business, I'd be earning comfortably over $150,000 a year, maybe over $200K, and doing that while still only publishing a book or so a year.

In the UK, I've only just wheeled to the end of a six-book deal with Orion (part of Hachette, the world's #2 trade publisher), and I'll probably take the same self-publishing route from here on. There's no huge pressure on me to decide, so I haven't decided.

Now that sounds kind of weird: a great long book on traditional publishing which ends up revealing I'm no longer traditionally published. Except that the reality is way more nuanced than that. For one thing, I am still traditionally published. In Germany, for example, my books are doing really well. They have the support of a brilliant editor and publishing house. They've garnered brilliant, and growing, critical coverage. They put nice wodges of cash in my pocket. In that market, traditional publishing has brought me everything I could have wanted, and more, and more.

Not only that. The glorious thing about today's publishing market is that it offers so many options to the writer. As it's turned out, my Fiona Griffiths series has done better self-published, but I have many more writing projects in me before I'm done. Some of those will want trad publication. Some will want to be self-published. Some may go by some exotic intermediate route. (Crowd-funding? Digital-first? Amazon Publishing? All these things have their specific strengths, their specific advantages.)

I do know a few things, however. First, I don't want to live in a yurt, eating sunlight. I don't want to struggle to pay the mortgage. I want some income that's independent of the vagaries of publishing. And when I do publish books, I want readers, I want sales and I want income. If that sounds very commercial (and, let's be honest, no one who chooses authoring as a primary career is all that commercial), I also want to write things that I enjoy writing. I won't engage with things that don't give me creative satisfaction. Even this book, practical and workmanlike as it is, has been a pleasure to write. I wouldn't want it any other way.

YOUR STORY

Your story is still to be written. There's loads you don't yet know about yourself, about your sales figures, about what really propels you. Here, nevertheless, are a few suggestions that you may find helpful.

1.   *Don't give up the day job*

The oldest adage and still the truest. You won't really know how your career is progressing until you've completed your first two-book deal and have started to talk about advances for the second. Even then, of course, huge uncertainty lies ahead of you, but, if your sales and advances are nudging upwards, at least you've avoided your first opportunity to sail straight on to the rocks of calamity. Writing (especially writing fiction) is perfectly possible to handle alongside a day job. If you have the kind of job that can be part-time, then go for it. If you need to, adapt your career to one that more easily permits writing. But that job, the real job – the one with things like payslips and pension provision and sickness and holiday pay – is a precious thing. It's not simply a safety net. It's a safety net you'll probably fall into sometime soon.

Even if your writing career flourishes and does well, it may well have gaps in it, caused by oddities in your publication schedule or anything else. If your publisher puts back the publication of your book by six months for some random reason, they won't even think about asking if that is going to cause difficulty for your finances, so your finances need to be robust enough to take the strain. Wait to be invited on Oprah, then give up the day job. Never the other way round.

2. *Marry for money*

Not everyone is fortunate enough to have the kind of day job which can easily accommodate writing. In such cases, you need to give even greater thought to creating that safety net. Assuming you haven't already been foolish enough to throw your life away for love, I'd urge you to marry someone obscenely wealthy. Choose someone whose personal habits can be endured for just long enough to accrue some decent alimony, then take the cash and enjoy the rest of your life. That's a safety net.

If you're soppily romantic about these things, you'll need to be a little more creative. You can think about all those classic writerly dodges – teaching, editorial work, journalism, translation, copyediting and the like – but bear in mind that these things are almost always poorly paid, because there's always a plethora of amply qualified writers queuing up to do them.

So if you can, think more broadly. Think of an occupation which suits your skills and your temperament and which can happily sit alongside your writing. Don't diminish the importance of this decision simply because you happen to value your time spent writing more than anything else. There may come a point at which your publisher no longer wants a book from you, your agent isn't returning your calls, and you have a gas bill sitting on the mantelpiece, shouting across the room at you in bossy red capitals.

3. Be promiscuous

Perhaps you see yourself as an author of women's sagas. Fair enough. If that's what you are, then plough that furrow to its end. But let's suppose your sales and your advances shrivel. Not your fault, just one of those things. Do you want to quit writing, or do you want to reinvent yourself? There isn't a right or wrong answer here. Different people will have different responses. But be aware that you *can* reinvent yourself if you want to.

The reinvention needs to be a real one. That is, if you wrote women's sagas under your own name, you are unlikely to be able to simply delete that identity and write the same kind of work under a different name. Almost certainly, you will need to write in new territory altogether, probably using your existing name, though your agent or publisher will tell you if you need to change it. I know an astrologer who also writes cookbooks. I know a literary author who also writes picture books. I know a screen-writer who also writes novels. I know a crime writer who also writes erotica. I know a poet who also writes crime. These different spheres of activity produce their own challenges, their own rewards. And the biggest hurdle to this kind of reinvention is always the same: a rigidity in the author's own view of who they are. Play with that view. It may be right. It may not be. You won't know until you start to experiment. Experimenting is fun.

4. If you see a door, kick it

A common outside view of the industry is that what matters is who you know, not what talent you have. I hope it's clear to you by now that that view is wrong. Talent is and has always been the single most important element in gaining access. Without it, you'll get nowhere. All the same, connections help, because you never quite know what they may lead to. My friend, the screen-writer-who-also-writes-novels, was working with a major international TV director. He was hungry for new projects and (because this is the film industry) needed them the day before yesterday in order to impress some affluent German investors. He asked her for ideas. She suggested my novels. He asked me for a treatment. I worked late that night and gave him three.

So far, nothing has come of that interest. There's at least a 95% chance that nothing ever will. All the same, a connection was made that wouldn't have been made had it not been for my friend. Equally, if you happen to know journalists, publishers, authors, agents, celebrities, film-makers, TV types and the rest, you need to nurture those connections. That doesn't mean getting creepy about it, but it does mean keeping some kind of inner Rolodex. It also, unquestionably, means being willing to push hard at doors, even if they're barely open. Often enough, you'll find yourself being welcomed – and it's most unlikely that anyone will be upset with you for trying.

It should also go without saying that one good way to nurture connections is to be as helpful as you can to others. If you can help make connections between authors, publishers, agents and whoever, then so much the better for others – and so much the better for you. Those you've helped will be that little bit more ready to help you in return.

5. Buy a bulldog

Not all professional authors have agents, but, if you don't have one, you should almost certainly get one. Agents aren't all as good as they ought to be, but they do know more about the market than you do or ever can. They know more about publishing. They know more about contracts and what can be negotiated. You need that knowledge, so don't think you don't.

6. Compromise your artistic integrity

There are things you want to write. There are things that the market wants you to write. The dead centre of the first circle is most unlikely to coincide with the dead centre of the second. You need to compromise. You're not sacrificing your immortal soul by doing so; you are shaping a product for a market. That's what you're paid to do. It's true that some of those compromises are painful. It's true that in some respects you may produce a less interesting book than the one you'd originally envisaged. At least half the time, however, the book that emerges from the compromise is a better one – cleaner, sharper, less self-indulgent. You won't feel that to start with, but you don't have to. Just go where the market leads you and write the most wonderful thing you can within those parameters. The best books in the world normally started out the same way.

7. Cultivate indolence

I know far too many professional novelists who, on completing a two-book deal, simply started off on book #3 or book #5, writing the whole darn thing 'on spec', just as they did with their very first manuscript. Sometimes this approach is unavoidable and you simply need to grit your teeth and get on with it – always bearing in mind the dreadful, but perfectly real, possibility that, as you're writing, the market will turn against you and the novel into which you've plunged so much work will be either unsaleable or saleable only for peanuts. At other times, however, it's possible to secure a contract before you've invested too much. Given how tough the market is, it's vital for writers to protect themselves against excessive wasted investment of time.

One of my non-fiction books, for example, was sold off the basis of a proposal that took me about a day to write. A previous, more ambitious and highly remunerative non-fiction project was sold off the back of a 10,000-word proposal. The same – sometimes – is possible with fiction too. In short, whenever you can, minimise risk before investing effort.

8. *Write with joy or don't write at all*

Lastly, if ever writing stops being a pleasure, if ever it starts feeling like *work*, then don't do it. Do something else. If you think of writing as a job, then it has to be one of the worst jobs ever invented: lonely, ill-paid, insecure, unpensioned, unpredictable, unthanked. Writing only makes sense if, like me, you think it's an amazing way to get paid for something that you want to do anyway. Just think about it! Getting *paid* to *write*! I can't even think of a suitable comparison for that, because there isn't one. I often find myself writing at weekends, bank holidays, and even at Christmas. I don't do this because I feel I ought to, but because my weekends, bank holidays and Christmases are usually pleasanter if I do. I never thought that about my past career (investment banking), nor can I think of any alternative career where the same might be true.

These feelings are common to most genuine writers. I know one fine young chap, for example, who wanted to take his laptop on honeymoon in order to work on his book proposal … until a wiser, older head told him that, if he wrote on his honeymoon, he'd be writing off his honeymoon. So keep the passion. If you lose it, move on.

CONCLUSION

Our revels now are ended. It seems a long time ago that your fingers withdrew astonished from that final full stop, and a lot of ground has been covered since then. Yet, in dealing endlessly with the *business* of writing, we have thereby chosen to ignore its soul. But the soul needs the final word. Gustave Flaubert put it like this:

> '*It is a delicious thing to write, to be no longer yourself but to move in an entire universe of your own creation. Today, for example, as man and woman, both lover and mistress, I rode in a forest on an autumn afternoon under the yellow leaves, and I was also the horses, the leaves, the wind, the words my people uttered, even the red sun that made them almost close their love-drowned eyes. When I brood over these marvellous pleasures I have enjoyed, I would be tempted to offer God a prayer of thanks if I knew he could hear me. Praised may he be for not creating me a cotton merchant, a vaudevillian or a wit.*'

He's right, of course, and yet he doesn't quite press the point home to its close. Writing is a strange game, because to do it right you have to put yourself to one side almost completely. It can't be you, or Flaubert, who sets those words down on the page. If it is, then you haven't yet reached the right creative depth. Perhaps you dissolve into the book, or the book dissolves into you. Either way, it's not like making an apple pie or a set of shelves.

At the same time, though, and just as you're pulling off your disappearing act, you are also highly alert. Your brain hasn't switched off. It's still thinking hard about craft, and sentences and word choice and the rest. Yet that brain of yours is both active and subservient. Subservient to *what*, I can't tell you, but it's no

369

longer quite the boss. If your book doesn't somewhat surprise you when you're done, then you haven't done it quite right.

The process changes you. Not hugely. Not so that your friends look at you strangely and ask you if you've found God or given up booze or started some new-fangled power diet. But it's a good sort of change, nevertheless.

An enlargement. A widening out. And that's why this job, this writer's life, is worth chasing, no matter how hard the going may be. This book gives you a road map for the path ahead. Actually following it is down to you. Your enterprise, your endeavour, your luck, your talent.

From one writer to another: good luck.

GET MORE HELP

As I mentioned, Jericho Writers has designed specific tools to help support you in your publishing journey. Here they are in all their glory:

> **Self-editing Pyramid** – A tool that helps you organise your editing process

> **Synopsis/Query Letter Builder** – Designed to help you create your query letter and synopsis in an hour

The simplest way to get hold of them is to go here and have us send them to you:
https://jerichowriters.com/getting-published-free-resources/

Don't forget, these tools are completely free and they're there to help.

ABOUT JERICHO WRITERS

If you've read this far, you'll already have gathered something about what we at Jericho Writers have to offer. But, just so you have everything in one place, we offer:

- A membership service. We have a whole ton of video courses, masterclasses, agent search tools, and more. Basically, once you pay your (fairly modest) membership fee, you get a whole all-you-can-eat-buffet of writerly goodness. If you want to know more, go to https://jerichowriters.com and hit Join Us. That'll tell you everything you need to know. Our aim is to offer more resources for less money than anyone else and to achieve that aim by a country mile.

- An editorial service. I've already told you all you need about that. Basically: we get one of our brilliant editors to read your manuscript, cover to cover, and tell you exactly where it's falling down and how to fix it. That's an awesome service, but don't go rushing out to buy it yet. You'll only get good value from the service if you've written your book, worked damn hard on editing it into shape, and are then looking for help with the final stages. That's where we'll be most helpful, most value-added.

- Courses. And mentoring. And pretty much anything else you might require. The purpose behind all these things is to help you write better and achieve your goals for publication.

- Events. This is where you get to meet authors and agents and publishers and self-publishing experts and everyone else you need to make sense of your career. The best event of all is our annual Festival of Writing (held in York,

England), which is inspirational, exhausting, amazing –
and a reliable creator of terrific book deals.

That's the business side of what we do, but we're here for
everyone, not just those with cash to spend. We also:

- Run an online writers' community. It's free. It's intelligent. It's superbly well informed. And it's extremely
  welcoming of people like you – that is to say, of all writers. You can find our community here:
  https://community.jerichowriters.com/
- Send out regular advice emails. About writing technique,
  publishing issues, self-publishing techniques and the market for books. These emails aren't salesy. They're there to
  help you solve the problems that you encounter now and
  in your future career. We have tens of thousands of readers and we get a ton of feedback telling us that people
  appreciate the help. You can sign up to that email list
  here: https://jerichowriters.com/sign-up-news-updates/

If you'd like to talk to me, you can. Readers often reply to my
weekly advice email and I try to answer everyone who writes in.

Finally, don't think that this book is all there is. We'll be bringing
out further titles pretty soon. They're all stuffed full of good
things, and your life won't be complete until you have 'em all.

Thanks for reading – and good luck!

Made in the USA
Columbia, SC
06 March 2021